NARRATIVES, POLITICS, AND THE PUBLIC SPHERE

For Liu

Narratives, Politics, and the Public Sphere

Struggles over political reform in the final transitional years in Hong Kong (1992-1994)

AGNES S.M. KU
Hong Kong Polytechnic University

Ashgate

Aldershot • Brookfield USA • Singapore • Sydney

Published by
Ashgate Publishing Ltd
Gower House
Croft Road
Aldershot
Hants GU11 3HR
England

Ashgate Publishing Company
Old Post Road
Brookfield
Vermont 05036
USA

British Library Cataloguing in Publication Data
Agnes, S.M. Ku
 Narratives, politics and the public sphere: struggles over
 political reform in the final transitional years in Hong
 Kong (1992-1994). - (Social & political studies from Hong
 Kong)
 1. Hong Kong (China) - Politics and government
 I. Title
 320.9'5125

Library of Congress Catalog Card Number: 98-74642

ISBN 1 84014 195 6

Printed in Great Britain

Contents

List of Figures

Acknowledgements

This book originated from my Ph.D. dissertation entitled 'The Narrative Making of Public Opinion', which was completed in Fall 1995. When preparing for the dissertation, I remembered embarking on my graduate study at the University of California, Los Angeles (U.C.L.A.) in 1989 with little idea of what I would end up in. The question of 'what cultural studies or cultural sociology is' had never occurred to me to be a significant and interesting one until one day I found myself caught knowing virtually nothing about the subject matter in my first paper for the course 'Culture and Society'. This was my first experience with Jeffrey Alexander in 1990, who later became the chair of my dissertation committee.

The completion of this book would not have been possible but for the intellectual guidance and support from, as well as the critical but sympathetic reading by the members of my dissertation committee – Jeffrey Alexander, Bill Roy and Ivan Szelenyi in the Department of Sociology, and Theodore Huters (who replaced Leo Lee) in the Department of East Asian Studies. During my stay at U.C.L.A., it was the Culture Club fellows who kept reminding me that I was not alone on the road to that 'flimsy' land of culture and that there was still a lot to be explored and done. I am deeply thankful for their intellectual stimulation, nourishment and comradeship. Besides, I would like to thank my current colleagues at the Hong Kong Polytechnic University for their thoughtful comments on the oral presentation of my work in the early stage of the research.

Last but not least, I owe a great deal to my husband, Liu, who has not only shown tremendous understanding and persistent support for me in my academic pursuit throughout the years, but also provided an invaluable basis for sustained intellectual dialogue and bombardment.

1 Introduction

In Hong Kong, in the midst of political and cultural changes during the political transition, the public sphere saw much contestation over the moral basis of political practices. Thus far, studies on local politics have focused mostly on the interests, the motivations and the positions of the state elites rather than the cultural and discursive forces that shape their practices. This has the effect of submerging the moral power of public discourse under the waves of top-level politicking. As a point of departure, this book will analyse, with reference to the controversy over Governor Patten's reform proposals in 1992-94, the political and discursive dynamics in the public sphere in Hong Kong in the final transitional years.

The Event

From a formal-legal point of view, the event under study started on 7 October 1992 when Governor Patten released a blueprint for political reform, and then developed through a number of episodes involving intense social conflicts over the legislation of the reform package, and finally ended with its successful legislation on 30 June 1994. Nevertheless, from a socio-cultural point of view, the reform proposals were not only a matter for politicking between the sovereign states or among the politicians but also an event engaging the moral and emotional responses of the local public. The whole event was politically and culturally significant in that it laid out a field of fierce political and cultural struggles in the final transitional years before China's resumption of sovereignty over Hong Kong closed the chapter of British colonial rule in July 1997.

Upon their release, the reform proposals were hailed with enthusiastic responses in the public (though they were not without their critics). By means of the proposals, the Governor was believed to be venturing the society into the sacred but prohibited terrain of democratic struggles vis-à-vis China – its future sovereign power. Many people, especially the democrats, looked upon the Governor as well as his proposals as a symbol of courage, vision and creativity, and therefore revived their hopes for the pro-democracy cause. In narrative terms, the release of the reform proposals developed instantly into a popular heroic romance, with Patten the protagonist seen as embarking on a quest for democratic autonomy vis-à-vis the Chinese government. Apparently, the final legislation of the reform proposals would signify a victorious ending as a fulfillment of the promises of the heroic-romantic beginning. However, the fact was, as the event developed over time, the public meanings of 'Patten' and his reform proposals changed in the process so much so that the story of heroic romance lost much of its initial colour and emotional charge. The question is, what explained the rather paradoxical development of the event – a victory without a sense of victory – at the end?

In this book, I am going to show how a symbolic force of the 'public' was at work in the public sphere which, through the initial construction of heroic romance, informed, guided and constrained political practices in the process of endowing cultural meanings upon the latter. Upon the release of the reform proposals, despite certain places of incoherence in the narrative construction of the event, the structure of heroic-romance, once consolidated in public discourse, persevered as a discursive force which 'demanded' Patten, his supporters and also the British side to stick to the initial line of action, or they would make a public mockery of themselves. In a significant way, the final legislation of the reform proposals, despite continual delay and attempts for diplomatic concession, testified to the discursive power of the narrative.

At the same time, there took place a process of narrative progression which changed the public meanings of the event in terms of the public's experiences with it. The narrative process could be conceived as one of de-heroization and de-romanticization, taking place through the interplay among the discursive force of the heroic-romantic construction, cultural-political conflicts among the local political actors, and also a number of contingent episodes involving Sino-British politics. Viewed from a wider historical perspective, the disputes over the reform proposals dramatized and intensified the conflicts that had gripped the whole society in the shadow of '1997'.

The Context: The '1997' Question, Changing Power Relationships and Local Struggles

The '1997' issue concerned the Chinese resumption of sovereignty over

Hong Kong in lieu of British colonial rule in 1997. In the early 1980s, in view of the prospect of the Chinese takeover, the society was roused to a state of anxiety and uncertainty over its political future. The problem was that, while most of the people would identify themselves as Chinese (or, Hong Kong Chinese), they were hesitant in, and even resistant to, embracing a Communist regime as their future sovereign state. Rather, they were quite contented with their way of life under British rule. The Chinese government, determined to resume its sovereignty, sought to win over the public by devising the 'One Country Two Systems' formula. What it meant was that, Hong Kong was to be returned to China and would at the same time be allowed a high degree of autonomy under Chinese sovereignty. On the face of it, this was a promising arrangment, but later events proved it to be too vague and general to be useful in resolving political conflicts.

On the part of Britain, as part of its decolonization scheme, it sought to install measures of a more representative democracy in the society, partly to save face after losing battles to China over the sovereignty issue and partly to forestall China's undue interference into the society in the future. In the meantime, China initiated the process of drafting the mini-constitution of Hong Kong – the Basic Law – which was a sign of China establishing its sovereign status in the society. In these two largely overlapped moments of politicking by the two sovereign powers over Hong Kong's political future, there took place in society a process of politicization which gradually gave rise to the formation of two loosely organized opposing camps, namely the pro-democracy activists and the conservative elites. The former were largely from middle-class and grassroots origins who had formed some kind of network among themselves through past participation in social movements since the 1970s. They, drawing on the value codes of democracy and autonomy, advocated an early introduction of direct election to Legislative Council. The conservatives were mostly socio-economic elites who, falling in line with China's prime concern with sovereign/ executive control, were against the advocacy of the democrats. The situation was further complicated with the outbreak of the Tiananmen incident in Beijing in 1989, which deepened the conflicts between the Hong Kong people and the Chinese government, between the democrats and the pro-China forces (including a portion of the socio-economic elites), and between the British and the Chinese governments. From this vantage point, the political history of the Hong Kong people in the transitional years would concern how they understood and coped with the uneasy tensions among the geo-political reality of imminent Chinese sovereign rule, their specific

Chinese/ Hong Kong identity, their striving for local autonomy, and the desires for preserving the good they had been enjoying in the existing system. It was against this larger politico-cultural background that public reactions to the Governor's proposals were to be understood. Still, the trajectory of the development of public opinion with regard to the event under study cannot be explained in full without attending to the specificities of the immediate political and cultural processes.

Existing Approaches to Local Politics

As I have stated at the beginning, academic and popular discourses on local politics have focused mostly on the interests, the motivations and the positions of the state elites rather than the cultural and discursive forces that shape their practices. Regarding the Patten controversy, Sum's article (1995) represents a brilliant first attempt in local studies to analyse the event in terms of two contesting discursive formations by the two sovereign powers as well as the concomitant process of alliance formation in international and local politics. In her article, based on a detailed study of publicized official discourses by the Governor and by the Chinese government, she finds that the rhetorical disputes between the two sides represented, rather than just a war or words, two competing discursive formations crystallized, respectively, around the two different themes of 'democratization' and 'pragmatic nationalism' whereby the Hong Kong people as subjects were positioned in such public discourses. These two discursive formations formed the rhetorical bases for mobilization of local support among different classes and groups through appeals to some imagined collective identities around the themes. In the discursive contestations, the two governments not only invoked specific value and moral claims to justify their own political projects and to downgrade the moral position of their opponents, they also resorted to specific discursive and political practices to enter and dominate the discursive space such as mediatization and intellectualization by Governor Patten, and displacement and legitimation by the Chinese government. Using a strategic-relational approach as her theoretical framework, Sum regards the agents' deployment of discursive strategies as mediating the relations between agents and structures — structures understood as 'structural constraints grounded in a specific articulation of the local, regional and global levels of economic, political and social orders' (p.69). In particular, she explains the event in relation to the larger changing political-economic context of British colonial rule in the society against a background of globalization and regionalization of capital, as a result of which 'the old colonial economic structure experiences the gradual hollowing out of colonial capital and is increasingly disarticulated from the clientelist power structure' (p.85). This picture about the hollowing out of the pre-existing colonial economic and political structure gives us a clue about the constraints Governor Patten was facing in his strategic choices for possible allies in society.

Sum's analysis has offered a very convincing and sophisticated explanation of how, on the one hand, discursive formations are the products of strategies, structural changes and conjunctural events on the global and local levels, and how, on the other hand, discursive formations in turn mediate the process of alliance formation through the construction of imagined identities around specific value themes. However, in focusing on the formation of power blocs clustered around the two sovereign powers, her analysis has been narrowed down to the discursive strategies of the two governments in their struggle for dominance as well as the formation of their allies. What has nonetheless been overlooked in her approach is the wider sphere of public discourse (other than the official public sphere) which, located outside the power centre, is rooted in the local context of public life. Such a sphere constitutes a dynamic field of political struggles between the dominant groups and the opposition forces who are entangled in the politics of domination, marginalization and resistance. Without taking into account this wider public sphere, Sum has therefore failed to attend to the cultural-political complexities and dynamics within a particular discursive formation. In particular, in her analysis, she has completely ignored the existence of a small group of pro-democracy activists who had faith in neither the Chinese government nor the British government. The size of this group might be small, but its persistent presence in the political arena and public sphere had kept alive critical tensions within the pro-democracy camp and exerted pressure on the Patten administration throughout the event.

My contention is that a discursive formation is formed not just through rhetorical appeals by the states or the hegemonic power blocs but also through a complex process of articulation between various domains of cultural and political idioms and modes of public discourse whereby the community of actors struggle to represent the collective ideals and experiences of local public life. By 'local', it does not mean an exclusive concern with local politics in lieu of a global horizon. What it suggests is that, instead of using a top-down approach as well as an outside-in perspective, we may look at the political context from the perspective of the particular political community concerned so as to understand how the various dominant and opposing strands of public discourse within the community come into a dynamic interplay among themselves in the process of discursive formation. For a more adequate approach to the cultural and political dynamics of discursive formation within a community of citizens, we should anchor our analysis within a conceptual framework about the public sphere as well as the cultural and political practices associated with it.

Theoretical Premises

Briefly put, a public-centred approach to the relationship between politics and public opinion requires (i) an acknowledgement of the centrality of the 'public' in the political life of a community, (ii) due attention to the discursive context out of which 'public opinion' is crystallized, and (iii) a strenuous emphasis on the subjective but shared experiences of the public in political processes.

Centrality of the Category of 'Public' in Political Processes

A public is embedded within and yet distinct from a political community. The latter, formed on the basis of legal citizenship, consists of multiple networks of associations among its members. A public, more specifically, is formed through a common communicative space within a political community i.e. the public sphere. The operation of the 'public' presupposes a collective consciousness of there being a certain kind of public sphere as governed by a certain conception about the boundary of legitimate-versus-illegitimate and credible-versus-incredible public discourses. As such, the notion of the public is at the heart of the political life of a community.

The first issue about the 'public' concerns whether, on the structural level, there exists in a political community a public sphere which stands relatively independent of the state and is strong enough to confront it by means of open discussions and criticisms among the citizens. Public opinion formed through such a sphere constitutes a powerful political weapon of the citizenry vis-à-vis the state. Habermas's theory of the public sphere ([1962]1991) provides a useful starting point for us to think along this line. Specifically, in his explanation of the emergence of the bourgeois public sphere in Western Europe, a structural feature stands out as the primary factor: the rise of capitalism. The rise of capitalism, alongside the development of the modern state, facilitated the growth of a private domain of economic exchange which took on a public relevance and an expanding infrastructure of social communication within the community of citizens.

The second issue concerns the institutional location of the public sphere. There have been two competing answers to this question. The first one, suggested by Habermas, is lodged within a conception of publicness which is essentially 'spatial' and 'dialogical' in character – the public as an assembly of individuals meeting in an open or public space where they discuss issues of general concern. The second interpretation, however, is based on a conception of openness which is divorced from specific locales while retaining the 'dialogical' element. According to this interpretation, the modern media, due to their visibility, take up the institutional role of a public sphere. Certainly, any endorsement of this second interpretation would have to take into account the question about the degree of autonomy of the mass media from the state and from the dominant interests.

Finally, the third issue concerns the cultural basis for establishing and undermining one's credibility in the public sphere. It is this cultural element that constitutes what I call *politics of public credibility* in the public sphere. Indeed power or politics has a material aspect as much as a symbolic one. As a matter of material interests, it inevitably involves a struggle over the distribution of societal resources. At the same time, politics is largely expressed through symbolism, which would endow it with symbolic meanings. In the public sphere, the politics of public credibility concerns the actors' ability to speak in the name of the 'public'. Such symbolic references have their sources of imagery in the cultural tradition of a society and the symbolic representations of the opinions of the public at specific times. As such, the 'public' as a symbolic force becomes the meeting ground between culture and politics. Recent development in the field of cultural studies has much to enlighten us on the interaction between cultural and political processes.

In relation to the issue of culture, a question arises as to whether the culture of the 'public' entails specific values, norms or codes that regulate the politics of public credibility. In principle, the culture of the 'public' in a political community hinges on its traditions and the opinions and sentiments its members would openly express. Nevertheless, if the concept of publicness is to entail an element of openness, the politics of public credibility may involve a struggle over the code of openness or transparency which is essential to the value of democracy. In other words, put in the modern context, the notion of the 'public' may have some significant implications on the question of democracy.

Discursive Formation of Public Opinion

Public opinion is neither a thing out there for us to find out nor a product of mechanical manipulation of the masses by the politicians. It is a discursive construction – the construction of what the people in a society believe to be the prevalent opinions in the society at specific times – which both shapes and is shaped by the culture and politics of the public sphere. Such a discursive construction of public opinion underlies three important theoretical assumptions. First, 'public opinion' as an imagined reference of collective sentiments and opinions is worked upon through numerous signification practices. In the final analysis, the meaning of a representation of public opinion is subject to the interpretation of the actors concerned such as the polling agents, the politicians, the public critics and the ordinary citizens.

Secondly, public opinion is embedded in public discourse. What it means is that, public discourse itself constitutes public opinion and allows the discursive space for the construction of 'public opinion' as the general image of the public. There is a tendency in the existing literature to treat public discourse and public opinion as two different entities, referring the former to the politics of articulation by the dominant groups and the social activists and the latter to the total sum of opinions of the lay people. These approaches overlook the facts that (a) public opinion can be expressed in different forms including open criticisms, opinion polls, protests and so on; (b) for public opinion to become a political force in politics of public credibility, it must be expressed through a public sphere; and (c) public discourses by the political actors and the opinions of the general public are engaged in the same discursive context.

The final point leads us to the third theoretical assumption, which is, the opinions of the members of a community are formed in relation to the discursive conditions under the symbolic 'public' can be performed. These discursive conditions include the kind of languages or vocabularies popular among the people, the meanings that certain commonly identifiable symbols carry, and the stock of sacred values and norms sedimented in a culture.

For one thing, for 'public' to be understood as a discursive force, it should not be taken as reflecting the existence of a homogeneous collectivity, but rather as referring to a set of different yet overlapping discourses on what is believed to be the existing versus the good/ bad order of social and moral relationships in one's society. The discourse of the public thus constitutes a sense of 'communality' not so much by homogenizing differences as by (i) interweaving into a public web of intertextual references (ii) the competing interpretations over what the collective 'we' consists in, (iii) which entails a discourse not only of commonness but also of relations. It is by means of the three concepts of intertextuality, interpretation and relationality that we may resolve the paradox of community-and-differences in public discourse.

The Narrative Context of Public Opinion

Public opinion is embedded in public discourse and a large part of public discourse takes the form of narrative. Narrative is a meaning structure that organizes the human experience of time by integrating the events in the past, the present and the future into a meaningful whole. Moreover, in progressing through time, it allows continuous revisions in the retrospective and prospective configuration of a sequence of events. Indeed just as an object or action may mean different things to us at different times, public opinion vis-à-vis an event or a public figure may change from time to time. Changes in public opinion, however, do not simply reflect fluctuations in whims or reflex reactions to outside changes, but underlie certain cultural logics that explain events in the form of story. In other words, public opinion develops in stories or narratives.

Narrative is a concept of both structure and processes. Existing narrative theories in cultural studies, drawing on the structuralist tradition, attend to the structural elements in narration while overlooking the temporal dynamics in narrative development. As an attempt to overcome the deficiency in structuralist approach yet without slighting the structured quality in narrative, Phelan's theory of narrative progression draws our attention to the experiential dynamics of reading structured but developing texts on the part of the readers/ audiences. This theory will be discussed and further developed into a framework that analyses the dynamic relationships between political action and public opinion.

The narrative making of public opinion, moreover, has to be understood against the larger discursive context. There are two levels of narrative in society: master narratives, which form the tradition or cultural repertoire of a society, and the specific narratives which the actors, drawing on the cultural repertoire, are constructing and reconstructing with regard to specific events as they unfold. Power relationships are enmeshed – either reinforced or challenged – in such narrative constructions which constitute the discursive formation in which 'public opinion' is embedded.

Discursive Structures in the Local Public Sphere

Public discourse, as a set of cultural practices in the public sphere, is organized around specific cultural codes while being couched in specific discursive (narrative) modes. In this book, three generic codes and three narrative modes will be identified as pertinent to our understanding of the cultural and political dynamics of the local public sphere, *namely the coded discourses of sovereignty/ nationalism, democracy/ autonomy, and stability/ prosperity, and the discursive modes of comic-realism, romanticism and cynicism*. On the part of the democrats, the discourses on democracy and autonomy have been framed partly in romantic (as well as romantic-ironic) terms and partly in cynical terms. A romantic mode of discourse accentuates a strong conviction in the conduct of combating for the ideals vis-à-vis the obstructing forces. In contrast, a cynical mode underlines a discrepancy between ideals and reality, with respect not so much to the constraints of reality as to the will, commitment and sincerity in those who have made a claim to the ideals. To the democrats, the political history of the society in the last decade had been about the people's growing aspirations for democracy and autonomy on the one hand and a concomitant experience of frustrations in their struggle on the other. In the 1980s, along with the state's incremental measures of a representative democracy, the Joint Declaration of 1984 promised a high degree of autonomy and democracy for Hong Kong, giving the people high hopes on their political future. Nevertheless, a bitter irony set in when subsequent development, especially over the drafting of the Basic Law, entailed 'a process of continuous erosion of the 1984 commitments' by both China and Britain (Davies, in *SCM Post*, 5 December 1992). In public discourse, while China (or state paternalism) was identified as the primary obstructing force in the pro-democracy struggle, a cynical sense of distrust also took root with regard to Britain's promise of moral commitment to democratization in the society.

On top of state paternalism, the struggle for democracy had to fight its way on another front, which is a culture of pragmatic submissiveness among the conservatives – part of an ever expanding pro-China alliance – as well as its accompanying discourse. *Pragmatic submissiveness* indicates both a tendency to yield to the force of authoritarianism with minimal resistance and a readiness to adapt oneself to the situation in such a way that one can both take advantage of it and stay on the safe side. To the conservatives, in their pragmatic mode of reasoning, given the reality of the resumption of Chinese sovereignty in 1997, the wise way of going about the situation is to co-operate with the future sovereign power on transitional matters so as to maintain stability and prosperity. It is with their pragmatic concern that they were more than ready to trade democracy and autonomy for peace with China. In the public sphere, drawing on a discourse of stability, they have expressed their concerns with order, harmony and smooth transition as opposed to disorder, conflict and unstable change. It was in such discursive terms that they have opposed democratic reforms that might jeopardize their established interests and/ or fall outside the orbit of China's intent.

In a nutshell, the discourses of sovereignty/ nationalism, democracy/ autonomy, and stability/ prosperity have structured to a large extent the way public contestations are undertaken whereas the discursive modes of comic-realism, romanticism and cynicism play a crucial part in shaping the ways the different discourses are articulated by the actors in the public sphere. It is, moreover, presumed that discursive articulation has played an important role in the process of political mobilization – alliance formation and fragmentation. It is also interesting to note that these discursive codes and modes, which are symbolic conventions, do not form stable constructions around particular actors but can be subject to different interpretations and re-articulations in the process of self-positioning and other-positioning. (For example, in the final stage of the event under study, while the leading democrats proclaimed themselves to be 'heroic' allies with the Governor, their more radical counter-parts saw in them a pragmatic readiness for compromises and concessions.) The controversy over Governor Patten's reform proposals, which spanned almost two years from 1992 to 1994, provided a fertile ground for studying the interplay among the different discursive forces in connection to the changing power alliances in the society at a time when China was just about to take over Hong Kong at the end of British colonial rule.

Lay-out of the Book

Building on the above premises and assumptions, I propose a narrative theory of politics of public credibility to explain how cultural and political processes shape public opinion (public discourse) on the one hand, and how public opinion (public discourse) influences political action in a continuous manner on the other. Chapters two and three are devoted to the elaboration of the theory dealing with the concepts of 'public' and 'narrative' respectively. In chapter two, I will review the different meanings of the 'public' in the Western literature with a view to developing a multi-level theory of the public. It is noted that the notion of 'public' has been juxtaposed against the concepts of 'mass', 'private sphere' and 'privacy', which thereby give rise to three different kinds of interpretation of the concept. Although the three conceptions are discussed in different theoretical contexts, they address one common question pertinent to the study of public opinion – the social organization of the communicative space within a political community.

The first interpretation has certain theoretical merits but is inadequate as a theory of the public. The second interpretation, represented by Habermas's work ([1962]1991), alerts us to the structural, institutional and discursive dimensions of the public sphere as a space for communication among citizens. However, due to his rationalistic conception of an ideal public culture, his main thesis is tied to the rather implausible 'public-mass' distinction. In the third and final interpretation, 'public' means 'open' or 'available to the general populace'. This interpretation connects itself to the idea of social action as drama or performance, which not only highlights the critical relevance of the media to the study of politics but also rightly orients us to the central role that culture plays in politics. Specifically, as Thompson has argued, the kind of visibility created by the development of mass communication, accompanied by processes of democratization, entails a new form of public accountability. Thus as I will venture to argue in chapter two, a more adequate theorization of the 'public' requires (i) a critical integration of the second interpretation into the third one and (ii) a re-conceptualization of the role of culture in the public sphere of politics. This will lead us from Habermas to the more recent development in cultural studies, and finally to a theory of politics of public credibility.

In chapter three, I will propose a theory of cultural politics which looks at the narrative contexts of the force the 'public'. In particular, I will add in the temporal dimension in our experience of public events by incorporating the three concepts of intertextuality, interpretation and relationality into a theory of narrative progression. The theory will be conceived in terms of three inter-related narrative components: thematic plots, characters and mood. Thematic plotting, mood creation and characterization are matters of interpretation by means of relational categories. In public discourse, relational juxtapositions often map out the moral underpinnings of what is sacred and what is profane, and hence who is right and who is wrong. Owing to competing and multiple interpretations, politics entails a reciprocal process of narrative construction and reconstruction among the actors. It is by means of such intertextual interpretations that the narrative context would capture the dynamics of change upon reciprocal actions, novel revelations, and retrospective reassessment as well as projective refiguration. Moreover, the idea of relative open-endedness about narrative development allows us to conceive a space for agency in the process of struggle and change. This new way of looking at the question of politics, I contend, will help us understand more about, on the one hand, how cultural and political processes intersect in the making of public opinion on an issue over a continuous span of time, and on the other hand, how, in a dramaturgical way, the changing collective imageries of 'public opinion' come to exercise their power over political action.

More specifically, since different ways of integrating the three components of plot, character and mood would constitute very different experiences with an event, for analytical purposes, I will delineate a classification scheme of four genres, namely romance, tragedy, comedy, and irony/ satire. Despite a possible western bias, the advantage for doing so is four-fold. First, a narrative genre integrates plot, character and mood in a most structured and unifying way. Secondly, the narrative genre as a form is meaning-laden in itself (White, 1987) while allowing an intertwinement with different thematic structures to produce the meanings of a narrative in all its structural and thematic specificities. Thirdly, it is able to integrate the concepts of structure and process in a way that is compatible with my theory of narrative progression. Finally, the whole system covers a wide range of narrative experiences by making fine nuances between apparently similar narrative structures.

Pertinent to the empirical case in this research, I will limit my theoretical elaboration to a particular instance – when an event starts off as a heroic romance. Given the relative open-endedness about narrative progression, it is conceivable that the subsequent course of development is open to different possibilities. In my theoretical explanation, the major variables include meaningful episodes, social actors and narratives (value themes, narrative forms and narrative cultures). A meaningful episode will be defined as an episode that contributes to the narrative development of the larger event by means of turn-making. It is usually the result, which may be intended or unintended, of human agency. Narrative configuration by the social actors results from the interaction between agency and the master narratives embedded in a culture. Narrative forms are limited by the narrative cultures sedimented in a society, and cultural themes are more or less prescribed in a culture, but their interaction opens the way for various possible combinations. The latter is where agency comes into the picture.

Social actors will be classified on the bases of their structural positions in the state-public nexus and their political stands. The social actors include three major categories: those representing the state(s), those representing the public, and those straddling between the public and the state. More specifically, the public refer to the commercial media, the political commentators and others who participate in public discourse such as polling agents, political groups and ordinary citizens. In this research, based on judgmental sampling, five newspapers will be chosen as the empirical referent of the public. Among the five newspapers, seven types of public critics will be identified based on their ideological positions. As for the semi-public actors, they will be divided into the pro-democracy camp, the conservatives and the pro-China camp.

In my work, the concept of narrative attains a special ontological and theoretical status, which dictates the use of what I will call a narrative methodology. A narrative methodology relies on the method of textual interpretation to analyse public opinion. More specifically, the idea of genre – narrative genre in particular – will be used to capture the changing part-whole relationship in public discourse. The method of analysis draws on the hermeneutic tradition and is developed out of a critique of empiricism. The question of validation and other methodological issues will be discussed in the methodological section in chapter four.

Based on the narrative theory of public credibility developed in chapter three, chapters five to eleven will analyse the political-cultural situation in Hong Kong as well as the chosen empirical case. In chapter five, I will first trace the historical development of the public sphere in the Hong Kong society. It will be found that while there had been a practice of public criticisms in the early days, a more general and inclusive public sphere did not develop in the society until the 1980s. The latter was a result of the interaction between structural changes, cultural processes and contingent events. Consistent with Habermas's theory, the growth of a capitalist economy was identified as a necessary structural factor for the development of a general public sphere. Pertinent to the particular case in Hong Kong, moreover, specific political and cultural processes were at work that shaped the character of the public sphere. In particular, the increasing mobilization of the middle class and the development of a new culture of the 'public' enhanced the role of the media as the public sphere and set in force the politics of public credibility which stressed the need for openness and democratic autonomy. Chapter six will delineate the immediate political-cultural context in the society wherein the politics of public credibility over the reform proposals were to unfold.

Chapters seven to eleven are the main empirical chapters. As an introduction to the empirical analysis, chapter seven will outline the event in terms of Sino-British politics. Chapters eight and nine will reconstruct the public discourses on democracy and stability in their respective narrative modes and chart their course of development in the early stages of the event. Chapter ten will analyse the empirical case as it developed over three stages. The release of the reform proposals was at first hailed by the public as a heroic romance with the Governor being the protagonist. However, as China began to take counter-actions, the event later underwent a process of de-romanticization and the Governor of de-heroization. The second stage saw the public divided into those who held steadfastly to the narrative of heroic romance and those who became more and more prone to a comic-ironic perspective. In the final stage, after months and months of struggles, the reform proposals were passed into legislation, but the general response at the outcome was neither thunderous applause nor deep anguish but one of ironic resignation. In light of such development, the following questions thus become prominent:

Stage I

(1) What were the narrative contexts that the people found themselves in before the release of the reform proposals?

(2) Who were the Governor's major supporters and how did he succeed to construct among them a narrative of heroic romance vis-à-vis China?

(3) Who were the Govenor's opponents and how did they discredit him? In what ways did the counter-narrative challenges bear on the ways the narratives would unfold in the later stages?

Stage II

(1) What were the counter-narrative actions taken by China and how did they change the meaning of the event so much so that the structure of

heroic romance was cross-cut with a realm of ironic realism?

(2) How did the force of narrative progression affect the actions, the public image and the self/other -positioning strategies of the political actors?

(3) How did the cultural and political processes interact in mobilizing the public into two opposing blocs? In particular, how did the comic-realists come to establish public credibility for an alternative line of narrative action to take?

Stage III

(1) What critical events took place in this stage that configured probable desirable or undesirable turns in the narrative accounts of the divided public whereby public opinion on the event was changed?

(2) What was the force of narrative progression in this stage that exerted constraints on or provided cultural resources for the political actors? In particular, what were the cultural and political processes at work that resulted in the final legislation of the reform proposals?

(3) How had the changing narrative configuration of the event change its meaning so much so that the general public responded to the legislation of the reform proposals with a sense of resignation?

In terms of research design, the empirical study will (1) analyse the narrative strategies of the actors and the public critics, (2) chart the course of narrative progression, and (3) correlate the force of the 'public' with the ebbs and flows in politics. Narrative analysis attends to the structural quality in public discourse and entails an inherently comparative logic – both between types and over time. Narrative analysis of public discourse on the Patten event will therefore proceed by making comparisons between the patterns of narrative structures of different public actors/ critics at different time points – the three stages as well as the sub-stages within each of them – and making tentative explanation about the process of change from one stage to another.

In the society, there have been a lot of public discussions on the event as it developed. While these public discourses constituted the very substance of the political culture and the cultural politics in the Hong Kong society, they have not been systematically documented and analysed in academic research. This research is intended to be a modest effort in this direction. It is one of the aims of the study to provide a way of understanding the narrative dynamics of the event from the perspective of the public by following closely the development of public discourses over a continuous period of time. In this connection, I seek to devise a theoretical framework to analyse the interaction between political and cultural processes in the unfolding of a public event. It is hoped that by way of such theorizing we may be able to arrive at some theoretical generalizations about the relationships between narrative structure and agency, between politics and culture, and between politics and public opinion. Moreover, as the political culture in Hong Kong is undergoing certain fundamental changes, it is also hoped that the study of the Patten event will shed light on the intricate relationship between democracy and the politics of public credibility in a society which is, hopefully, changing from paternalistic authoritarianism to increasing democratic consciousness.

2 Theoretical Approaches to the Public Sphere

When we understand images and texts as public, we do not gesture to a statistically measurable series of others. We make a necessarily imaginary reference to the public as opposed to other individuals. Public opinion, for example, is understood as belonging to a public rather than to scattered individuals. (Warner, 1992: 379)

This chapter is concerned with the notion of 'public' as well as its conceptual place in a theory of public sphere. In academic debate, much confusion develops around the concept in the current usage of the term. In one context, it defines a structural domain; in another context, it refers to a space of sociability; in others, it implies a locus of human agency; and in some others, it underlines a mode of orientation in social interaction. Moreover, in each of these usages, debates on the theoretical import of the concept as well as its empirical referents underscore contradictions and ambiguities that beg a range of questions. For example, does the public sphere lie outside or inside the market that has conventionally been defined as a private domain? Is the 'public' a realist category referring to concrete people or is it a 'phantom' (Lippman, 1922) having an imaginary existence instead? Does it connote rationality or irrationality? As I will show in this chapter, the confusion around the concept arises out of its multiple and often inconsistent meanings that are derived from three different yet overlapping dichotomies posed on different planes of analysis. The three dichotomies are public versus mass, public (sphere) versus private (sphere), and publicness versus privacy/secrecy.

The three interpretations of the notion of public, albeit being proposed and discussed in different theoretical contexts, address one common question that is pertinent to the study of politics – the institution of public communication within a political community. In the first interpretation, a public is conceived as a self-organized community of interacting people in contrast to a mass of disparate and passive individuals. The second interpretation is based on a notion of the public conceived in spatial terms. In particular, Habermas's book ([1962]1991) that addresses the question of the public sphere in relation to state power, the institution of the market economy and the practice of public discourse in modern society presents a most comprehensive piece of work on the notion. In the third and final interpretation, 'public' means 'open' or 'available to the general populace'. What is public is therefore what is 'visible or observable, what is performed in front of spectators, what is open for all (or many) to see or hear or hear about' (Thompson, 1990:240). As it stands, the three sets of dichotomy have been posed on quite different planes of analysis the relationship among which is yet to be more clearly articulated. It is the aim of this chapter to tease out the different layers of meaning of the concept, especially those embedded in Habermas's work, with a view to developing an alternative, integrated framework to analyse the interrelationship between politics, culture and the public sphere.

In my critique, I will argue that the public–mass distinction is flawed on the presuppositional level, and that Habermas's main thesis, due to his rationalistic conception of an ideal public culture, is tied to this rather implausible public–mass distinction that impoverishes his otherwise rich conception of the public sphere. In Habermas's framework, moreover, the public–private divide in terms of the state– non-state distinction falls short of specifying the characteristics of the public. In going beyond the simple domestic– non-domestic distinction, his approach has avoided the residualistic conception implicated in much of the family studies literature; however, without conceiving the notion in its own terms, the meaning of the public appears inconsistent and imprecise in his framework. In this chapter, I propose that the notion of public be conceived as indicating the membership organization of citizenship, and that it be accordingly theorized on three different levels of analysis – structural relations, institutional location and discursive practices. It is on these three levels that I will take issue with Habermas's theory of the public sphere at length.

On the face of it, the third interpretation may seem to be the most trivial of the three. None the less, if we look at it on a deeper level, it actually connects itself to the ideas of social action as public drama or performance, and of politics as cultural politics and identity politics. For the 'public' here would indicate a mode of orientation or practice specific to the public sphere. In this regard, media publicity, due to their publicness, relative accessibility and symbolic capacity, plays an indispensable role both in linking together the members of a political community in a common discursive field and in defining the political and moral boundary of publicness. This way of interpreting the notion offers a fruitful way of understanding the relationship between culture, politics and the public sphere. The emerging field of cultural studies has much to offer in this respect. As we will see, a more adequate theorization of the public requires a critical integration of the second interpretation into the third one, with a re-conceptualization of the notion in its own terms and an accentuation on the role of culture in the public sphere of politics. Towards the end of the discussion, a theory of politics of public credibility will be proposed as an attempt to capture the political and cultural dynamics of the public sphere in modern society.

The 'Mass–Public' Distinction and its Discontents

In some of the earlier traditions of sociology and political theories, it has been held that the emergence of mass society in the modern era has eclipsed the public of reasoned opinions. In such an interpretation, the public is conceived as an active, organized collective agent in politics as opposed to a passive mass of disparate individuals. A number of theories on mass society are premised implicitly on such a distinction of mass versus public wherein the public is either seen as a thing past or presupposed as an unrealizable ideal in modern times (Dewey, [1927]1946; Mills, 1956; Arendt, 1958; Adorno and Horkheimer, [1947]1977; Sennett, 1974; Dewey, 1985).

Within this tradition, Mills' discussion of mass society (1956) brings out two significant issues pertinent to the study of the public sphere of politics, namely, the social organization of the communicative space within a political community, and the extent of autonomy of the political community vis-à-vis the state or other authoritative institutions. In a mass, he explained, the communication and realization of opinion is by and large controlled by the authority. The mass, with far fewer people expressing opinions than receive them, becomes 'an abstract collection of individuals who receive impressions from the mass media'. A public, on the contrary, is organized through an arena for open communication that stands autonomous from the authoritative institutions and is readily accessible to all.[1]

Mills' distinction of the two concepts has the merit of underlining the important idea that a public is an interacting public, hence a locus of human agency, that is formed within a complex system of institutional nexus. Nevertheless, in taking the public as a historical given and focusing on the transformation from public to mass, his analysis fails, on the one hand, to specify the structural factors and the historical processes leading to the formation of the public, and fails, on the other, to give a satisfactory account of how a public is often not a structural given but has to be continuously shaped through struggles. As a result, by means of the dichotomous distinction, the public is idealized as a historical given whereas the mass society is relegated to 'an abstract collection' of disparate and passive individuals.

On the presuppositional level, moreover, I hazard that there could be no such thing as the mass per se. The problem is that, the concept of mass represses the possibility of human agency, hence being incapable of conceiving the complicated political and cultural processes at work in the multiplicity of discursive practices. Drawing on Thompson's critique of the 'culture industry' thesis,[2] I suggest that the conceptualization of the mass is founded upon an internalist fallacy, that wrongly assumes that the people will become a mass when they are treated as such by the state (or the market). On this point, Williams' view is worth-quoting:

> There are in fact no masses; there are only ways of seeing people as masses ... What we see, neutrally, is other people, many others, people unknown to us. In practice, we mass them, and interpret them, according to some convenient formula ... Yet it is the formula, not the mass, that is our real business to examine. (1958:289, 293)

In this light, even granted that a community of people might understand themselves as a passive, faceless mass, the very consciousness of the people themselves being such a mass would have to be founded upon certain complicated cultural and social processes of interaction. In this connection, Baudrillard (1985) goes to the extreme in claiming that 'the silent majority' is the only referent still functioning in politics in the postmodern era. In taking the silence of the majority as a sign of deliberate agency on their part, he turned the previous argument upside down by a sleight of hand. This, however, still presents an inadequate understanding of culture as well as the complex articulation between culture and politics in human practices. As Alejandro (1993) is apt to point out, politics requires 'a vocabulary that legitimizes itself through a complex web of symbols and authorities that are the referents of the political, and far beyond the "silent majority"' (p.208). In short, the notion of mass, whether in its more conventional conception or in its postmodern guise, remains as an unsatisfactory category.

In sum, the public–mass distinction is flawed on the presuppositional level while the notion of public is yet to be more adequately conceptualized and explained. None the less, as far as the question of agency is concerned, Mills' definition of the public entails a more plausible assumption that people are not passive receptors of messages coming from the outside, but are engaged in communication, not just with the intimate few around them, but also with all those belonging to the same political community. This then raises the important questions of what is it that enables the people of a community to communicate among themselves as a public, and what are the defining features of a public as opposed to a non-public? For an adequate answer to these questions, we need to look for a different interpretation of the notion, and look into the symbolic as well as institutional nexus of public life in modern society.

An Engagement with Habermas's Theory of the Public Sphere

The second interpretation defines the public as basically a sphere or domain of social life as opposed to the private. Early family research conceives the private and the public spheres in terms of the domestic– non-domestic distinction (Stacey 1981). In other words, the family is private and everything outside it is public. This definition is problematic because it offers a residualist conception about the public sphere and underscores a conflation between levels of analysis. The fact is that, the public sphere is not just a sphere outside the home, but one that designates specific spatial locations on the one hand and entails specific set of institutional arrangement on the other. A more precise definition of the public is needed to differentiate the public sphere from both the domain of market economy and the domain of state authority.

A Socio-historical Account of the Bourgeois Public Sphere

Habermas's book on the public sphere ([1962]1991) is a significant first attempt to explicate the relationship between politics, culture and the media in terms of a multi-levelled understanding of the notion of public. On the one hand, he conceives the public in spatial terms i.e. as a public sphere, and locates the public sphere in structural terms, identifying the bourgeois public sphere as part of the private realm of civil society[3] that is distinct from and yet related to the public realm of state authority. As part of the private realm, it was constituted by private people as opposed to public officials and was founded upon the capacity of the civil society of private people to organize itself independent of any imperative from the state. Situated, moreover, as an interface between the private realm and the public realm of state authority, the bourgeois public sphere put the state in touch with the society through the vehicle of public opinion, that is based on rational-critical discourse. Precisely, the purpose of his study of the bourgeois public sphere is to explore the social and cultural bases within the private realm of society for the development of an effective rational-critical discourse whereby political disputes may be arbitrated. It is on this cultural level that Habermas, on the other hand, gives to the notion of public a different meaning that, as we shall see later, is anchored in the critical theory tradition.

Historically, Habermas identifies the bourgeois public sphere as the product of certain long-term processes that took place between the late Middle Ages and the eighteenth century. In general terms, the rise of capitalism, alongside the development of the modern state, had helped establish in society a private sphere of commodity exchange that could none the less take on a public relevance – 'civil society' understood in a narrow sense. As commercialization reoriented productive activity from the old basis of the (private) household economy 'toward a commodity market that had expanded under public direction and supervision' (p.19), there emerged a new stratum of bourgeois forming a sphere as distinct from both the state and the domestic domain:

> On the one hand, the society now confronting the state clearly separated a private domain from public authority and ... on the other hand it turned the reproduction of life into something transcending the confines of private domestic authority and becoming a subject of public interest .... (p.24)

Significantly, these processes of change were at the same time facilitated by and reshaping the context of social communication for public life, especially in terms of an expanding infrastructure of social communication among the people (the press, reading societies, coffeehouses and salons). Public discussions were conducted in salons and coffeehouses; ongoing debates on political issues were developed in the independent press. Opinions crystallized in these public forums became a political force or weapon in that the new stratum of bourgeois as well as those involved in professional and journalistic writing 'readied themselves to compel public authority to legitimate itself before public opinion' (p.26).

For Habermas, the basic question is, to what extent can the opinions guiding political action be formed on the basis of rational-critical discourse? This is a salient issue as conflicting interests will arise among the actors out of their economic and other differences. In his liberal vision of the public sphere, he identifies the importance of rationality and universality in democratic political practices rather than reduce politics to simply the clash of power interest. Specifically, he points out a number of institutional principles distinctive about this kind of public discourse, namely a disregard for personal status, a self-defined domain of common concern and general accessibility (inclusiveness). Indeed the very idea of the public is based on the notion of a basic general interest, the discourse about that would not be distorted by particular interests:

> For as a public they were already under the implicit law of the partiy of all cultivated persons, whose abstract universality afforded the sole guarantee that the individuals subsumed under it in an equally abstract fashion, as 'common human beings', were set free in their subjectivity precisely by this parity. (p.54)

While this political public sphere of rational discourse came into being in the context of economic changes, it had its precursor in the patriarchal conjugal family and the literary public sphere, that cultivated a subjectivity 'capable of relating to literature and oriented toward a public sphere'. In particular, the 'literary experimentation with the psychology of the humanity common to all' (p.171) helped institutionalize a form of rational-critical discourse among private individuals that could be carried over directly into political discussion.[4]

Habermas's book is an ambitious attempt to study the historical development of the bourgeois public sphere in terms of its social-structural basis, cultural-integrative aspect and political function. In his account, the growth of the capitalist economy is identified as an important structural factor for the emergence of civil society and hence the development of the public sphere. More specifically, his historical study brings to the fore the institution of mass communication as 'a formative factor' in the development of public life in modern societies (Thompson, 1990). By and large, the bourgeois public sphere of critical-rational discourse was founded on commercial capitalism, facilitated by the development of an independent press − that was free from state censorship − and had its cultural nourishment from the literary and intimate spheres.

The Role of the Bourgeois

In Habermas's framework, the civil society in early capitalism in Europe is conceived as a private realm that engaged the activities of private individuals bearing the double identity as property owner and 'homme'. These private individuals referred to a new stratum of bourgeois people or capitalists who became the real carrier of the public. As he puts it,

> The fully developed bourgeois public sphere was based on the fictitious identity of the two roles assumed by the privatized individuals who came together to form a public: the role of property owners and the role of human beings pure and simple. (p.56)

The role of property owner in a market economy secured for the bourgeois people a space in society for activities that, extending from economic to political kinds, did not come under direct state control whereas that of 'homme' helped cultivate a practice of critical-rational discourse among these people that then shaped public opinion vis-à-vis the state. In other words, it was on both the economic and the cultural levels that the capitalists played a primary role in the formation of the early public sphere.

In this connection, the state, by means of its mercantilist policies, unintentionally played a part in mobilizing the newly emerged capitalists into a self-conscious collectivity − the public − in opposition to the state:

> In this stratum, that more than any other was affected *and* called upon by mercantilist policies, the state authorities evoked a resonance leading the *publicum*, the abstract counterpart of public authority, into an awareness of

itself as the latter's opponent, that is, as the public of the now emerging *public sphere of civil society.* (p.23)

In so far as the state administration was involved in the regulation of commercial-entrepreneurial activity, mercantilist policies such as those relating to taxes and duties became the major target of public criticisms by the capitalists. This explained how the rise of capitalism, in conjunction with the development of the modern state, established in society a private sphere that could nonetheless take on a public relevance. This in turn explained how the capitalists became the major carrier of the public in those days.

Moreover, the capitalists, with both their financial resources and their reading ability, contributed to the development of another important element of the early capitalist commercial system, that was the press. The early journals published news on wars, harvests and commerce that at first developed as an informative complement to commercial development and later themselves became commodities in the market system. As it developed, the press assumed an additional, political function in serving as a forum for open debate about public matters such as state policies.

Habermas has accounted for the emergence of a public sphere that stood independent of state control. The capitalist economy in general, and the capitalists in particular, played a crucial part in facilitating the growth of a public sphere as such. However, a question arises as to how far the bourgeois public sphere defined by Habermas could claim to be a sphere of the public. As Eley (1992) has pointed out, Habermas's account of the public sphere neglected 'the extent to that its institutions were founded on sectionalism, exclusiveness and repression' (p.321). As a matter of fact, the capitalists at that time were facing two ways in their role, one progressive and the other fixative, if not regressive:

> [T]he participants in the bourgeois public always faced two ways in this sense: forward in confrontation with the old aristocratic and royal authorities, but also backward against the popular/ plebeian elements already in pursuit. (p.321)

In this light, the capitalists arose as a competing power bloc in place of the old aristocratic authorities without really transforming the power structure in society to a genuine democracy. The bourgeois public sphere bore the mark of publicness in being a non-state sphere that took state policies as its major concern, but in so far as it was confined to a particular stratum, it should best be conceived as a sectional-public sphere. My contention is that, only when it is re-defined as such then will we be able to look into the process of struggle within the civil society of different class-based, status-based and other kinds of groups in the formation of a more generalized public sphere.

Does the Public Sphere Belong to the Public or the Private Domain?

As we can see, in terms of the public—private dichotomy, the meanings of the public in Habermas's framework are anchored on two different levels of analysis — namely spatial location and structural relations. In rather paradoxical terms, the public sphere is conceived as a public space instituted in the private realm of civil society. Such a paradoxical usage of the notion of public in his theory none the less indicates conceptual imprecision and inconsistency in definition. In part it shows the persistent influences of two contradictory political legacies on modern thought — the Roman empire and ancient republicanism — that understands the public, respectively, as state sovereignty and as the political community of citizens (Garcelon, 1997; Weintraub, 1997). In part it epitomizes the metanarrative of Anglo citizenship theory — in terms of the state/public versus market/private duality — that has dominated political and academic thinking about democracy since the seventeenth century (Bobbio, 1989; Somers, 1995a, 1995b). Such a duality does not sufficiently specify the defining characteristics of the public.

My contention is that, the state is a public domain but it is not the defining feature of the latter. Rather, it is in being a specific membership organization[5] — citizenship — that the state is conceived as such. In this light, the public domains should include both state and civil society. Both the state and civil society are political organizations in terms of citizenship. It is within the public domains of citizenship, then, that state and civil society are to be further distinguished from each other in terms of the state-non-state dichotomy. The market is also accessible to all, but in so far as 'the consumer' constitutes a status of single individuals rather than membership of a political community, the market does not fall within the category of the public in structural terms (but may be taken as a quasi-public domain).[6]

While public institutions and spaces in general are identified as those belonging to the state and / or civil society, the public sphere is conceived as originating, more particularly, in the non-state public domain of citizenship, that is, civil society. It originates there for it is where one's sense of membership is derived from day-to-day practice. In other words, it is as a member of civil society and national community rather than as state subjects that people participate in the public sphere. Institutionally, the public sphere is none the less intertwined with the state and the economy in various ways. The state may provide certain constitutional safeguards for the effective operation of the pubilc sphere (for example, freedom of association and freedom of speech) without controlling the latter, or it may intervene into the sphere by means of differential relationships with the different social groups in society. In some extreme cases, it may exercise outright control over civil society so much so that the public sphere becomes suppressed. The market itself is not equivalent to civil society or the community but perhaps provides the socio-economic infrastructure needed for the emergence and development of a politically autonomous communicative network among the citizens and communal members.

As far as politics is concerned, it remains analytically important that the (political) public sphere is conceived as growing out of civil society whereas civil society is defined in terms of citizenship rather than in class terms. In Habermas's book, however, he failed to understand civil society in such terms. Specifically, with his rather narrow and overly economistic conception, civil society was conceived as a private realm that engages the activities of private individuals bearing the double identity as bourgeois and homme. With such an understanding of civil society, the result is that, as Cohen and Arato (1994) have pointed out, Habermas fails to 'find an adequate locus, even in principle, for the activity of the citizen' (p.220).

Recent historical studies by Zaret (1994, 1996) have challenged the class-centred analyses by Bendix (1977), Gould (1987), and Habermas ([1962]1989) that linked the initial appearance of democratic ideas to 'class interests of the bourgeoisie' or to 'an extension of aristocratic privileges that involved alliances between the aristocracy and bourgeoisie'. Instead of identifying the bourgeois as the carrier of the public, Zaret (1996) located the origin of the modern public sphere in a novel communicative practice among the wider populace – printed petitions from political associations. In England, prior to the widespread use of printing, the right to petition established only a privileged and restricted form of direct communication to those in power. It was with the economic and technical development of printing that direct petition began to take the form of printed petition. In a significant way, this novel practice altered the culture as well as the scope of political communication: 'Out of practical experiences with political petitioning emerged new ideas that attached unprecedented authority to public opinion in politics' (p.1535). Indeed it is the appeal to the anonymous authority of a larger audience in society — the public — that characterizes communicative practices in the public sphere. In other words, the symbolic reference to the public in political discourse lays the cultural basis for the practice of citizenship in modern society.

The Question of Culture

On the cultural level of analysis, Habermas's book is concerned the germ of rational-critical debate in the public sphere as well as its subsequent eclipse. It is on this level that his analysis of the changing nature of public discourse is found grafted essentially onto the public–mass distinction. In a way, Habermas shares with Mills' concern about the institution of public communication that is central to the practice of democracy. Given his greater linguistic emphasis, his major concern is to explore the social and cultural bases within the private realm of society for the development of an effective rational-critical discourse whereby political disputes may be arbitrated and also the changing conditions that led to the final degeneration of the public sphere of rational-critical discourse.[7] It is with this concern that his analysis appears as an arduous elaboration of Mills' 'mass versus public' framework from a socio-historical perspective. He sets out to establish that the meaning and material operation of the 'public' has changed over time, in accordance with changes in the nature of the public sphere. In a nutshell, the public sphere had developed from (i) one of publicity of royal or manorial representation before the subjects in the Middle Ages to (ii) the bourgeois public sphere of rational-critical debate among private citizens in the 18th and 19th centuries, and then degenerated into (iii) a sphere of manipulative staged publicity thereafter. Depending on the nature of the public sphere, 'public opinion' would take on a different meaning, either as the object to be molded in the service of particular persons and institutions or as 'a critical authority in connection with the normative mandate that the exercise of political and social power be subject to publicity' (p.236).

Regarding his approach to culture, on the one hand, Habermas locates identity primarily outside the public sphere – in the private realm of the conjugal family as 'humanity's genuine site'. On the other hand, he idealizes the culture of the bourgeois public sphere in rationalistic terms and treated symbolic representations as both external and inferior to such rational discourse. Concerning the nature of the kind of critical-rational discourse he conceived, Habermas distinguishes between the public and the non-public in terms of a two-fold dichotomy: rational discourse versus private interests, and rational discourse versus symbolic identification. The juxtaposition of rationality against instrumentality and against non-rationality is premised on a theory that conceives a rational discourse as stripped of any instrumental concern and symbolic references. Debate in the bourgeois public sphere was presumed to be governed by 'universal rules', that, in being objective and strictly external to the individuals, did not so much constitute their identities as secure space for the development of their subjective interiority.[8] This tends to empty the public sphere of the substance of meaning and subjectivity. In so doing, he impoverishes the notion of the 'public' as the ground for collective self-understanding and for cultural politics. This presents a failure on the part of Habermas to see how politics is as much about culture as culture is about meanings and identities embodied in symbolic forms (Alexander, 1991; Alejandro, 1993; Chaney, 1993; Peters, 1993; Robbins, 1993; Calhoun, 1994; Cheah, 1995).

Very often, people participate in public discourse with a sense of community on the one hand, and diverse, distinctive self-identities on the other; and in the process of public communication, they may develop new understanding about themselves, the different others and the community as a whole. However, in emphasizing the universal rules and the common humanistic principles that governed critical-rational discourse, Habermas tended to slight the substantive relevance of a society's culture – tradition, history, collective memories and values – to public discourse. In emphazing, moreover, the general common concern that transcended individual differences and particularistic considerations such as gender, class, race and party, he side-stepped the issue of how the latter may come to be excluded or talked about in the public. Thus, as Calhoun suggests (1992), instead of bracketing differences, Habermas should have theorized in more positive terms 'how the public sphere incorporates and recognizes the diversity of identities that people bring to it from their manifold involvements in civil society' (p.3). Indeed politics in the public sphere is, to a large part, about the question of identity. The notion of identity or subjectivity involves an intricate relationship between a sense of communality and a sense of intra-communal, or even personal, diversities, that calls forth a due theoretical emphasis on the constitutive role of culture in our public political life. (This is an issue I will dwell on in my later theoretical elaboration.)

In a nutshell, in Habermas's conceptualization, the ideal public sphere is at once-de-politicized and de-culturalized. It is with this thin notion of the public that, in his neo-Marxist framework of late capitalism, he credits culture as well as the media very little autonomy in contemporary society and saw the political and economic sub-systems as possessing an irrepressible force that overruns the domain of communicative action. He explains the degeneration of the public sphere into one of manipulative publicity in terms of the development of capitalism. On the one hand, the structural separation between the private realm and the public realm broke down in that the tendency towards a concentration of capital intensified class interests, that, together with an 'institutionalized promise of universal accessibility' of the public sphere, resulted in a re-politicization of the public sphere together with increasing state intervention into the private realm.[9] (By 're-politicization', Habermas meant that the public sphere has become the playing field of politics among classes with conflicting interests rather than an authority for it.) On the other hand, the pervasion of the market principle into the mass media has transformed a public of rational debate to an enlarged one of 'culture-consumption' (p.161). In this view, the attempts to affirm or reshape identities through public action are degenerative intrusions due to growing inclusiveness and to interest-based manipulation of opinion by means of symbolic identification.[10]

The problem with this account of the degeneration of the public sphere is that it is based on a conception of symbolic representations as mere camouflages of interests (sheer politics) and as distortions of rational discourse. In this regard, Habermas's approach to the 'public' under-theorizes the symbolic and collective basis of public discourse, and hence the centrality of lived culture and community in public life. In section three, I will argue that the late-Durkheimian critique on the question of community lays the foundation for a more culture-sensitive theory of the public yet without necessarily committing a fallacy of culturalism.

To sum up, Habermas specifies the historical processes that brought about the emergence of the bourgeois public sphere in Europe. In his historical study, the rise of capitalism stood out as a prominent structural factor that facilitated the growth of a private domain of economic exchange that took on a public relevance, and also the expansion of the infrastructure of social communication within the community of citizens. It is this idea of a public sphere being located within particular social structures and developing out of specific historical processes that provides us with an anchorage point to think about the structural and institutional dimensions of the public. However, Habermas's approach to the culture of the public sphere tends to slight the significance of symbolic representations in public discourse and of the media in democratic processes. In particular, the notion of critical rationality, that associated the group of reading and reasoning bourgeois with the public, illuminates little on the cultural and political dynamics in the public sphere in modern society. What we need in place is an approach that allows us to look into the particular political and cultural processes at work that shape the specificities of political struggles, which is to have a great impact on the character of the public sphere today. Of particular interest to us is the issue of how and how far democracy is (not) being established in the process of struggle in relation to the public sphere. In this regard, the third interpretation of the notion of public offers a promising way out, even though it is yet to be further substantiated as a theory. The next section will take a further look at Habermas's theory in connection with the third interpretation.

Publicity, Openness, and the Public Sphere

The third interpretation of the notion of public juxtaposes publicness or publicity against privacy/ secrecy.[11] What is public is what is visible or accessible to all as opposed to what is restricted to a tiny minority or some particular individuals or groups. Such an understanding of the public can be found in different analytical frames such as the public versus the private (Fahey, 1995), the open versus the secret (Bellman, 1981), and the front stage versus the back stage (Goffman, 1959). Under this interpretation, while the specific meanings of the notion are variegated – ranging from a mode of orientation and a zone of social life to an ideological device – they all conceive the public/non-public divide as a cultural and political construction rather than as a clearly defined institutional structure. For instance, in feminist scholarship, the notion has been understood as zones of human life that cut across the conventional distinction between public sphere and private sphere (Marks, 1994; Fahey, 1995), or as a cultural image used to enforce gender segregation in society (Garmanikow et al., 1983; Hansen, 1987; Lopata, 1993). In political sociology, one of the concerns has been with the relative visibility and invisibility of power in the modern state such as the amount of state secrecy (Babbio, 1989; Thompson, 1995; Ku, 1998a). In this third interpretation, unlike the second one, the notion of public is not defined in spatial terms, yet somehow it underlies a specific spatial meaning in terms of some open and shared space in a community where publicness is embedded. In this regard, the media could be seen as embodying a distinctive quality of publicness on both the institutional and the cultural levels. This third interpretation of the public does not necessarily contradict the first one but opens up the debate about how and how far the modern media may be taken as a general public sphere for democratic practices (Habermas, [1962]1989; Gitlin, 1978; Hall et al., 1978; Hall, 1982; Calhoun, 1992; Garnham, 1992; Fraser, 1993; Thompson, 1990, 1995; Dalgren, 1995). Among critical theorists, questions are raised as to whether the media, due to their commercial character as well as hegemonic relationship with dominant groups in society, could function as a sphere for critical and rational discourse. This argument contains certain grains of truth, but in being predisposed to a social-structural mode of theorization, such an approach falls short of grasping and spelling out the cultural and political significance of the publicist quality of the media. My contention is that the media embody an element of publicness in two distinctive ways that have to do with the concept of openness in two related senses of the word – openness versus restrictedness, and openness versus secrecy (Ku 1998a). Turning to critical theory as a point of departure, the following will elaborate these ideas in the context of Habermas's theory of the public sphere, partly as a critique of and partly as an attempt to reformulate it.

Habermas's book on the public sphere ([1962] 1989) does not define the public in terms of openness, yet the idea that openness (in both senses of the word) forms an integral part of the public sphere is implicated in various places. First, on the institutional and cultural levels, publicness is embodied in three institutional criteria in public discussion, one of that is the norm of general accessibility or inclusiveness – 'openness' in the first sense. (The other two are an adherence to the principle of critical-rationality versus status consciousness, and an unprivileged interpretation of the domain of common concern via the commodification of culture products.) In the public sphere, 'everyone had to *be able* to participate' (p.37); but in idealizing the critical-rational nature of discourse conducted in public spaces like salons and coffeehouses, his analysis underscores the oversight that such places for face-to-face discussion are in theory open to anyone but are limited in public accommodation and hence accessibility. According to Thompson (1990), this interpretation of the public sphere is lodged within a conception of publicness that is essentially spatial and dialogical in character – the public as an assembly of individuals meeting in an open or public place where they discuss issues of general concern. In his elaboration, Habermas nonetheless appears to be well aware of the existence of a larger public, that the bourgeois circle was conscious of being part of, that extends beyond the immediate locale of the debating individuals:

> The public of the first generations, even when it constituted itself as a specific circle of persons, was conscious of being part of a larger public. Potentially it was always also a publicist body, as its discussions did not need to remain internal to it but could be directed at the outside world .... (Habermas, [1962]1989:37)

Here, Habermas apparently acknowledges the relevance of media publicity as a feature of the public sphere. However, like others (Bendix 1977 Mayhew 1984; Wuthnow 1989), he conceives the press at that time as carrying out a publicist function for certain activities such as coffee-house discussions, rather than as a social institution having a cultural logic of its own. As I will argue later, due to its publicist nature, media discourse necessarily encompasses the whole citizenry as the 'imagined community' participating in the same discursive context. The media hence become a sphere *of* the public. As a corollary, media discourse necessarily calls forth the imagined 'public' as the prime symbolic reference whereby politics in the public sphere is conducted.

In Habermas's account of the bourgeois public sphere, there is a second context in that the notion of publicity cropped up as an important element in the process of political struggle against the state. In the monarchical states of medieval and early modern Europe, state affairs were conducted largely in the closed setting of the court. Habermas contrasts this practice of state secrecy with the principle of publicity through the press. His historical analysis gives an account of how the press played an indispensable role in the successful struggle against the privilege of secrecy of Parliament in Britain, eventuating the historic transformation of the form of the state in Europe. Through media publicity, not only were parliamentary debates opened up for public scrutiny, but political actors might actively appeal to the public for support in times of internal dissension:

> ... it took the new relationship of Parliament to the public sphere that ultimately led to the full publicity of the parliamentary deliberations to bring about a qualitative difference from the previous system ... The minority that did not get its way in Parliament could always seek refuge in the public sphere and appeal to the judgment of the public. (Habermas [1962] 1989:63)

Clearly, with the emergence of civil society, media publicity has played a prominent and indispensable part in the process of the democratic reformation of the state. In this light, we may go one step further in presuming that to the extent the concept of public sphere entails an element of openness, concomitant with the development of modern media is a democratic struggle for openness versus secrecy in state politics.

This is perhaps not the place to go into the details of the complicated historical processes that have shaped the struggles for state openness. Nevertheless, based on Zaret's (1994, 1996) in-depth historical analysis of the rise of the notion of public, I hazard that the struggles against state secrecy that took place in the early modern period had been deeply connected with a cultural process that marked the change from a discourse of deference to a discourse of democracy. Before the rise of the public sphere, the right to petition was a privilege that allowed people to communicate directly, and hence non-publicly, with the state authority. This kind of privileged, non-public petition was pervaded by deferential rhetoric that 'portrays petitioners as 'humble' suitors who 'pray' and 'supplicate' for relief from grievances' (1996:1514). This contrasted with later petitioning practices that, as a result of the development of printing, 'invoke or imply popular will as a source of authority.' This observation not only lends force to my presumption that the development of the media has been concomitant with a democratic struggle against state secrecy and political privilege, but also gives support to my argument that politics in the public sphere entail a need to make constant reference to the symbolic 'public'.

At this point, we may conclude that on the question of democracy, the political and cultural implications of the notion of openness, that has remained under-theorized in Habermas's framework, are indeed far-reaching. As an open discursive space, the historical significance of the public sphere lies not so much in it being a sphere for critical-rational discourse, as Habermas conceives it to be, as in it being (a) a sphere of the public (b) having been deeply involved in the process of democratic re-formation of the state (Ku, 1998a).

For one thing, struggles against state secrecy and political privilege are democratic in substance whereas the invocation of the public is democratic in form. Here a question arises as to whether the symbolic reference to the public, which is democratic in form, must necessarily entail a democratic content. In theory, with an increasing democratic consciousness of the right and power of citizenship in the ever globalizing world, it is highly likely that the discourse of community would incorporate a democratic discourse of the public. In reality, however, the public of a political community may be represented through democratic, non-democratic or even counter-democratic discourses and practices, depending on the history and culture of the particular community (Ku, 1998b).

Culture, Politics, and the Public Sphere – An Alternative Framework

Citizenship Struggles, State, Civil Society, and Public Sphere

Citizenship originates not only in the modern state but also in the domain of civil society, which refers to the 'community' side of the nation–state construction. In modern democracies, state authority can no longer be taken for granted but has to be established in large measure by continually invoking the consent of the people. As Calhoun (1995) has succinctly pointed out, in modern society, the state no longer defines the political community directly, but perhaps 'interactively' (to put words into his mouth), for 'its legitimacy depended on the acquiescence or support of an already existing political community' (p.235). Apparently, state and civil society constitute two quite different political institutions which underscores possible tensions and dynamism in the relationship between the people and the state over the meaning, form and scope of citizen participation.

Both state and civil society are citizenship institutions but they entail different logics of operation. The state, with its massive bureaucratic, legal and political machinery, has monopolized the power to define the formal boundary of citizen membership. Unlike the state, the civil society of discourse and association is not a formal membership organization; nevertheless, it constitutes an indispensable form of political community from which one derives (and to which one attaches) a sense of membership, togetherness and common belonging. As a concept associated with the state, citizenship is primarily about formal status and rights. However, as a concept associated with civil society, it is at once about practices, identities and struggles among the people as citizens (Alejandro, 1993; Somers, 1993). While public institutions and spaces in general are identified as those belonging to the state and/ or civil society, the public sphere is conceived as originating, more particularly, in the non-state public domain of citizenship, that is, civil society. It originates there for it is where one's sense of membership is derived from day-to-day practice. In other words, it is as members of civil society or national community rather than as state subjectts that people participate in the public sphere.

Politics over Public Credibility

By means of publicity, the public sphere is able to involve the whole community of citizens as symbolic participants in the same context of public discourse. That is, in encompassing the whole citizenry as the 'imagined community'[12] participating in the same discursive context, public discourse necessarily calls forth the 'public' as the prime symbolic reference whereby politics is openly monitored. The 'public' conceived here indicates neither a sum of individual opinions among the citizens nor a kind of empty rhetorics manufactured by the politicians without solid grounding in the culture of a community. Rather, it refers to *a realm of imagined reference to what is regarded as publicly relevant, reasonable and respectable*. It is a realm of imagination but it is rooted in the culture of a community. It delineates a realm of the symbolic that marks off the domain of the publicly credible from that of the publicly incredible. In this regard, it would be better to conceive the public sphere as embodying a cultural force of the symbolic public as such rather than what Habermas believes to be an idealized principle of critical rationality (or a less-than-ideal element of irrationality). In a similar vein, Thompson (1995) has made a sustained argument that the kind of visibility created by the development of mass communication, accompanied by processes of democratization, entails not only power display but also a new form of public accountability, that is very different from that managed as royal display before the subjects in the Middle Ages.[13]

In the public sphere, while members in the community, in terms of ground rules, are equally eligible for participation, what different people say and do in the sphere do not necessarily carry the same moral force. In Habermas's ideal conceptualization, critical rationality is the norm or criteria for discursive practice; under this rule, those who are able to present a rational and most convincing argument will win the debates. The notion of critical rationality is meant to lay down a normative principle whereby disputes may be arbitrated in a democratic way. However, rather ironically, the notion in Habermas's formulation, as a number of scholars have pointed out, is acultural and even counter-democratic in that it assumes the then mode of debate – one represented predominantly by white, middle-class male – as an ideal universal norm without adequately taking into account the lived cultures of a particular community and also the multiplicities of discourses among different subaltern groups within the community. As a result, the ideal public sphere is de-politicized and de-culturalized. In this section, drawing on the growing body of works in cultural sociology, I seek to propose an alternative concept of public credibility to capture the political and cultural dynamics in the public sphere. Such a concept will be elaborated in a theory of politics of public credibility to explain how the symbolic 'public' shapes politics while being shaped by them.

Contrary to Habermas and many other social theorists, cultural sociologists emphasize the semiotic basis of social life and also the relative autonomy of culture as a symbolic system (Durkheim, [1912]1965; Sewell, 1985; Alexander, 1988, 1990; Kane, 1991). In very brief terms, the symbolic system of culture has an internal logic within it that structures cultural and moral meanings in terms of differences, oppositions and relations, for example, the famous late-Durkheimian dichotomy between the sacred and the profane. As a system of moral significance, culture not only gives meanings to action but can also shape it. In Geertz's words, it is both a model 'of' and a model 'for' action (1973). The culture system is relatively autonomous in the sense that its internal structure has a certain degree of tenacity about it that renders itself a causal force over action. Nevertheless, to the extent that culture is constituted through concrete practices, it is not completely immutable to changes and may be transformed in the course of action (Kane, 1997).

Drawing on the arguments by cultural sociologists, I argue that at the heart of the public sphere is a cultural force of the symbolic 'public' that both gives shape to politics and is itself shaped through political practices. The symbolic public is understood, to reiterate, as a realm of imagined reference to what is regarded as publicly relevant, reasonable and respectable as it is defined within a particular community at a particular time. In so far as the public sphere is a sphere of the public, discursive practices in the public sphere would concern one's ability to speak and act in the name of the 'public'. In the public sphere of politics, what different people say and do would carry different moral weight depending on how far it is perceived as falling in line with the 'public'. The 'public' delineates a realm of the symbolic that marks off the domain of the publicly credible from that of the publicly incredible for and through political practices.[14] *Public credibility* is an evaluative claim, by the public of citizens, of moral status and authority about particular actors, institutions or the whole government on the basis of their public presentations and performances at specific times.[15] It is a moment-by-moment evaluative claim which is established in and through a discourse of community that consists of a set of discursive themes, codes and narratives about the values, traditions and experiences collectively remembered, treasured, lived out and celebrated in a community. In this light, just as public credibility is established through a discourse of community, it can be undermined through a discourse of anti-community that profanes or contravenes shared beliefs.[16] (One good example may be found in the increasingly prominent idea of political correctness that guards against any intentional or unintentional act of discrimination against any kind of people.) It is in essence a moral force; under the force of the symbolic 'public' as such, it is required that the actors be able to conduct public discourses and shape their course of action in line with the moral boundary of publicness – that may be re-defined in the process – so as to keep up their public credibility. This is what I call politics of public credibility. Put together, we may understand the public sphere as *the shared communicative space within a community where politics as politics of public credibility are conducted.*

By 'public', it does not mean that cultural meanings are uncontested and unchanging; rather, the diverse or even conflicting meanings are interwoven into a web of publicly coded discourses that makes public contestations possible and necessary.[17] For example, for a political actor entrusted with a certain degree of power and authority, whether an act done in private (for example, an extra-marital affair) should bear public relevance or not, and whether those regarded as relevant to public concern are believed to be publicly acceptable and respectable or not are often a matter of much open dispute. The stronger the civil society is, and the more political freedom is allowed in it, the more likely that public contestations will take place. In the face of open challenges, there is always a need for the actors to maintain or increase their public credibility. In this way, media publicity helps in the continuous operation of the symbolic 'public' in the political process. In day-to-day practice, the multiple discourses in the public sphere simultaneously constitutes and invokes the authority of the 'public' as a symbolic force that informs and shapes political struggles.

In public discourse, the symbolic reference to the 'public' as well as the social basis for public credibility has its sources of imagery in (a) the store of symbols and symbolic representations in a culture, and (b) the symbolic representations of public opinion at particular times. The public of a political community may be represented through democratic, non-democratic or even counter-democratic discourses and practices, depending on the history and culture of the particular community. Values, beliefs and meanings are embodied in symbols and symbolic representations that, given their lived meaningfulness, furnish the powerful cognitive, emotive and evaluative means by that people make sense of social reality and define their sense of self. Public life is embedded in a thick web of symbolic meanings, and it is often through dramatization of characters and events that they become a compelling force in the politics of public credibility. Political actors, as public figure, are looked on as symbolic characters performing in the innumerable public dramas that constitute the lived context of public life. Along this line of thinking, Chaney (1993), drawing on Klapp (1962), describes the presentation of identity for public figures as a performance staged out of dramatic resources that is 'liable to be ruptured or to be re-framed in ways that they might or might not be able to control' (p.148). As public symbols, none the less, the actors' character is no mere fantastic construction or inauthentic make-believe; quite to the contrary, it has a substantial existence in public life:

> it is the wealth of tangible detail we know about the lives of celebrities, it is the consistency with that their personal relationships are caught up in the web of public identity, all of this gives them an existential reality that is perhaps more substantial than everyday experience. (p.145)

In this light, publicity itself must entail a process of symbolic representation of identities. In publicity, as Warner (1992) points out, 'we are given a stake in the imaginary of a mass public in a way that dictates a certain appeal not so much for (a particular person) but for the kind of public figure of that he (or she) is exemplary' (p.391). Through their symbolic identities, public actors can provide a means of identification for the people belonging to the same political community. Thus to ask about the kinds of identification required or allowed in the sphere of publicity is to understand both the meaning structure through that a collective identity is constructed and the wider symbolic conditions under that the 'public'can be performed.

The Paradox of Community cum Differences

At this point, a question perhaps arises as to how we may reconcile the time-honored paradox of differences with communality. To resolve this problem, we need to conceive the 'public' not so much as indicating sameness in an essentialist sense as referring to a discursive construction of a collectivity out of lived experiences. In fact, in adopting a discursive conception of the public, we will be in a better theoretical position to conceive differences as part and parcel of the discourse of community. Firstly, within a discursive framework, it becomes conceivable that the definition of community could become a matter of politics involving different or even conflicting interpretations. Indeed a large part of politics is about the struggles over the interpretation of what the collective 'we' consists in. The construction of a collective 'we', that is juxtaposed against a 'they' or an outsider, is a central cultural mechanism whereby symbolic and political boundaries are maintained between groups of people. Hence the construction of a collective identity. This is often achieved through some recurrent symbolic representations of the common past, present and future of the people concerned and also of the common culture that they have shared. As such, it is not only a symbolic community of shared history, tradition and memories, but also a moral community of shared values and beliefs. Owing to divergent interpretations, the substantive meanings of the 'we' image are nonetheless subject to both conflicts and change.

Secondly, I propose that the continuous definition of the collective 'we' entails not only a discourse of commonness but also a discourse of community in relational terms, both socially and morally. Indeed it is the idea of relationality that allows us to grapple with the question of differences by conceiving the community as organized around contrasts and related differences. In the public sphere, especially in certain dramatic moments of conflicts and crises, actors are often understood not only as socially differentiated groups or categories but also as morally distinct yet deeply related characters who join together to advance the action line of a narrative or drama. More specifically, Klapp (1962, 1964) speaks of social values in relation to the socially produced images of hero, villain, victim and fool that connote respectively the ideas of praise, condemnation, sympathy and ridicule. Put in relational terms, a moral order may be conceived as an order of juxtapositions between certain moral types such as hero (heroine) versus villain, villain versus victim, hero (heroine) versus fool, and so on and so forth. In day-to-day happenings in the public sphere, it is quite inevitable that a process of moral typification will take place that imbues social relationships with moral meanings, hence the status of public credibility. For example, in social movements fighting for certain citizenship rights vis-à-vis the state, the citizens concerned are often presented as the victims of the policy of the state who incurs social injustice in protecting the interests of particular classes at the expense of the general populace. Or, in feminists movements fighting against gender inequalities in society, the activists usually present women as being disadvantaged, hence victimized, under a patriarchal system in that men are more privileged. Hero/ heroine and villain are two extreme categories that suggest, respectively, very high versus very low public credibility; the category of fool lies somewhere in between on the scale of public credibility for it is associated with stupidity or incompetence rather than moral vices; finally, the category of victim is less an indicator of credibility status than a pointer to the existence of villain. Apparently, moral characterization in such differential or relational terms constitutes a crucial cultural mechanism in the public sphere whereby one's public credibility is established or undermined.

Thirdly, while we understand that the stock of public symbols in use remains hermeneutically bounded to the experience of a society, different groups may have different interpretations or articulations of the meanings of these symbols, and as such public discourse is often an amalgamation of 'dissimilar meanings ... worked into systems of interacting symbols' (Geertz, 1973:209). In other words, a public interpretation of the collective 'we' will present itself as a structured social dialogue with the competing interpretations in the form of intertextual references. It is this dialogical aspect in the form of intertextuality that forms another basis for the formation of imagined community. For example, in public discourse, while the actors have their own self-positioning strategies (for example, positioning themselves as heroes/ heroines in contradistinction to their opponents), they will be further looked on by the others as embodying the moral qualities of true heroes (heroines), just fools or even villains. In the final analysis, it is the 'public' of intertwined discourses by multiple actors that determines the moral meanings, hence the status of public credibility versus incredibility, of the public characters as well as their action.

In sum, in politics of public credibility, discourses in the public sphere constitute a sense of community not so much by homogenizing differences as by (i) interweaving into a public web of intertextual references (ii) the competing interpretations over what the collective 'we' consists in, (iii) that entails a discourse not only of commonness but also of relations. Substantively, the 'public' constitutes a meeting site between the discourse of community and the discourse of democracy, which may or may not overlap with each other in empirical situations. Through media publicity, the competing interpretations of the order of moral relationships in society presented by different social actors will constitute the symbolic 'public' that subjects the political actors concerned to the continuous test of public credibility.

Discursive Construction of Public Opinion

Finally, just as the culture of 'public' is conceived as a realm of lived experience of a political community, public opinion, by the same token, must be understood as a dynamic but structured meaning system which has its roots in the culture and history of a society. In a hermeneutical sense, public opinion represents the concerns, the worries, the hopes and the beliefs of the people in a community at a specific time. In this sense, public opinion is no different from public culture in its essential quality, except that it is often referred to as a time-specific crystallization of the diverse opinions of the public as they are expressed in various forms. In other words, it is a more self-conscious discursive construction of what one believes to be the prevalent opinion in society at a specific time, rather than simply 'a collection of individual opinion' as the empiricists would have us believe.[18] While the diverse opinions of the public form the basis for the construction of public opinion, these diverse opinions must also be understood in relation to the discursive conditions under which the 'public' can be performed. As Dalgren (1995) put it,

> The common notion of opinion as simply something existing in people, to be captured by multiple choice questions, is indeed misguided, for it ignores the dynamics whereby meaning circulates, is acted upon, and revised, to result in political interpretation and will formation. (p.21)

The significance underlying such a discursive conception of public opinion is three-fold. First, it understands public opinion as both shaping and shaped by the culture and politics of the public sphere. Indeed politics would become a rather mechanical and straightforward business if politicians could either manipulate public opinion completely to their own advantage or simply go to find out what the state of public opinion were and then curry favour with it. The truth is that, that different political actors would draw on the same symbol in public discourse such as 'democracy' or 'national interest' does not necessarily follow that they would be looked on by the public as equally credible in making a claim to it. If there is a nuance in public reception, then why? As Kertzer (1988) points out, though a politician may manipulate symbols and rites, s/he does not totally control them, because 'they have a history of connotations and emotions for the people who look on' (p.90), and because the people have 'their own material experiences, which are themselves perceived in good part through a symbolic filter' (p.5). This leads us back to the notion of symbolic identification.

   Secondly, a discursive conception of public opinion brings to the fore the fact that public opinion is not a thing out there for us to find out, for it will alter its shape when seen from different angles or represented in different modes. Indeed 'public opinion', as a discursive construction, is worked upon through numerous signification practices, by the political actors, the polling agents, the media and so on. In asserting this ontological as well as epistemological position, I do not mean to deny the value of opinion polls, but to contend that opinion polling, with its own mode of operation, (i) may result in different patterns of responses pending the ways the questions are framed, and (ii) is one only discursive form, among others, whereby public opinion may be represented. While the arithmatics got from the multiple-choice format gives a quick and handy summary of the orientations of the people, the most vivid representation of the *lived* quality of public opinion, as I will argue in the next chapter, takes the form of narrative discourse or narrative dialogue, which is also capable of accomodating numerical highlights.

Thirdly, as a logical extension of the second claim, a discursive conception helps put into light the idea that any kinds of presentation of public opinion, including numbers, are symbolic in nature. Just as a symbol has the properties of 'condensation', 'multivocality', and 'ambiguity' (Kertzer, 1988), 'public opinion' as a symbolic representation lacks a single precise meaning but embodies a diversity of meaning. As such, the symbolic value of public opinion data, as Herbst (1993) has pointed out, will emerge only in the context of public discourse: 'It is only in the context of political discourse and ritual that the true rhetorical value of numbers becomes apparent' (p.29). It applies to not only polled opinions but also other forms of opinion expression. This then brings us back to the first premise that, public opinion, instead of being simply the sum of individual opinions, is constructed in and through a specific public sphere. Indeed, in day-to-day politics, the image of the public depicted through the media often becomes a most important reference point whereby the political actors, the media and the public itself understand the collective views and sentiments of the people (Bogart, 1972; Lang and Lang, 1983).

The symbolic nature in the presentation of public opinion is further complicated by the fact that public opinion may be expressed in different ways, ranging from special columns (in the printed media) or direct interviews to street protests or opinion polls publicized through the media. Given the diversities of the modes of public opinion expression, it is not unusual, though not very often, to find in public discourses a discrepancy between the author's own moral position attached to a set of sacred symbols and the proclaimed 'public opinion' or 'popular will' that is attached to another set of values. Nevertheless, no matter how conflicting they are, they will often be accomodated in the same sphere of public discourse in the form of intertextual reference or dialogue – specifically in terms of the centre-periphery juxtaposition. (I will elaborate this idea also in the next theoretical chapter.) What I am suggesting here is that instead of finding out public opinion in an empiricist fashion, we must devise a framework as well as a method to analyse the dynamics involved in the public sphere of discursive formation in which 'public opinion' is embedded.

Still, there is the question of change. What explains the temporal dynamics in politics in that the meaning of an event or of a person could change over time. For instance, it may be that a certain position held by a certain group was looked upon as daringly progressive at a particular time, but the same position held by the same group was regarded as cowardly conservative at another time, or vice versa. The questions are, what constitutes the moral force of the 'public' at a particular time and what explains its changes over time?

In brief, my mode of theorization will share with the late-Durkheimian formulation that 'community' has a real existence in terms of the relatively structured quality in the culture and the material organization of our social life, and that it is being continually reproduced through processes of ritualistic enactment. Nonetheless, my theoretical strategy will depart from this culturalistic tendency by highlighting the facts of continuity and consistency in communal life on the one hand, and of heterogeneity, conflict and change on the other. This will require an adequate theorization of (i) 'action' in all its symbolic and material relevance, and (ii) the temporal quality in action as well as communal life. 'Narrative', I venture to argue, is the fundamental symbolic form whereby the temporal dynamics of public life is experienced; and for this reason, it is the chief discursive mode whereby public discourse is conducted. 'Narrative' as a symbolic form ties together our emotional and moral experience of time, events, characters/ relationships in a most coherent and powerful way. In the next chapter, I will incorporate the theory of the public into a theory of narrative progression.

Notes

1. See Mills (1956), pp.303-4.
2. See Thompson (1990), p.116.
3. The definition of the concept 'civil society' is itself subject to dispute even within the Hegelian-Marxian tradition. While Hegel defines civil society broadly as all the spheres of society juxtaposed to the state, Gramsci (1971) includes family and politics in it but not the capitalist economy. In a different vein, Habermas sees the private realm as comprising both the domain of market economy ('civil society' understood in a narrow sense) and the intimate sphere of personal relations anchored in the conjugal family. For detailed discussion of the concept, see Cohen and Arato (1994), Chandhoke (1995) and Hall (1995). For a review of the liberal conception of the public-private distinction, see Benn and Gaus (1983).
4. Habermas ([1962]1989), pp. 36-37.
5. The term 'membership organization' here is borrowed from Brubaker (1992) but it also conntes certain meanings which are quite absent in his definition. In his book, he argues that the modern nation-state forms not only a territorial organization but also a membership organization with a set of formal membership criteria as well as institutional practices differentiating a citizen (insider) from a non-citizen (outsider). He has focused on the formal or state-endorsed aspect of membership; nevertheless, from both a conceptual and a historical points of view, citizenship originates not only in the modern state but also in the domain of civil society, which refers to the 'community' side of the nation-state construction.
6. If it is unsatisfactory to define the public-private divide in terms of the state – non-state dichotomy, it becomes doubtful as to whether it is a necessarily fruitful undertaking to conceive the market as belonging to the private domain. If the notion of the public has been found ambiguous, the meaning of the private as a structural category is in fact even less distinct.
7. The bourgeois public sphere is not a universal given, but was the product of certain long-term historical processes, which Habermas located between the late Middle Ages and the eighteenth century. By and large, the bourgeois public sphere of critical-rational discourse was facilitated by the development of an independent press, which was free from state censorship, founded on commercial capitalism and had its cultural nourishment from the literary and intimate spheres.
8. Ibid., p.54. Regarding this, Calhoun (1994) has poignantly criticized that Habermas 'presumes that the private sphere provides it with fully formed subjects with settled identities and capacities' (p. 23).

9.   Ibid., p.145.
10. Ibid., p.206 and p.221.
11. For discussion on the conceptual distinction between privacy and secrecy, see Warren and Laslett (1977).
12. In his discussion on television and the public sphere, Dahlgren (1995) suggests moving from the category of private audience to citizen in the sense of a public of interacting social agents. In a similar vein, Skogerbo (1990) emphasizes the image of the citizen in place of the consumer. For the concept of 'imagined community', see B. Anderson (1983).
13. J. Thompson (1995).
14. This position comes close to Chaney's idea (1993) of the public being 'a rhetorical figure, both as a mode of address and as a form of social being' (p. 127). See, also Robbins (1993), for his remarks on the newly accentuated relationship between culture and the public sphere.
15. The conception of politics as public performance is based on a dramaturgical understanding of culture. For an exemplification of the dramaturgical tradition, see Goffman (1959) and Turner (1974), Chaney (1993).
16. Durkheim's late work (1965[1912]) on religion presents an insightful analysis of the internal structure and processes of culture in terms of the sacred–profane dichotomy and on the basis of communal experiences. For pioneering efforts in developing a late-Durkheimian theory on culture, see Alexander (1988) and Kane (1991).
17. In a similar vein, Fraser (1995) suggests 'replacing the homogenizing, ideological category of 'community' with the potentially more critical category 'public' in the sense of a discursive arena for staging conflicts' (p. 192).
18. For illustration of the empiricist tradition, see the early works by Klapper (1960), and Lazarsfeld and Gaudet (1948).

3 Narratives and Politics

As I have discussed in chapter two, the notion of public sphere presupposes the existence of a public in the form of what Anderson (1983) calls an 'imagined community'. It refers to the largest possible communicative space within a community of citizens wherein public discourse is conducted in the name of the public. For 'public' to be understood as a discursive force, it should not be taken as reflecting the existence of a homogeneous collectivity, but rather as referring to a set of different yet overlapping discourses on what is believed to be the existing versus the right order of social and moral relationships in one's society.

In this chapter, I am going to add in a 'time' dimension in the political process which looks at the narrative contexts of the force the 'public'. Such narrative contexts would map out the moral underpinnings of political authority, status, and relationships in a community. They would also capture the dynamics of change upon reciprocal actions, novel revelations, and retrospective reassessment as well as projective refiguration. This new way of looking at the question of politics, I contend, will help us understand more about, on the one hand, how cultural and political processes intersect in public discourse on a theme, issue or event over a continuous span of time, and on the other hand, how, in a dramaturgical way, the changing collective imagery of public opinion as it is represented in and through public discourse comes to exercise a symbolic power over political action.

This chapter consists of three sections. The first section introduces the concept of narrative and analyse the narrative structure of public discourse. The second section discusses the mechanism of symbolic mediation of political relationships – power, authority, status, solidarity and differences – in terms of the notion of narrative genre. Finally, the third section elaborates a theory of narrative progression in more dynamic terms, theorizing a particular instance in which an event starts off as a heroic romance and then develops into an irony. In my theoretical elaboration, I explain how in the public sphere, the changing narrative construction of events hinges on the interplay among three factors: (i) the value themes or codes prevailing in the community, (ii) the modes of narration used in public discourse, and (iii) the mobilizational strategies of the political actors.

Narrative, Experience, and Meaning

Recently social scientists, drawing on cultural theories, have focused on the symbolic structures and processes underlying cultural formation. In particular, the concept of narrative[1] which indicates a specific kind of meaning structure has attained increasing theoretical significance in a number of areas of study, such as collective mobilization (Hart, 1992; Couto, 1993; Fine, 1995), class formation (Somers, 1992; Steinmetz 1992), identity construction (Alexander and Smith, 1993), news convention (Schudson, 1982), cultural meanings (Kane, 1994; Somers, 1995), the construction and resolution of crisis (Jacobs, 1996), and the creation of social solidarity (Jacobs and Smith, 1997). In most of these works, the concept has been applied to show how events are selected into and interpreted as meaningful constructions which in turn contribute to identity formation and enable social action. While the application of the concept produces insightful works, one problem, nonetheless, with the concept in the diverse ways it is being used lies in a lack of specificity about it. As Sewell (1992) has succinctly pointed out,

> One (problem) is that they use the term narrative to signify many different things: a universal category of human cultures, conventions of storytelling, epistemological and ontological assumptions, accounts of life experiences, ideological structures intended to motivate the rank and file of social movements. Although each of these uses makes sense in its particular context, one sometimes feels that using *narrative* to cover all of them dilutes the meaning of the term ... If the term *narrative* is to retain analytical bite, we probably need to be more attentive to what is specifically narrative in the texts and practices under study. (pp.486-7)

In this light, this chapter proposes a way of understanding narrative which will attend to both its structural quality and its temporal dynamics. The following section will discuss these two aspects in greater depth.

Temporal Dynamics in Human Experiences

> Time becomes human time to the extent that it is organised after the manner of a narrative; narrative, in turn, is meaningful to the extent that it portrays the features of temporal experience. (Ricoeur, 1985, p.3)

Temporality is a primary dimension of human existence. Our sense of self, on both the individual and the collective levels, is always founded upon some forms of unifying grasp of the happenings in the past, the present and the future. In more concrete terms, the experience of how we come to be what we are now is essentially a story of certain meaningfully connected events and people. As Ricoeur (1985) put its, 'It is in telling our own stories that we give ourselves an identity. We recognize ourselves in the stories that we tell about ourselves' (p.214). In this sense, stories or narratives are not only told but lived (MacIntyre, 1984; Carr, 1986; Kerby, 1991; Somers 1994).

Narrative is a meaning structure that organizes the human experience of time by attributing significance to individual actions and events according to their effect on the whole (Barthes, 1975; Culler, 1975; Fisher, 1987; Polkinghorne, 1988). In Ricoeur's metaphor, narrative is a thread that unites otherwise disparate happenings into the significance of a development, a directionality, or a destiny. It not only delivers over the past but also mediates our aspirations and desires, imaginatively expressing a possible future with its attendant joys and hardships. Within a narrative frame, a single event is often experienced as having a specific temporal structure which unfolds itself as a story through a chain of small episodes. For instance, to a straightforward question like 'why do you take social work as your career' or 'why did you get married', it is not unusual that the answer would entail a configuration of a set of episodes and characters into a storylike nexus involving temporal, thematic and emotional connections among them. Extending Geertz's example of the wink that we discuss in chapter two, we may add in a temporal dimension which connects the symbolic meaning of the gesture to a background context of foes turned friends in a relationship. In this case, the gesture does not simply indicate friendliness or wittiness in a general sense, but signifies a specific joyful turn of readiness and initiative for reconciliation. It is this special temporal quality that gives our experience an added sense of depth.

In a more profound way, the temporal quality in human experience can be understood as one of extended awareness. That is to say, our experience of time is not simply successive but integrative.[2] While the meaning or significance of an episode is produced by the part it plays in relation to other episodes in an unfolding event, a particular event, together with other events, will form part of a larger, still developing story which constitutes our sense of a changing yet continuous self. In terms of temporal development, the realm of meaning is continuously enlarged by new experiences which at the same time deepens our understanding of old experiences. As we progress through a host of events, each new situation is construed as a revised configuration of the entire sequence up to that point, which would also lead to revised expectations of the outcomes. In more analytical terms, as a temporal experience, our understanding of events is always informed both projectively and retrospectively (see Leitch, 1986). On the one hand, authoritative insight is always retrospective in the sense that later judgments, made in the light of new experience, can overturn earlier judgments. Indeed prior events and causes are so only retrospectively, in a reading back from the end. On the other hand, Leitch, drawing on Fish (1980), argues that it would be misleading to analyse narrative solely from the perspective of later comprehension, for 'everything a (reader) does, even if he later undoes it, is a part of the 'meaning experience' and should not be discarded'. In fact, a reading of a story text is always guided by a prospective sense of its teology. In Brooks's words, this is 'anticipation of retrospection' what remains to be read will restructure the provisional meanings of the already read. This projective sense of teleology, which is itself contingent and timebound, gradually becomes retrospective as more of the story passes into one's own past.[3]

In a nutshell, the realm of meaningful experience integrates, moment by moment, recollections of the past, perceptions of the present and expectations about the future.[4] As such, the meaning of a specific event will change as its relations with or significance to other events changes, as parts of a continuously enlarging whole.

A word of clarification. To say that human beings experience the temporal dynamics of social life in the form of narrative does not amount to saying that our experiences with the numerous episodes and events will necessarily form into a coherent whole. There is no denying that confusion and inconsistency are a fact of life, and I have no intention of theorizing away their existence. What I am proclaiming here is that we human beings, out of our need for understanding the host of episodes and events surrounding us, do have a narrativizing inclination; and it is absolutely conceivable that in the very search of narrative coherence, we would feel confused when we find it rather impossible to integrate an event into what we believe to be an intelligible story.[5] That is to say, confusion or ambiguity forms an intrinsic part in our narrative experience rather than being outside or contrary to it. It is our task, then, to theorize the dynamics and varieties found in our narrative experience.

The Narrative Structure of Public Discourse

In the public sphere, a discourse is usually a discourse on a cultural theme, social issue or political event, which is constituted in an intertwinement between cultural codes and narrative modes. Alexander and Smith (1993) conceive discourse as sets of binary codes which members use to typify, define and symbolically locate other actors and institutions. Jacobs (1996), drawing on Alexander (1992), further argues that codes have an analytic autonomy which are only made concrete by being specified and elaborated into narratives. In this section, I am going to explain how narrative form is meaning-laden in itself (White, 1987) while allowing an intertwinement with different thematic structures to produce the meanings of a narrative in all its structural and thematic specificities.

Narrative meaning consists in the significance the events have for the narrator in relation to a particular theme (Culler, 1975; Kermode, 1979; Bruner, 1986; Polkinghorne, 1988; Somers, 1994). A theme is not only cognitive in nature but also has a deep moral meaning which can best be captured by means of the late-Durkheimian frame of 'the sacred versus the profane'.[6] From this dichotomous or relational scheme comes the whole elaborate structure in human cultures of good versus bad, right versus wrong, high versus low, bright versus dark, strong versus weak, so on and so forth. In essence, this is a scheme of moral relationality (binary moral codes) the specificities of which may, upon interpretation, change over time and vary between groups within a society. In terms of narrative structure, plot is the temporal projection of such thematic structures whereas character play the dual role as the symbolic embodiment of the themes and as actor propelling the thematic plot forward.

Plot, character and mood are analytical components in a narrative that form an inter-related whole. Different ways of integrating the three components with regard to certain events constitute very different narrative experiences. It is then our theoretical task to delineate some sort of classification scheme that will encompass the diversities in our narrative experiences as far as the current state of knowledge allows us. In this chapter, I will draw on the system of narrative modes developed in the Western tradition consisting of the four genres of romance, tragedy, comedy, and irony/ satire. Despite a possible western bias, the advantage for doing so is four-fold. First, a narrative genre of this kind integrates plot, character and mood in a most structured and unifying way. In drawing on two of the four genres in their explanation of political culture, Jacobs and Smith (1997) argue that '(g)enre gives force to representation, making narrative events concrete by linking temporal and spatial relationships to a plot and its characters' (p.67). Secondly, the narrative genre is a meaning-laden discursive form which at the same time allows an intertwinement with different thematic structures. Thirdly, it is able to integrate the concepts of structure and process in a way that is compatible with a theory of narrative progression that I am going to develop. Finally, the whole system covers a wide range of narrative experiences by making fine nuances between apparently similar narrative structures.

In terms of affect or mood, these narrative modes can be explained as temporal expressions of emotional attachments of desire and then fulfillment (romance, comedy), of grandeur and then dignified pathos (tragedy), and of hope and then ridicule or repugnance (irony/ satire). In comedy, the essential element of plot is reconciliation or the restoration of order involving a hero/ heroine seeking to achieve this and an obstructing character standing in the way of the action. The obstacles to the hero/ heroine's will form the action and the overcoming of them the comic resolution. In romance, the essential element of plot is adventure or quest (say, the establishment of a new order) involving conflicts primarily between a charismatic protagonist and a villainous antagonist, and secondarily between a cowardly fool and the romantic-heroic protagonist: 'Characters tend to be either for or against the quest. If they assist it they are idealized as simply gallant or pure; if they obstruct it they are caricatured as simply villainous or cowardly' (Frye, 1957:195). The beginning in romance sees the courageous hero/ heroine challenging the existing order in a most exhilarating manner and the ending the victorious celebration of the romantic cause against the assault of reality. A tragedy may be understood as an unfulfilled romance. In tragedy, the hero/ heroine provokes enmity or inherits a situation of enmity, and the return of the avenger constitutes the catastrophe. The tragic hero/heroine is very great in contrast with other characters, but there is something on the side of him/ her such as accident, necessity or circumstance that causes his/ her downfall. (In this sense, a tragic hero/ heroine is a heroic victim.) It is with this tragic structure that a sense of pathos is created at the end, which makes light of the response of moral indignation and hence emotionally blurring the sacred-profane distinction. Finally, irony represents a gap between the way things ought or have expected to be and the way they are or turn out to be. *Victimization* is a distinctive theme in irony, which presupposes a certain kind of intended or unintended villainy in some actors. Irony can be divided into comic-irony, romantic-irony and satirical irony, which have different kinds of affective responses going with them such as disappointment, deep despair, repugnance, ambivalence, and a sense of helplessness developing into indifference. Comic-irony and romantic-irony refer to the gap between reality and the respective comic and romantic projections whereas satirical irony points to a more militant form of irony – cynicism – based on a lack of faith in what the others claim to be a comic or romantic cause. As a militant irony, satire often presents itself as a parody of comedy or romance. In most instances, what a satire needs is not only a villain vis-à-vis a victim but also a fool (naive follower) vis-à-vis a mock hero/ heroine – the dingier the hero/ heroine, the sharper the irony.

The Idea of Narrative Progression

In the public sphere, do events display the qualities of the actors involved or those of the audience? Literary and cultural theorists such as Leitch (1986) and Phelan (1989) who insist on the 'transactional' or 'rhetorical' nature of storytelling would see them as inseparable, for either would be incomplete without the other. A public event's tellability, as their arguments may imply, is based on its audience's narrativity.[7] For instance, the pathos of one's failure or mishap may be implicit in the text, but only a sympathetic audience can release it. In particular, Phelan's theory of narrative progression attempts to sensitize the analysts to the *experiential dynamics* of reading a text without slighting its structured quality. His theory is meant to show 'the way texts work on readers and the way readers may exercise power over texts' (p.74). Thus as a critique of structuralism, which emphasizes the formal features of a text, his model is double-layered in that it conceives the text as containing not just the patterns of tensions and resolutions central to plot development, but also the audience's responses to those patterns:

> The concept of progression assumes that the narrative text needs to be regarded as the fusion two structures: (1) the narrative structure per se ... or what I call the pattern of instabilities and tensions; and (2) the sequence of responses to that structure that the text calls forth from the authorial audience. (p.115)

With regard to the second point, Phelan calls our attention to the emotional quality of experience. Indeed human emotions are very powerful forces for emotional states are as much evaluative as affective – the affect of, say, hope, shame, anger, anxiety or joy indicates what we value dearly and hence potently influences our judgement and action. Thus as Taylor (1985) has pointed out, emotional experiences are not only the result of interpretive emplotment but also the occasion for it.[8] The important implication is that, people are not just passive spectators of scripted events, but play an active part in shaping the specific narrative form of these events while responding to them.

In terms of emplotment, for instance, the audience's role is not limited to responding to the movement of the plot. What is more engaging, according to Phelan, is the 'accompanying sequence of attitudes' that the audience is asked to take toward the pattern of conflicts and tensions. In plot development, the opening event at the beginning establishes a conflict or a promise around a theme, which inclines both the actors and the audience to wonder in what way the conflict will be resolved, or how the expectations it arouses will be fulfilled. The power of the middle lies in its guiding the desires or fears aroused by the beginning while making a desired ending a matter of degree of possibility. Finally, the ending will be judged as to whether it fulfills the promise of the specific complications. In this light, audiences are not passive spectators but play an active part in their affective evaluation of the events. It is the development on thematic structure along with the 'accompanying sequence of attitudes' that indicates what an event really means to the people – whether it will be regarded as morally uplifting, pretentious or 'no big deal'. This is what I mean by narrative mood.

Characters are the agents that advance the plot while engaging the emotions of the audience. As the embodiment of thematic values, they are inevitably embedded with moral meanings. Klapp (1962, 1964) speaks of social values in relation to the socially produced images of hero (heroine), villain, victim and fool, which connote respectively the ideas of praise, condemnation, sympathy and ridicule. Typification by these relational codes entails strong social approbation and disapprobation and is therefore a chief means by which individuals can feel themselves and others to be different members of the same moral collectivity. Besides the thematic function of characters, the mimetic component in characterization, i.e. a character's attributes as well as their bearing on his/her actions, plays an important part in narrative progression. Drawing its strength from the emotional involvement of the audience that comes from viewing the characters as plausible persons, the mimetic component will influence their judgements, expectations, attitudes and desires about the characters and the conflicts they face:

> The pattern of judgments, fears, hopes, desires, expectations, and so on that typically but not exclusively cluster around the mimetic component is as much a part of the dynamics of reading as the sequence of actions in which the character participates. (Phelan, p.115)

In most but not necessarily all instances, the mimetic traits could perform thematic functions.[9] A progression may develop different thematic functions from different attributes, which will work together as part of the narrative's exploration of a general theme. As such, the audience will have to consistently reposition their mimetic engagement into a broader thematic context.

Thematic emplotment, mood creation and characterization are matters of interpretation in terms of relational categories. What seems to be a sacred ideal, a heroic act, or a joyful moment may look profane, foolhardy (or even hideous), or worrying to others. Thus it is not uncommon to find the existence of competing or conflicting interpretations of the 'same' set of events. Plot development is therefore complicated by the fact that the plot of action is propelled forward by numerous sub-plots of action by actors who find themselves playing different roles in a plot or who are configuring different plots of action around different themes. In public discourse, these different interpretations of relationality will get intertwined in that they may be conjoined with, embedded into or made to alternate with one another (see Prince 1982). In the course of events, it is by means of this kind of intertextual complications that new themes or new plot lines will emerge which then change the meaning of the opening event as well as the subsequent happenings.

In sum, narrative is a concept of both structure and processes. Our cognitive, emotional and moral responses are framed within narrative structures which are always informed retrospectively and projectively. My contention is that it is with a due emphasis on the temporal dynamics of experience with reference to the full range of its moral as well as emotional quality that we will be able to explain and demonstrate 'the way texts work on readers and the way readers may exercise power over texts'. This is particularly pertinent to our understanding of the dynamic relations between politics and public opinion.

A narrative, which incorporates the cognitive, affective and evaluative dimensions into our social experience of time all at once, is a dynamic account of moral order and moral relationships. A narrative in a particular mode such as romance or irony not only indicates what we value and how we define our relationships with others at a particular time, but also captures the changing meaning of events, situations and relationships at different points of time. Indeed it is only from a narrative perspective that we can talk of causal changes, new realizations, growth or deterioration of hopes disillusioned, aspirations fulfilled, weakness accepted, trust betrayed (hence friends turned foes), convictions found doubtful, so on and so forth. Without narration the past would sink into an obscurity of forgetfulness wherein everything becomes equal (Kerby, 1991). Without narration, the past would sink into an emptiness of irrelevance which has no bearing on the present or the future. In *The Great War and Modern Memory*, for instance, Fussell (1975) demonstrates very well how the narrative mode of irony, which arose from 'a collision between innocence and awareness', was prevalently used to achieve the people's strongest recollections of the Great War. It was by applying to the past a paradigm of ironic action, he explained, that 'a rememberer is enabled to locate, draw forth, and finally shape into significance an event or a moment which otherwise would merge without meaning into the general undifferentiated stream' (p.30).

A thematic discourse, as a coded structure put in specific discursive forms, has a certain degree of stability; yet at the same, as a set of concrete practices instanciated through time, it is full of tensions and is subject to narrative reconstruction in the political process. The idea of a 'moving structure' – premised on the notions of continuous projection and retrospection – that renders a developing story a structured and yet relatively open-ended configuration. As such, *genre classification is not the imposition of a ready-made structure on an independent set of events, but consists in a dialectic process that takes place between the events and the construction of plot, characters and mood all at the same time.*

Narrative, Community, and Conflict

Community and Solidarity

Carr, drawing on Hegel, maintains that a community exists not only as a development, but also 'through the reflexive grasp of that development when its members assume the common "we" of mutual recognition' (1986:130). A community understands itself in terms of its values and various kinds of symbolic representations; in relation to their values and concerns, people understand their collective life within a time frame, relating the present to the past (origins, traditions, causes and precedents) and to the future (expected and/ or desired outcomes). In public discourse, it is within the narrative frames that its histories and its present situations are understood, and that collective expectations are created.

In an innovative attempt to relate narrative to communal formation, Jacobs and Smith (1997) discuss two solidaristic forms in terms of two narrative genres, namely romance and irony. Romantic narratives are a utopian discourse which 'assume the existence of powerful and overarching collective identities that can unite persons in the pursuit of this utopian future' (p.68). While such a narrative constitutes a unifying force within a community, the other side to such a form of communal solidarity is nonetheless authoritarianism which tends to marginalize minority voices in the wider society. A most conspicuous example is the nationalist ideology. Irony underlies a reflexive consciousness which 'provides the critical distance from which the contingency and limits of the present are revealed, and through which possible futures are made available for negotiation at individual and collective levels' (p.71). Irony subverts totalizing discourses; however, it is not without a danger of nihilism which inhibits the expansion of solidarity. In view of these potentials and dangers inherent in romance and irony, the authors therefore propose for a balance between the two forms of discourse in the public sphere as a way to achieve a solidary, reflexive and tolerant political culture.

The conception of narrative form as a basis for communal solidarity has been espoused by Jacobs and Smith (1997). Building on yet extending their arguments, I would contend that narrative is not only a unifying force but also a divisive one. To understand the complex relations between community and differences-in-community, we need to bring in the manifold classification of narrative genre as they, in their interaction with different cultural codes, are being specified in the public sphere of communal discourse.

Narratives grow out a social milieu; they reflect and augment its values and concerns, including the limits and opportunities posed by the cultural and the social environments. There are two levels of narrative in a society, namely master narratives and event-specific narratives. The former refers to the culturally embedded ways of historizing about the society. This comes close to Taylor's conception that 'we already have incorporated into our language an interpretation of what is really important', which points to the extraindividual narratives-beliefs-ideologies that form the very core of any society.[10] Event-specific narratives are instanciation of the master narratives which are constructed and reconstructed with regard to specific events as they unfold. In a society, while some common value frames are essential for social integration, conflicts usually take place at the sub-cultural and the social levels. I propose that a society's general values are subject to different narrative interpretations by different social actors with divergent interests. The social actors would have at least one master narrative as their dominant frame of reference, which may be articulated with other master narratives in different ways. The multiplicity of narratives in a tradition allows for multiple framing or coding of an event within the cultural context.[11]

Political conflicts, be they over ideal or material interests, often express themselves as conflicting narrative accounts between social actors. In the public sphere of politics, where actors are judged in terms of public credibility, they must be able to make the best articulation of the society's sacred or central values and concerns and present themselves to be the honorable heroes/ heroines in their specific narrative interpretations of the issues at stake. Owing to competing and multiple interpretations, politics entails a reciprocal process of narrative construction and reconstruction among the actors. Precisely the idea of relative open-endedness about narrative development allows us to conceive a space for agency in the process of struggle and change. In the following, I will theorize the dynamics between narratives and political conflicts in the struggle of establishing one's public credibility and undermining that of the opponents. In the next section, I will, with specific reference to a typical instance, theorize the progressive formation of the force of the 'public' out of political struggles as well as its power over the positioning and re-positioning of the actors.

Political Conflicts as Narrative Differences

Analytically a society would have on the one hand the *centre–periphery* nexus as the institutional structure of its material power, and on the other hand the *sacred–profane* classification as the moral underpinnings of its symbolic power.[12] In modern society, the state institution usually forms the power centre which the elites have greater access to whereas the majority of the people in society stay in the periphery. The political elites in the centre by no means form a homogeneous entity, and neither do the non-elites in the periphery. As such, the political public sphere becomes an arena for constant conflicts not only between the centre and the periphery, but also among the elites within the centre as well as different parts of the periphery. Sacredness refers to a society's collective commitment to certain ideals embodied in some material objects such as flags and constitutions which 'can be seen by all, understood by all, and represented to all minds' (Durkheim, [1912]1965, p.27). The sacred as a collective force has a critical social dimension in that there always exists a kind of gravity that inclines the centre into the realm of sacredness. Where centredness has the cultural correlate of sacredness, it will be looked upon as a legitimate authority. If, on the contrary, it carries the cultural emblem of profanity, a legitimacy crisis is likely to arise, which will start off a process of purifying or re-sacralizing the centre by replacing it with a new one. The Watergate event in the United States in the 1970s, for which the President was removed from office, was a case in point (Alexander, 1988). More drastically, the numerous revolutionary movements in history such as the French Revolution in the eighteenth century and the waves of incidents in Eastern Europe in the late twentieth century bespoke the attempts to establish a new politico-cultural order altogether.

The political world constitutes a moral and social order with its attendant pattern of socio-cultural relationships. It has a logic of ordering as well as a logic of development of its own which can be characterized in narrative terms. The sacred–profane basis of authority branches itself out into the comic–romantic realm vis-à-vis the ironic realm, with the latter underlining a sense of realism about the distribution of material power and also a concern with material interests. In many instances, that the centre or part of the centre is challenged is not so much because it loses its sacredness or legitimacy as because it loses its credibility. Both legitimacy and public credibility are evaluative claims, by the public of citizens, of moral status of the political authorities on the basis of their public presentations and performances at specific times. Nevertheless while legitimacy is defined in absolute terms in opposition to illegitimacy on the institutional level based on the sacred–profane distinction, public credibility is a matter of degree, measured against particular actors, institutions or the whole government, which may vary from moment to moment within the scope of legitimacy. Indeed an authority is constantly evaluated in terms of its public credibility which hinges on how well it is able to articulate, within the sacred realm, the various or even conflicting concerns of the public such as the relations between economic progress and ecological preservation, and between democracy and liberty. Where a good balance or integration between the conflicting value claims is achieved, high public credibility is likely; on the contrary, where a divergence is shown, low public credibility is more probable. From the distinctions between the symbolic and the material bases of power, and between legitimacy and public credibility, we may derive a two-dimensional scheme of the narrative context of power (see

Figure 3.1 below).

Figure 3.1 The Narrative Basis of Credibility Status

	Legitimacy	*Illegitimacy*
High Credibility	Romance, Comedy	X
Low Credibility	Irony	Irony
Mixed Credibility Status	Tragedy	X

Romance and comedy entail different kinds of narrative ideals and different courses of action to take whereas irony and tragedy bespeak two different reactions to what is perceived as an undesirable order. As a rule, high public credibility is represented through romance or romantic-comedy and low public credibility through irony. Tragedy is one form of irony which presents a paradox of refusal and acceptance of the crumbling down of a developing romance. In romance or romantic comedy, a desired order is achieved or restored by the hero/ heroine whereas the antagonists are defeated or the blocking characters are reconciled. Pride or confidence is the keynote in mood. In irony, it is the absurd that reigns, which points to a perceived discrepancy between the realms of idealism and of realism. The smaller the discrepancy is, the lighter the irony will be, and the more probable that the perception of power stays in the 'legitimate/low credibility' realm. On the contrary, the greater the discrepancy appears, the more militant the irony will be (satire), and the more likely that power is perceived as illegitimate. Finally, the 'illegitimate/high credibility' realm and the 'illegitimate/ mixed credibility status' realm represents two cases of impossibility for illegitimate power can only go with low credibility status.

The public sphere is an arena for constant conflicts of various kinds, depending on the centre-periphery relations and also the status of authority of the centre. Where the centre has been able to maintain high public credibility through a narrative of romance or comedy, it poses no great problem for the state to contain any challenges from the periphery. The event of any such conflicts as it unfolds will take the shape of a comedy, at the end of which the centre is able to bring about a comic resolution i.e. the restoration of the desired order. In a situation where the centre has secured low public credibility, the reverse will likely be the case in which challenging forces from the periphery seek to override the centre (romance). Nationalist struggles and social movements usually take the form of romance. In other instances, more profound political conflicts exist where the centre or the core part of the centre finds itself in a desired state of triumph − of stable control over the society (comedy) whereas some elites together with a significant portion of the periphery find the existing order absurd or wicked but, due to a lack of material resources, are in no position to overturn it (irony or satire). This sense of ironic consciousness is quite common in a lot of politically closed societies where the citizens often respond to the state with a sense of helplessness or cynicism. (It is no wonder, then, that black humor appears to be particularly prevalent in totalitarian societies.) Nevertheless, in such ironic situations, there is always a potential for a romantic turn − the occurrence of an event which erupts into a social drama of quest and confrontation. A heroic romance will take shape in the event of mobilization against the centre by some charismatic leaders who are able to muster up popular support.

By and large, political conflicts are expressed through characterization within specific narrative modes. Characterization forms the chief instrument through which the actors maintain themselves separate from, hostile towards and convinced of their moral and political superiority to the others. It is often the case that the challenging forces will present themselves as heroes/ heroines fighting for a better cause whereas the challenged power will discredit them by characterizing them as trivial or absurd fools or as dangerous villains. This kind of moral juxtaposition in characterization − heroes/ heroines versus villains, and heroes/ heroines versus fools − in turn gives rise to other kinds of social and moral relations such as admirable or abhorable comrades, allies and supporters. In the public sphere of politics, whoever are able to successfully present themselves in heroic terms and project a better order around themselves while undermining the public's trust in their opponents will carry the stamp of public credibility.

It must be noted that while the political actors play a major part in the drama of action, the ordinary citizens as the audience play a no less important part in it. Narrative progression as a public force hinges on the dynamics between the way the political drama works on the audience and the way the audience exercises their power over the drama. In the public sphere, the audience's cognitive, moral and emotional responses or the political actors' idea of their responses will become the imagined force of the 'public' that guides political action. The reference to the 'public' has its sources of imagery in (i) the store of sacred symbols and meta-narratives in a political tradition, and (ii) the symbolic representations of the opinions of the public at specific times. Public opinion in its turn is formed within specific narrative contexts informed by both public discourses and the people's own lived experiences. All in all, the force of narrative progression as the force of the 'public' will change the meaning of an event or a person over time, which inclines the actors to continually reposition themselves with regard to the new situation. For an adequate explanation of the interplay between politics and public opinion, we need to develop a double-layered model of narrative development which takes into account the action of the political actors and of the general public. In this section, I have discussed how politics can be understood as narrative conflicts between different social forces; in the following, I will add in the dimension of audience response to explain the political and cultural dynamics involved in the narrative development of the force of the public.

Narrative Progression of the Force of the 'Public'

A prevalent political narrative thrives on public opinion, which is by no means stable and consistent over time. In their struggle for public credibility, the political actors must know how to capitalize on the current public concerns and sentiments so as to gather enough social momentum for their narrative action. The specificities of public concerns and sentiments in turn depend on three factors: (i) the value themes or codes prevailing in the community, (ii) the actions or mobilizational strategies of the political actors, and (iii) the preferred modes of narration in public discourse. In the process of political struggles, as a result of the interaction of the three factors, the public's consequent narrative configuration and re-configuration of the events will be crystallizing the very dynamics of the force of the 'public' that guides political action in the sense of providing the actors with a moving symbolic map for location and direction.

The Beginning

In the public sphere of politics, for a perceived ironic situation to turn into a romance, the hero (heroine) must be seen as acting within or stepping into the 'not-yet-realized' sacred terrain of the aspirations of the public. If the desire for a change in the political order has been fervent, and the charismatic leader is seen as strong enough for the quest, the narrative of irony is likely to breed romanticism among the public. *Romanticism*, as a kind of narrative culture, presents itself as a strong conviction in the spirit and conduct of combating for the ideal. It sees a distinct line between the sacred/ good and the profane/ evil and condemns those who show a lack of moral courage to affirm the dividing line and fail to stand strong on the side of sacredness. In the hide tide of romanticism, the event of *charismatic mobilization* will establish a specific instability that becomes the generating moment for the development of a whole new narrative possibility.

A narrative of romantic heroism, just like other narrative modes, is founded upon the three narrative practices of thematic emplotment, characterization and mood construction. Thematically, it develops itself as a romantic projection of a new order around a sacred value. As a quest into the sacred realm, the rhetoric of heroic romanticism would require the noblest diction about the protagonist as well as his/ her actions. Thus the challenge is for him/ her to engage the public on the mimetic and thematic levels sufficiently to make them care about his/ her choice both for what it means thematically and for the protagonist himself/ herself. It is this sense of heroism in characterization that colors the narrative with a mood of splendor and exhilaration, of hopes and promise. The early stage of the student movement in Beijing in 1989, in which the student leaders presented themselves and were portrayed as the romantic hero in a narrative of hope, is a case in point. (In fact, it was because the movement was portrayed in such romantic terms through the media that it was soon able to mobilize support from various walks of life in the cities on a national scale.) At the same time, the moral force of the 'public' in romance would require the identification of an antagonist who will be associated with profanity, as representing the wicked forces in society. The more villainous they are seen to be, the stronger the sense of heroism will be felt about the protagonist's quest. The more heroic the quest looks, moreover, the more likely it is that those who hesitate or refuse to join it will be typified as cowards who lack moral courage. The thematic structure in romance may be elaborated as follows:

Sacredness	vs.	Profanity (villainy)
liberation		repression
vision		expediency
justice		injustice

Sacredness	vs.	Profanity (inadequacy)
resistance		subservience
courage		cowardice
idealism		pragmatism.

Nevertheless, even though there are sufficient forces for a narrative of heroic romance to take shape in the beginning, *the subsequent course of development is open to different possibilities*. A narrative which starts off as a romance may have a comic ending (complete romance), a tragic ending or a satirical ending. In the same example of the student movement in Beijing in 1989, to many people, what began as a romantic social movement turned out to be an ironic tragedy in which the movement was completely crushed by the state. It was tragic because the romantic heroes (heroines) could not carry their cause forward due to the state's bloody crackdown. It was ironic because even though the regime had lost its legitimacy, it continued to rule with even more repressive measures. From another perspective, nonetheless, some read the events in a different ironic light. To them, some of the students leaders actually showed themselves to be naive idealists or even easy waverers (mock heroes/ heroines) rather than true heroes/ heroines. This use of ironic narrativization may indicate a quick shift from a romantic reading to a parody of it at an early stage, or a change from a tragic reading to an ironic realization at a very late stage. Indeed narrative interpretation is never a straightforward matter, for the outcome of an event depends to a large extent on the perceived complications of the beginning, which opens itself to different possible paths of development of the middle, which in turn points to different possible closures for the ending.

Figure 3.2 The Narrative Mapping of Politico-cultural Conflicts

SOCIAL RELATIONS	Periphery/ Fragments of Centre	vs.	Centre
NARRATIVE CONFLICTS | Event: Mobilization |	Irony	vs.	Comedy
PUBLIC DRAMA			
(i) Narrative Challenge	Romance: [hero/ heroine	vs.	— villain]
(ii) Counter-narrative Action	— [villain/ mock hero		Irony: comic hero/ heroine]
(iii) Narrative Reconstruction	Romance/ Tragedy/ Irony	vs.	Irony/ Comedy
CREDIBILITY STATUS	(variable)		(variable)
POWER RELATIONS	(variable)		(variable)

From the Beginning to the Middle

The narrative development of an event is seldom straightforward and without incoherence. As a matter of fact, it is always complicated by (i) *the counter-actions and counter-narratives* made by the 'antagonist' as well as its supporting forces, and (ii) the existence of *undercurrents* that serve to undermine the prevalent narrative. Just as the romance characterizes the antagonist as villainous, the antagonist would usually intervene in the course, mobilizing every cultural and material resource available to discredit the hero/ heroine and to trap him/ her in a difficult or fragile position. In public discourse, the antagonist will propose a counter-narrative of irony or satire, portraying the protagonist as a mock hero/ heroine instead. A mock hero/ heroine is one who has been playing the role of a hero/ heroine but is in fact a fool or a villain, who is unable to carry the cause through (due to a lack of resources or the need of circumstance), unaware of the possible negative consequences of his/ her action, or insincere about the quest altogether. The sharpest irony comes in when it is found that instead of fulfilling the promise of romance the people have expected of him/ her, the hero/ heroine is actually leading them to hell chaos or victimization. In such instances, irony will usually be found embedded in a comic-ironic discourse of chaos versus order, or a satirical discourse of distrust versus faith, the thematic structures of which are respectively coded as follows:

Comic-irony	vs.	Comic-sacredness
chaos		order
extremity		moderation
non-cooperation		reconciliation
inflexibility		resiliency
naive idealism		pragmatism
Satire	vs.	Presupposed Sacredness
hypocrisy		honesty
conspiracy		uprightness
hideousness		honorability
victimization		benefaction.

Among the public, there may be a portion of people who strike the same comic-ironic chord with the antagonist even though they are not themselves the main target of romantic challenge. Having taken a narrative perspective different from that of the romanticists, they will probably not respond to the event of charismatic mobilization with romantic enthusiasm, but with cautions, reservations or even oppositions. Yet by the force of narrative progression, in the event that the narrative of romance has become prevalent in public discourse, hesitations would mean cowardice or a lack of moral vision whereas outright oppositions would probably mean unwarranted villainy. In such a dilemma, they are left with three alternatives: (i) to side with the antagonists at the risk of losing public credibility, (ii) to support the romanticists in order to show they are on the side of the public, which actually contradicts their own initial position, or (iii) to articulate an alternative narrative around a different theme which is also central to the political life of the people.

From the Middle to the Ending

How far the antagonist's counter-narrative or the non-romanticists' alternative narrative can work successfully depends to a significant extent on whether it can capitalize on the existing undercurrents in society. To the extent that the structure of romance could be cross-cut with a realm of *ironic realism*,[13] some characters would be alert to the realistic aspects of life like the presence of danger and conspiracy, which will threaten the unity of the romantic mood. In such a situation, I would contend, at least three kinds of reactions are possible among the public, which are rooted in three different kinds of narrative cultures: (i) defeatism, (ii) cynicism or (iii) persistent romanticism. Defeatism is a variant of ironic realism which presents itself as an expectation of defeat. It may be a result of certain painful or depressing experiences of failures in the past, or based on a conservative judgement of a lack of material resources needed for a possible victory. In a developing romance, such an attitude may generate a tragic turn. *Cynicism* is rooted in a culture of distrust,[14] which is often the product of learning from their society's history. In some cases, it is expressed as an attitude of distrust about the good will of the 'romantic hero', which makes way for all sorts of conspiratorial thinking. In other cases, it is expressed as a foresight about the kind of dangerous situation that the 'romantic hero' is leading the society to. Among the cynics, the radical romanticists tend to distrust the 'romantic hero' without distrusting the romantic cause whereas the most skeptical cynics believe in neither the character nor the cause. If defeatism or cynicism becomes increasingly prevalent, the people will be expecting and hence preparing for an ending in which the hero (heroine) is defeated either by the weight of the circumstance albeit preserving his/ her greatness and dignity (tragedy), or because he/ she fails to prove himself/ herself adequately trustworthy (irony). Both of these attitudes would certainly undermine the romantic aspect of the protagonist and draw the people away from supporting him/ her in the quest.

For those who hold the third kind of attitude i.e. persistent romanticism, they can ill afford to back down from the romantic cause because if they do so in the face of challenges, they will be making a mockery of what they themselves have been advocating. Moreover, since they have believed in the cause with a strong sense of conviction, they will be worried that if defeatism or cynicism becomes prevalent in the public, it will deal a detrimental blow to the romantic cause. Thus in order to continue with the cause, they may play the role of either the heroic protagonist or the unyielding supporter/ ally of the protagonist. They will try to convince the public of the honesty of the protagonist/ themselves while contrasting it with the villainy of the antagonist. However, in the event that the protagonist they first supported fail to prove himself/ herself clean and honest, they may separate the protagonist from the romantic cause to be pursued and themselves take up the role of hero/ heroine in a new narrative. This presents a possibility that the more romantic cynics join hands with these persistent romanticists in the struggle for a new political order.

As a matter of fact, for a developing romance to gather enough social momentum so as to persist to its presupposed ending, it is necessary for the audience to see the heroic action not only as essential and genuine but also as a feasible and sustainable project. In other words, a romance must develop itself into a plausible romance in order to sustain its public credibility. In the event that protagonist fails to strike a good balance between the two realms of idealism and realism, the romanticists may, by the force of narrative progression, be ridiculed as naive idealists or rash fools. The following two-dimentional scheme relates sustained public credibility to the context of narrative practices.

Figure 3.3 The Narrative Context of Sustained Public Credibility

	Sustained Public Credibility	
	High	*Low*
Narrative Context (Thematic Plot)	{Plausible Romance} Sacred Central Feasible	{Irony} Profane Peripheral/ Irrelevant Impossible
(Moral Character)	Strong Honorable Upright Truthful Courageous Idealistic	Weak/ Strong but wicked Hideous Conspiratorial Hypocritical Imprudent Naive
(Affect and Mood)	Bright Hopeful Confident Glorious Joyful	Dark Gloomy Fearful Shameful Repugnant

Conceivably, the intention for a narrative of romantic heroism may fail, in varying degrees, to stand up to its challenges. Nonetheless, while a counter-narrative of ironic mockery may undermine the narrative of romance, it itself is not adequate for establishing public credibility. If there comes a situation where the romantic narrative is undermined without an adequately credible alternative narrative being articulated, the public will be left in an ironic situation of absurdity, confusion, uncertainty or directionlessness. If, however, some social forces are able to articulate an alternative narrative, they may be able to make a significant turn in the development of the event. Their action as well as their account may take the shape of a comedy an attempt to restore the disrupted order to its original state or to bring forth a new ending of reconciliation. Depending on the strength of the undercurrents and on their ability to articulate a better narrative of plausibility and desirability, they may (i) get themselves further and further marginalized by the force of the 'public', (ii) bring about a shift in the major narrative line in public discourse, or (iii) facilitate a process of social polarization between the romanticists and the comic realists.

In the first case, if the romantic narrative remains strong, the comic realists will be seen as making themselves the icon of public disrespect or even ridicule, further alienating themselves from the public. In the second case, in which the romantic narrative has been severely undermined, the force of the 'public' will certainly have the meanings of the events and the characters changed. For example, the 'romantic hero (heroines)' and the romanticists will likely become mock heroes (heroines) in an ironic narrative of incredibility whereas the 'cowards' i.e. the realists, will become the new heroes (heroines) in a new narrative of comedy. As a different kind of narrative culture, *comic realism* celebrates flexible pragmatism and regards compromise and co-operation as the most desired attributes that will bring about a result of reconciliation and/ or restoration of order. In its high tide, it will give rise to a strand of comic optimism, which tends to look at the bright side of a situation that may contribute to comic development. Finally, lying between these two extremes is a case where the comic realists and the romanticists are in a position of more or less comparable public credibility. While the former will demand the romantic protagonist to concede for what is believed to be a better order, the romanticists will probably stand firm on their cause to fight against any self-defeatism. A process of social polarization will take place when the two sides take as their enemies those on the opposite side and also those who apparently do not side with them. In such a situation, the force of the 'public' would require a very delicate balance between the conflicting demands arising from the different narrative perspectives. For instance, the 'romantic hero' may be demanded to concede without yielding. In either case – whether s/he concedes or s/he does not, the irony is that s/he will become less than what s/he has first appeared.

The Ending

In structural terms, a prevalent narrative which begins with a strong sense of heroic romanticism will end either as a romance or as a tragedy. Nevertheless, the theory of narrative progression dictates that the complications of the middle – with the counter-actions taken by the opposing forces in a context of narrative undercurrents – will make the ending open to various other possibilities. The ending can be comic in the sense of completing the initial quest, but it may not signal a romantic fulfillment if too much irony has preceded. As such, it may become a mundane 'romantic' comedy without a romantic hero (heroine) and without any mood of a glorious victory. The ending can also be comic in the sense of reconciling the conflicting forces in a new order; it may signal a comic or a comic-ironic fulfillment, depending on whether the new centre has a close affinity with the sacred realm. Finally, the ending can be totally ironic in that (i) the 'romantic protagonist', whether or not in the centre, has stepped out of the sacred realm, and/ or (ii) the 'antagonist' remains in the centre without learning to attach itself to the realm of sacred values. Be it a comic, tragic, romantic or ironic ending, it will be the beginning of another narrative yet to develop.

Notes

1.   For further discussion of the notion of narrative, see Husserl ([1928]1964), Barthes (1975), Culler (1975), Ricoeur (1985), Carr (1986), Fisher (1987), White (1987), Polkinghorne (1988), and Smith (1994).
2.   Husserl ([1928]1964) explains the difference between the ordinary representation of time and the human experience of time. White (1987) differentiates narrative from the chronicle, which simply lists events according to their place on a time line. Ricoeur (1985) believes that the exploration of narrative can provide a still deeper understanding of the transition from within-time-ness to historicality.

3.   Brooks (1984) draws an analogy to chess playing. In playing a game of chess, we are normally not interested merely in the outcome, nor in a linear sequence of events, but in the process whereby a teleology emerges from apparently contingent events. For a review on the recent literature, see W. Martin (1986).

4.   According to Husserl, our temporal existence is characterised the 'living present', a present that contains, as Augustine long ago pointed out in his *Confessions*, a present of things past and a present of things to come. See Kerby, 1991, p.19.

5.   See MacIntyre 1981.

6.   In his late stage, according to Alexander (1988), Durkheim develops a theory of secular society that emphasized 'the independent causal importance of symbolic classification, the pivotal role of the symbolic division between sacred and profane, the social signficance of ritual behavior, and the close interrelation between symbolic classifications, ritual processes and the formation of social solidarities'. Sacredness is treated as an outgrowth of the human concern for meaning and order, and as a focal point for the institutionalization of power and control. For the wide-ranging applications of these ideas, see the edited volume by Alexander (1988).

7.   Scholes (1982) defines a narrative as 'a text which requires and rewards narrativity', indicating a practice of narrative constructin by the audience. Similarly, Chambers (1984) argues that meaning is not inherent in discourse and its structures, but is contextual – 'a function of the pragmatic situation in which the discourse occurs'.

8.   Taylor (1985) explains that emotions have a life history, for they change during the course of our developing understanding. For instance, the emotional states of hope and despair, and of doubt and belief make sense only against a background emplotment.

9.   The fusion between the mimetic and the thematic functions of character nonetheless varies in degrees. If a narrative establishes Ms. X a character with a central trait, and then orchestrates the progression around the influence of that trait on her actions, which at the same time guides the audience's judgments of those actions, the mimetic and thematic functions of the character will become virtually interchangeable. In other instances, a character's thematic functions may not fully define the multiplicity of his/her traits, which nonetheless do have an impact on the audience's emotional and moral response to him/her.

10.   See Kerby 1991.

11.   Embedded in this theory of multiple narrative frames is a notion of multiple dualities. I intend to go beyond a simple dualistic model of culture on the empirical level without abandoning it as an analytical construct.

12.   For an elaborate explanation of the notions of 'centre' and 'periphery' as well as the symbolic and material dimensions in the distinction, see Shils (1972), and

Chan (1998).
13. Ironic realism is an alertness to the weight of the dark side of reality such as obstruction, suppression and danger.
14. Goldfarb (1991) defines 'cynicism' as 'a form of legitimation through disbelief' (p.1). He further distinguishes between two kinds of cynicism, one more optimistic and the other pessimistic: 'Satirists and social critics with political ambitions reveal the distance between social ideals and social practices in hopes of instigating changes in social practices. Modern (mocking) cynics reverse this critical impulse. They satirize or raise doubts about social critics and their criticism, and about the possibility of social change. The distance between ideals and realities discourages rather than encourages efforts to enact change or reassert fundamental principles' (p.20).

4 Methodology

From Hermeneutics to Narrative Analysis of Texts

Narrative analysis takes as its central problematic the actor's subjective experience of time. Narrative is not the only form of human experience, but insofar as it forms a constituent part in the realm of meaningful experience, narrative is an ontological condition of being. In Carr's words, stories are 'told in being lived and lived in being told' (1986:61). In my work, the concept of narrative attains a special ontological and theoretical status, which dictates the use of what I will call a narrative methodology. A narrative methodology which attends to the temporal dynamics in the actor's subjective experience is a specific application of two major hermeneutical principles: (i) the focus on text or discourse as the linguistic objectification of the internal, subjective state of a collectivity, and (ii) the interpretation of text in terms of the part-whole relationship – the 'hermeneutical circle'.

Textual Interpretation

The realm of meaningful experience has its objectively comprehensive expression in text, which is largely but not exclusively in linguistic form. It is true that every text has its own author, but what is presented in the text is the 'said' rather than intended meaning. To conflate between a mere intention to do something and the concrete accomplishment of that intention is to commit what Wimsatt and Beardsley calls an 'intentional fallacy' (Hirsch, 1967:11). Thus instead of probing into the actor's internal mental state, textual analysis focuses on the objective or textual meaning inscribed in the text one produces.

The task in textual interpretation is to grasp the deep meaning of the text as a whole. This interpretive approach is in contradistinction with the traditional method of content analysis. The latter, rooted in empiricism, assume that the frequency of items can be taken as a valid expression of the objective meaning of the text that contains them. The problem with this approach to meaning is that it tends to be atomistic, decomposing the text into its individual elements and disparate parts.[1] Atomistic approach of this sort will have the effect of repressing the kind of holistic significance of a text that lies beyond the meanings of single words. I propose that the meaning of a text does not lie in single words or phrases, however frequent they are used, but in the connections between them or the structure of the text as a whole. For instance, irony or sarcasm seldom announces a position that is inherent in the denotative meanings of words themselves. Comic ideal and romantic ideal cannot be distinguished without referring to the narrative context that an ideal is embedded. A sense of irony about an outcome cannot be captured by means of the victory-defeat distinction. Tragedy presents a case of paradox that has to be understood as an ironic turn from romance. In this light, it is absolutely conceivable that one understands every single item in a text but still misses the point. As White (1987) argues, 'One might understand every sentence in a story and still not have grasped the point. One might be able to explain why and how very event in a sequence occurred and still not have understood the meaning of the sequence considered as a whole' (p.50). That is to say, the deep meaning in a text is larger than the summation of the words used.

As a critique of empiricism, hermeneutics and structuralist approaches to textual analysis focus instead on the meaning of the whole text by highlighting, respectively, the part-whole relationship and the schematic structure in culture. As it has been well-known, the relationship between the parts and the whole is one of dialectics. The 'whole' is a principle for generating parts, and full understanding of an individual part presupposes understanding of the whole. While the whole is able to retain its integrity and completeness even if not all of its implications have been articulated, it must be understood from individual parts and their combinations. In the same spirit, the semiotic concept of coded structure expresses the claim that the whole is constituted by the relations between the parts. In this light, 'genre' is at once a hermeneutic and semiotic concept. On the one hand, the 'genre-bound' character of understanding is a version of the hermeneutical circle – of the dialectical relationship between the parts and the whole.[2] The idea of genre entails a sense of the generic whole by means of which an interpreter can understand any part in its determinacy. On the other hand, generic classifications are always made in terms of distinctions and interrelations among each other.

Given the genre-bound character of texts, on the methodological level, interpretation has to proceed as a continuous dialogue between theoretical typologies and empirical materials. Generic classification or typological distinction, as Walton (1992) points out, involves certain theoretical assumptions pertinent to the research problem:

> The act of making 'typological distinctions', of constructing a property space
> based on key considerations that 'frame' the case, involves theoretical choices
> about the causal forces that distinguish and critically affect the case. (p.124)

A research usually starts with a set of theoretical assumptions about certain
phenomena which may be developed into a scheme of typology for
descriptive and explanatory purposes. Nonetheless, what the typology
consists in is essentially a hypothesis which is subject to revision upon
incompatible evidence during the research process. In this research, I have
proposed a four-fold scheme of narrative genres as a more or less
exhaustive typology. By 'exhaustiveness', I do not mean that the typology
should not or need not be revised in any fundamental ways. What I mean is
that it covers a wide enough range of, while making nuances between, our
narrative experiences as far as the present conceptualizations allow us.
Certainly, pitched on a very general level, the typology needs to be
substantiated, enriched and even modified in the light of specific empirical
materials. (The question of validity will be discussed later.)

Furthermore, while a narrative methodology of this kind takes issue
with the empiricist approach associated with the survey method, there is, to
reiterate, no denying that opinion polls do play a role in the functioning of
society. If it is the empirical character of public opinion that we attend to, I
propose we adopt a discursive approach by taking opinion polls as one
discursive form whereby public opinion is represented. Indeed statistical
displays are types of discursive events that are rendered meaningful by
rhetorical devices used to construct them. Moreover, it is in public
discourse that people make selective references to the polls as indicating the
state of collective consciousness at specific times. A textual interpretation
of public opinion should therefore concern itself with the question of how
opinion polls, as well as other forms of public opinion expression, are
shaped, interpreted and then constructed in political discourse as the public
opinion of the day.

A Narrative Approach to the Part-Whole Relationship

While the part-whole relationship can be retained in the idea of genre, a
static conception of genre is unable to put into light the temporal dynamics
in the part-whole relationship. A part is not only a part of a static whole at

one point of time, but also a part of a temporally unfolding whole. As we have discussed in the previous chapter, the concepts of 'narrative' and 'narrative progression' help explain how the parts are integrated into a structural whole not only at one point of time but also continuously over a span of time. As such, narrative analysis of text, which seeks to reconstruct the underlying narrative structures in discourse, is a most appropriate methodological strategy to capture the part-whole relationship in discursive practices.

In my scheme of typology, narratives are classified into four genres, each of which integrates plot, character and mood into a unifying whole that conveys specific meaning. Each of which, moreover, entails specific structural progression from the beginning, through the middle, to the end. In short, the typology allows for a dual comparison between the discourses of different actors at one point of time, and between the discourses of the same actor at different points of time. In my theory of narrative progression, the idea of a temporally unfolding whole is captured in the conception of narrative genre as a 'moving structure'. For example, it is by means of structural progression that an initial romance may develop into a tragedy or fulfilled romance.

The methodological implications of such an approach are three-fold. First, any attempt to trace the changes in public opinion must make reference to a narrative model in lieu of a linear model or a fragmentation model of time. A linear model of time takes time as calendar and clock time. Typical in many longitudinal studies, temporal development is divided into equal time slots over which the curve of public opinion change is to be charted. In this model, public opinion is often assumed to be an dependent variable caused by some external forces such as structural changes and important events.[3] In a fragmentation model, similarly, there is little sense of continuous development of an event over time. Episodes and events are treated as disparate happenings which may or may not have an effect on public opinion. The temporal dimension is reduced to a simple 'before-and-after' logic. A most typical example can be found in the experimental design by the 'minimal effect' theorists in early communications research. In these two models, the measures of time are either linear or discrete, and public opinion changes are conceived as being caused by some independent variables external to public opinion.

The narrative model of time, in principle, takes into account the actor's moment-by-moment integration of the related episodes and personages into a continuously unfolding whole. Put in another way, it pays attention to the actor's subjective experience with time in a 'cumulative' sense – a process of extended awareness through continuous retrospection and anticipatory projection. Episodes and personages are meaningfully connected insofar as they carry certain symbolic significance in a narrative experience. It is the changes in their symbolic meaning that constitute changes in public opinion. Thus instead of measuring public opinion at regular intervals or in fragmented ways, the narrative model charts the narrative progression of the force of the 'public' in terms of the notion of stages. Indeed just as a complete narrative structure has a beginning, a middle and an ending, the temporal development of an event as well as of public opinion vis-à-vis the event may be divided, at least, into three stages. Granted that the beginning of an event is identified, the second and the third stages will be defined in terms of the significance certain new episodes have – either on the furtherance of the narrative towards its anticipated ending or on the constitution of a structural turn from the initial narrative. In short, a narrative model looks at time on the basis of the meaningful connectedness between episodes and events in terms of the notion of stages.

The second methodological implication is that the proposed method of narrative analysis allows for a certain degree of integration between the case-oriented strategy and the variable-oriented strategy.[4] According to Ragin (1987), the former attends to the complexity of specific historical cases whereas the latter seeks to test theoretically derived hypotheses so as to produce generalizations across a large number of cases. In this light, the notion of narrative genres is both useful in illuminating the process of discursive construction with regard to specific events and capable of offering certain theoretical generalizations. On the one hand, narrative analysis focuses on the specificities of the development of an event by following closely the continuous interaction between politics, culture and public opinion with regard to the event. On the other hand, granted that the typology is constructed in a highly general level, continual dialogue between the theoretical typology and the empirical case may give rise to generalizations that have certain theoretical implications. Such generalizations would have to take into account and distinguish between the contingent and context-dependent factors and the more general explanations that may be applied across the board.

Thirdly, regarding the issue of casing,[5] the narrative approach both delimits the boundary of an empirical case and allows it to be transformed in the research process. On the one hand, the four-fold typology is used to draw conceptual (as well as experiential) boundaries between cases. Cases falling within the same type are assumed to be the same in terms of their basic defining features. On the other hand, as Abbott argues (1992), 'transformation in attributes can be so extreme that a case which began as an instance of one category may complete a study as an instance of another' (Abbott, 1992:64). Under the present typology, cases starting as romance may diverge in the process of events so much so that they develop into different narrative genres. While the narrative approach sensitizes us to such divergent development by making nuances between types, a methodological problem is that inappropriate weight may be given to cases where either an expected factor is not found (Cullen 1989) or that an unexpected factor appears. The risk is two-sided. First, as Vaughan (1992) points out, the approach may assign the cases a special theoretical status when they may be cases where the occurrence of an expected factor has a low probability. Secondly, it may overlook or give undue weight to cases where the occurrence of a particular factor has a high probability. The questions of sampling and weighting will be discussed in relation to the present research question in section two.

The Question of Validation

The question of validity in interpretive methodology hinges on three issues, namely the credibility of the source of evidence, the degree of correspondence between the researcher's interpretation and the subjects' experience, and the admissibility of evidence. In the first place, for an explanation to be a valid account of the experience of the actors, it must rely on sources which document their lived experiences or their actual discourses. In my research, the media are not just a source of evidence, but have a significant theoretical status as the public sphere of political discourse. The newspaper editors and columnists are themselves part of the audience (citizens) actively participating in public discourse out of which public opinion is crystallized. In public discourse, it is certainly the 'said' rather than the intended meanings that count. While every text has its own author, public discourse proceeds by means of intertextual exchange, which again tends to relativize authorial coherence. Chaney (1993) has put this idea in a most succinct way:

> As publics are reflexively constituted in forms of communication which relativize authorial coherence, so the 'voice' of that communication becomes less that of specific authors or editors and becomes more that of the mode of communication in itself; or more precisely the phenomenological stance of the implied reader of that mode of communication. (p.136)

Given the textual as well as intertextual quality in public discourse, textual interpretation of political or popular discourses in the media will be a most valid approach to study public discourse.

Still, a second methodological question arises as to the validity of the researcher's own interpretation. As Cohen has pointed out, the same text can belong to different groupings or genres and serve different generic purposes, pending on how the audiences receive it. If a text is open to multiple interpretations by its audiences, the problem then is, on what grounds does a researcher, who is only one of the many audiences of a text, claim validity to his/ her interpretation? In fact, an interpretation must be an interpretation made from a certain point of view. According to Hirsch, textual interpretation implies a choice that is required not by the nature of written texts but rather by the goal that the interpreter sets himself/ herself. In my research, while asserting the ontological status of narrative, I am far from making the claim that there is a universal way of experiencing time. Not that I do not have the knowledge about it, which is certainly true, but that such a claim would be charged with essentialism. In my theory of narrative progression, I bring in a set of narrative genres for theoretical purposes that I have already explained. Certainly, the four-fold narrative genres are subject to revision upon theoretical criticisms and incompatible evidence.

Granted that an interpretation is a theoretical hypothesis supported by evidence, the   third question is what should the criteria be for the admissibility of evidence. Drawing on Hirsch's discussion (1967), I propose three validity criteria, namely *coherence, correspondence* and *relevance.* Coherence dictates that an interpreter posit a whole meaning in reference to which the meanings of the parts cohere with one another. This procedure is circular in that the whole text is derived from the meanings of the parts which are themselves specified and rendered coherent with reference to the text as a whole. Given this kind of circularity, coherence becomes a janus-faced concept. On the one hand, circularity makes it difficult for the public to alter their constructions, and as such consistency or inter-text reliability will serve as a validity check for the interpreter. On the other hand, this very kind of circularity also makes it difficult for the interpreter to alter his/ her own conception in the interpretive process even in the face of contradictions. In order that the latter problem be avoided, an interpretation must be checked against the second criterion of correspondence: it must account for each linguistic component in the text. The point is to alert an interpreter to possible conflicting evidence. Correspondence nonetheless should not be taken as the most important criterion, for an interpretive hypothesis need not explain all the evidence that comes along. The admissibility of evidence is ultimately determined by the criterion of relevance: 'Evidence must be accepted as relevant whenever it helps to define a class under which the object of interpretation can be subsumed, or whenever it adds to the instances belonging to such a class' (Hirsch, p.197). In this context, irrelevant evidence should not be defined as evidence that does not fit into a pre-conceived class; rather, it must be defined as evidence that adds no new information and therefore may be omitted on the ground of repetitiveness. Taken together, the interpretive process of narrative construction should go like this: when small-scale plausibility judgments about the disparate details are consistent with the generic hypothesis, the former will be established as an instance of the theoretical type or pattern; when they conflict with each other, the former may overturn the latter on the ground of adequate weight.[6]

Research Design

Theoretical Logic in the Research Question

This research seeks to study the dynamic interaction between politics and public opinion with regard to a specific event in Hong Kong: the introduction as well as legislation of the Patten proposals. In terms of theoretical significance, the empirical case represents a specific instance in which a romantic beginning develops into an irony at the end.[7] In my theory of narrative progression, narrative development is conceived to be open to different structural possibilities depending on the interaction between the initial narrative structure, the prevailing narrative culture(s) in society, and the mobilizational strategies of the political actors involved. In a counter-factual sense, the empirical case, given its romantic beginning, could have developed into a fulfilled romance or a tragedy other than an irony. In this light, this research is a study of how the romance was made possible at the beginning, and how, out of the three structural possibilities, two were closed off and one was actualized in the course of the event.

Defining the Variables

Politics has both a public and non-public dimension, and this research focuses on the former i.e. politics of public credibility in the public sphere.

The study is contented with a narrower focus as such in part because the non-public dimension of politics is not quite accessible to the researcher, and in part because the political and cultural processes that are involved in the formation of the force of the 'public' is a research subject in itself. 'Public opinion', which includes the various symbolic representations of public opinion in public discourse, refers to the symbolic force of the 'public' that both constitutes the substance of politics and regulates the material aspect of politics. It is embedded in public discourse which embeds narratives. In this studies, the major variables include *events* and *episodes*, *actors as well as their political relationships, credibility status*, and *narratives* (value themes, narrative forms and narrative cultures). An event does not have a clear-cut empirical boundary, for it is often made up of numerous episodes which are related to another event. As such, the definition of an event is an arbitrary undertaking, which is decided on the basis of the research question in hand. In this research, the event is defined as a social drama which started on 7 October 1992 when Patten the new Governor released his reform proposals without China's prior approval, and then developed through a number of episodes or small events involving social conflicts over the scheduled legislation of the proposals, and finally ended with the completion of the legislative process on 30 June 1994. The choice of the beginning and the ending is thus made first because they form a relatively coherent story and secondly because their juxtaposition highlights the fact of irony in a most dramatic way. Finally, a meaningful episode will be defined as a small event that contributes to the narrative development of the larger event by means of turn-making. It is usually the result, which may be intended or unintended, of human agency.

Social actors and political relationships will be classified on the bases on their structural-institutional position in the state–public nexus and their political stands. The social actors consist of three major categories: those representing the state (the Chinese government, Governor Patten and the Hong Kong government), those representing the public (media personnel, political commentators, polling agents and citizens participating in media-related activities), and those straddling between the public and the state (political party members and individual politicians sitting in the Legislative Council through all kinds of election). In terms of their political stands, these actors may be classified in terms of a few conventionalized categories – categories that have been used in public discourse in Hong Kong – which also indicate the relationships of political alliance and differentiation. The conventionalized categories are the democrats (or the pro-democracy camp), the conservatives and the pro-China camp; and within the pro-democracy camp, it may be further divided into the mainstream (leading democrats), the more radical and the moderate fragments.

For one thing, these are the events and the actors understood in their social forms emptied of their moral meaning to the people. My theoretical point is that it is through narrative discourse that they become culturally significant and meaningful. Narrative, through the interplay between genre and value theme, gives shape to political relationships, specifies the basis of and indicate the degree of credibility status, and indicates the discursive force of the 'public'. Narrative configurations by the public and the political actors result from the interaction between agency and the master narratives embedded in a culture.[8] As far as the latter is concerned, narrative forms are limited by the narrative cultures sedimented in a society, and cultural themes are more or less prescribed in a culture, but their interaction opens the way for various possible combinations. This is where agency and contingency come into the picture.

Logic of Research

Given the research focus, the more concrete tasks in this study consist in (1) deciphering the changing narrative contexts presented in the public sphere, (2) situating within these narrative contexts the self-conscious references to collective subjectivity in public discourse such as 'we feel that', 'the people generally believe that', ' most of the Hong Kong people find that', and (3) relating these discursive developments to the public action of the political actors to see how far they exert power and influence on each other. As it is the process of change from one stage to another that needs to be explained, a comparative method has to be devised. The latter will be done by way of narrative analysis.

Narrative analysis has an inherently comparative logic. It takes into account the changing shape of discursive development at different points of time yet without abandoning the idea of structure. It is with the idea of 'moving structure' that we will be able to make comparisons between the pattern of narrative structures at different time points, which will then allow us to arrive at some kind of tentative causal analysis about the dynamic relationship between politics and public opinion. In a sense, narrative causality is no different from variable-oriented causality in that they are both established on the criteria of correlation and temporal sequence. In another sense, the two are fundamentally different in that variable-oriented causality is prone to isolate variables in its emphasis on the third criteria of the lack of spuriousness whereas narrative causality stresses the meaningful connectedness among events and people. In this research, I will pay special attention to the questions of temporal sequence and meaningful connectedness in addition to the criterion of meaningful connectedness. Correlation will be established when public opinion and the actor's justification of his/ her own public action strike resonance in one way or another. Temporal sequence will be followed closely by (i) dividing the whole event into three progressive stages, which correspond to the most generic plot structure of beginning, middle and end, and (ii) attending to the sequential logic within each stage. Pertinent to the empirical case under study, I propose two theoretical hypotheses to guide the empirical research:

(1) In a situation perceived as romantic-ironic, a heroic romance will likely take shape in the event of charismatic mobilization.
(2) While the progression of the event towards a particular ending is impelled by the structural logic in the developing romance, it is likely that obstructing forces will set in to undermine the romance, and hence creating a situation of crisis or deep conflict. These obstructing forces come mainly from those who have had little faith in the romance. They include the antagonist targeted in the romance, those who hold a comic position about the pre-existing order, and those who do not trust the romantic hero/ heroine.
(3) The development of the event into an irony is a result of the interaction between the actions of the initial hero/heroine, the actions taken by the opponents and the different kinds of ironic realism existing in the society, namely tragic defeatism, cynicism and (comic) pragmatism. In particular, for the legislation of the reform proposals to become an irony, the initial romanticists must have adopted a cynical-romantic position about the event.

Narrative analysis of texts will proceed by way first of a reconstruction of the major master narratives available in the cultural repertoire, and then of detailed examination, with close reference to the texts, of the repetitions and variations of these meta-narratives in their specific instanciation in public discourse. For the reconstruction of master narratives pertinent to our concern, empirical materials will be drawn from discourses conducted in the major newspapers in the 1980s and the early 1990s, with special attention to the post-Basic Law period. The formal endorsement of the Basic Law in early 1990, which put an official end to the five-year dispute over it and which took place just a few months after the Tiananmen Square incident in Beijing, was a significant event in the political history of Hong Kong. Specifically, as the Basic Law has been looked at as a symbolic configuration of very differently understood historical processes, it is highly relevant that the narratives constructed around it will shed light on the narrative contexts for the Patten event which was to take place just two years after it. For public discourses related specifically to the Patten event a number of newspapers will be chosen as the unit of observation.

Unit of Analysis and Sampling

The theoretical unit of analysis in this research is public discourse. Public discourse forms a web of intertextual references between competing interpretations over what the collective 'we' consists of, which entails a discourse of both commonness and relational differences. In other words, it is the web of intertextual references and competing interpretations in public discourse that should form the unit of analysis. As such, in sampling, we must take into account both the range of discursive positions in the different media and the relative weight of each position as representing the totality of public discourse.

In this empirical study, I will, based on judgmental sampling, rely on five major newspapers, four in Chinese and one in English – *Hong Kong Economic Journal, Ming Daily, Express Daily, Success Daily, and South China Morning Post (SCM Post)* (English). It is true that the five newspapers that I choose do not delineate the entire boundary of the public sphere in Hong Kong, yet they can claim a high degree of representativeness on four grounds. First, they are quite comparable in terms of their market-oriented character and wide readership – in terms of readership, they all belong to the top ten category. Secondly, as they have different target readers and different editorial positions, which may be classified respectively as middle or upper-middle class/ liberal, middle class/ centrist-conservative, lower or lower-middle class/ centrist-conservative, lower class/ centrist-conservative, and upper-middle class/ liberal, the five of them together cover a wide ideological spectrum and can therefore claim representativeness of the ideological diversities in the press of Hong Kong. Thirdly, these newspapers as market-oriented enterprises provide an open arena for the expression of diverse opinion by people outside the media personnel, which thereby expands the scope of ideological positions allowed in the press. Indeed quite a number of newspaper columnists have labored to offer sustained public criticisms, some falling in the mainstream and some staying in the periphery. As far as the periphery is concerned, more radical criticisms can be found among the five newspapers, especially in *Economic Journal*. Finally, the press in Hong Kong as a whole, as compared to specific radio and television programs, are less susceptible to change and therefore provide a relatively stable arena for public discourse.[9]

Out of the five newspapers, two belong to the liberal category and three to the centrist-conservative category. In order to strike a balance between them, I will add in the democrat-critics. Still, insofar as these six elements stand for the mainstream positions, I will include, among the public critics, the pro-democracy cynics as representing a discursive position at the periphery. The whole sample will therefore consist of the following seven elements:

(a) democrat-critics (e.g. M. Ng *in SCM Post*, Chai Sun in *Economic Journal*)
(b) *SCM Post*
(c) *Economic Journal*
(d) *Ming Daily*
(e) *Express Daily*
(f) *Success Daily*
(g) democrat-cynics (e.g. T. On and W.Y. Wong in *Economic Journal*)

Some may criticize that the sample is limited in that it does not take into account the two politically significant newspapers, *Wen Wei Daily* and *Dao Kung Daily*, which serve as the mouthpieces of the Chinese government. The exclusion of these papers may be justified on two grounds. First, they are financed and run by the Chinese government and therefore fall outside our definition of the public. Given our research focus on public opinion, it is how the Hong Kong public conceive the Chinese government rather than the Chinese government itself that is our major concern. Secondly, despite their exclusion, the relevance of the two papers has been taken into account in that the pro-China stance among the press is included in the sample (most obvious in *Success Daily*), and that it stands to reason that some of the published materials in the two state-run papers, in so far as they are important sources of news about the Chinese government, are also made known through the market-oriented papers by means of intertextual references.

The decision to include three rather than two elements in each of the liberal-democratic and the centrist-conservative categories is based on three considerations. First, it enhances representativeness of the sample. Secondly, it allows us to check consistency among the different elements in each category. Finally, the more elements we have for a category, the greater chance there is for us to spot variations in the subsequent development of a particular narrative beginning. Indeed given the similar ideological position the elements have, it is highly likely that they belong to the same narrative type in the first stage of the event. For this reason, in addition to inter-category comparison, intra-category comparison over time will provide us with some interesting but unexpected empirical evidence, which will shed new light on our theoretical construction. In view of this, however, a methodological problem arises as to the possibility of differential weighting between the sub-categories.

Weight of Evidence

In this research, I have combined a qualitative approach with a simple quantitative measure by including seven categories of public critics in my sample. In a nutshell, the greater the number of critics adhere to a particular narrative, the greater the force of the 'public' that the narrative is supposed to carry. This, however, must be considered in relation with the actual construction of 'public opinion' in public discourse. In particular, as opinion polls form an important basis for the construction of public opinion, focus will be put on the discursive structure of the surveys, the interpretation of the results and the way the results are highlighted in news and other media discourse.

Regarding the problem of opinion polls, for the purposes of cross-referencing, both publicized-cum-interpreted and non-publicized results will be studied. Among the press, *Ming Daily* and *SCM Post.* had commissioned some agencies to do regular polls, the results of which were continually published for their news value. Another important source is the Social Sciences Research Centre of the University of Hong Kong. The Centre has published a summary report of its poll findings. The design was both longitudinal and cross-sectional. In particular, the results for the tracking question of 'how satisfied you are with Mr. Patten's policy speech' were continually reported in the media to show the changes in public opinion. There were other polls on more specific questions, some of which were published and some not, but all of them were useful for cross-referencing.

Still, as pointed out previously, the creation of sub-categories within a category in the course of narrative development may generate the problem of unequal weighting between the sub-categories. On the question of weighting, it has to be pointed out that in the present research, 'representativeness' does not necessarily mean having equal numbers in each sub-category; rather, it is the difference in the size of the categories as they develop that will provide more useful information about the relative weightiness of particular narratives in public discourse. In other words, in order to check the amount of variations over time, balanced weighting between categories needs to be done only at the beginning and differential transformation among the sample elements forms the very focus of the research.

Notes

1. See Scott, 1990, p.147.
2. According to Hirsch, a genre or a type is an entity with two decisive characteristics: (i)it is an entity that has a boundary by virtue of which something belongs or does not belong to it, and (ii) it can be represented by different instances with different contents of consciousness. See Hirsch, p.78.
3. This is similar to what Abbott (1992) describes as the population/ analytic approach: 'If we represent each case at each time by a point in a variable space, finding the plot is a matter of connecting the dots of $time_1$, $time_2$, etc.' (p.65)
4. In his book, Ragin (1987) discussed and compared between the two methods.
5. A thorough discussion of this issue can be found in the book co-edited by Ragin and Becker (1992).
6. See Hirsch, p.198.
7. An event can be taken as a case of a variety of things. According to Walton (1992), the choice of a particular casing strategy is decided on 'the explanatory advantage produced by formulating a case in one way of another'.
8. Master narratives form part of the tradition of a society which are themselves the cumulative product of historical agency. As the work of agency, they are in principle subject to transformation; yet as a structured tradition, they are usually rather resistant to change.
9. During the Patten event, there emerged a television programme which the sacred but prohibited terrain of democratic struggles vis-à-vis China – its anchored very daring criticisms against the different political actors, especially the Chinese government. This programme, which was refreshing and uplifting, stood out as an exemplary pioneer in political programmes in

the electronic media. However, the programme, despite its popularity, did not last long. It was speculated that political considerations were involved in the broadcasting corporation's decision not to resume it.

5 Historical Development of the Political Public Sphere in Hong Kong

Hong Kong remained a capitalist and undemocratic city-state under British colonial rule. In the early days, consistent with Habermas's analysis, the growth of mercantile capitalism, alongside the formation of the (colonial) state, was an important structural factor for the development in society of a public sphere which operated independently in the non-state domain of market exchange but was nonetheless oriented towards the state. The press already made their appearance in those days serving commercial purposes at first and later developing a political function of open criticisms about state policies. If we follow Habermas's argument, we may arrive at the conclusion that the capitalists constituted the carrier of a public sphere which held the power of the undemocratic colonial state in check. This is true in one sense, but taking a departure from Habermas's logic of reasoning, what I am going to argue in this chapter is that the mercantile public sphere in those days was a sectional-public sphere formed on the basis of class and racial distinctions. Such an exclusive discursive sphere was developed in a context where the society had been deeply divided between people of different classes and races. The process of evolution of the public sphere in the society is a question deserving serious historical study based on judicious collection of evidence. This, however, goes beyond the scope of concern of the present research. In this chapter, for contextualizing purposes, a brief outline of the historical development of the political public sphere will be presented. More specifically, I hazard that a more general public sphere did not emerge until the 1970s and 1980s.

My argument is that while capitalist development continued to play a part in the process, particular political and cultural processes had shaped the specificities of political struggles which had a great impact on the character of the public sphere today. These included the expansion of education and increasing politicization of local issues (such as constitutional reforms and public housing). In stating their editorial opinions on particular issues, the commercial press began to appeal to the general public while presenting themselves as the voice of the public. Specifically, in the 1980s and the 1990s, the newly emerged middle class played an important role in the struggle for political inclusion, which effected the formation of a public that was to get increasingly involved in a politics of public credibility. Concomitant with this struggle was the rise of a new culture of the public which stressed openness, accountability and representativeness, which thereby enhanced the role of the media as the public sphere.

Political Communities, Economy, and the Press in the 19th Century

In the early days, Hong Kong, as a colonial city, saw the co-existence of two disparate political communities in the society – one that was rooted in mainland China but sprouted in Hong Kong and the other that gradually grew out of local politics but was predominated by the merchants, especially the British merchants. In accordance with the development of the two political communities, the early press in the society fell into two major categories – Chinese political papers and English commercial papers – both of which became some open discursive spheres whereby public criticism against the state(s) was forged. Generally speaking, the early press in Hong Kong bore the stamp of a public sphere in several ways, but they were limited in terms of membership and accessibility.

Traditionally, the territory had been used by the Chinese dissidents as a place of refuge or as a hatching ground for reformist or revolutionary activities in the Mainland. These Chinese activists developed a strong network of political communication among themselves. In particular, the early political newspapers were founded mostly by these Chinese dissidents who used the papers to advocate their political beliefs. The development of political press had its heyday amidst the upsurge of the reformist and revolutionary movements in China by the turn of the 19th century and during the Japanese occupation in 1937. On the whole, these political press had served to institutionalize among the Chinese activists a practice of open criticisms against their government.[1] However, by its very nature, this public arena had a transient existence which did not take root or belong to the local community. They generally did not survive long for economic reasons, which were attributed to their failure to strike political resonance among the local residents.

Within the local community, there had developed a strong non-state run economic domain of trading activity, and the commercial press emerged and grew under such development. The growth of the commercial sector was attributable to two factors. First, it was the British colonial policy, which targeted primarily at economic gains, to limit the role of the government to 'the encouragement but not the control of enterprise', serving the interests primarily of the merchants.[2] To begin with, Britain's occupation of the Hong Kong island in 1842 and the Kowloon peninsula in 1860 was driven largely out of commercial considerations.[3] Owing to its geographical feature and location, Hong Kong was used as an entrepot for trading with China. Decreeing that Hong Kong should be a free port, the British colonial government limited its role to 'the encouragement but not the control of enterprise', serving the interests primarily of the merchants. Thus from the beginning of its rule, the state already adopted a laissez-faire approach to the development of the economy, leaving the market to run on its own while using every administrative and political means to protect the market. This facilitated further the growth of a merchant class as well as a non-state economic sector, which was not only independent of the state but was strong enough to stand opposed to state policies (Chiu, 1994).

In such a context, the development of the entrepot trade in the society not only created demand for commercial news among the merchants, but also made available the capital needed for the running of the press industry. The early commercial press began primarily as shipping and market sheets. Later papers featured a commercial news section while expanding the scope of newspapers to include political news and commentaries (Lam, 1977; Clayton, 1980).

Secondly, as Chiu (1994) observed, the development of bourgeoisie predated the formation of the colonial state, resulting in them being a dominant class in society. As a result, business power formed an 'institutional hindrance to the state's financial capacities to intervene in the marketplace' (p.26). The merchants had continually waged battles against the government on the issue of taxation and other fiscal measures. As early as 1894, it was out of an intent to influence the government's way of taxing and spending that the merchants began to demand constitutional reforms in the Colony (Chan, 1989).

From the very start, the British merchants had had a great deal of say in Britain's policy vis-à-vis Hong Kong. While the government was acting with the Queen's authority, the merchants, rather than merely subjects, assumed a role of sanctioning and overseeing it. On the public front, they often formed a strong voice against the government's unfavorable decisions.[4] In particular, the early English press, started mostly by the British merchants, became the arena where the merchants openly criticized state policies.[5] Noticeably, this arena showed a number of features that were characteristic of an early public sphere. First, it was founded on the basis of a set of interests which transcended 'the confines of private domestic authority'; secondly, it institutionalized an opposition between state and (civil) society; thirdly, it practiced political criticism. The public arena formed among the merchants was strong vis-à-vis the state, but it was limited to the English-reading cum business circle.

As a matter of truth, the earliest public sphere among the European merchants, which was of limited accessibility, was itself founded upon a society of polarized class positions which developed partially along race lines. Indeed the historical development of the civil society in Hong Kong may be summarized as one of continual struggles for political equality among people of different races and classes. According to Chan (1989), the manner of Hong Kong's acquisition established both mercantile dominance in the society and British supremacy over the natives. The foreign community in the 1850s was characterized by 'snobbery and a spirit of exclusiveness' (p.42). Many exclusive clubs such as the Hong Kong Club were established as centres of sociability among the European merchants. Membership criteria were made strict to ensure that only the rich European males could join the Club. In other words, club membership was a badge of high social status, which built not only on class differences but also racial (and gender) distinctions.[6] In the political arena, moreover, the British merchants, in order to protect their own interests, demanded greater say inside the government. In 1850, as an act of 'compliance', the Governor appointed two British merchants as unofficial members into the Legislative Council, which up to then comprised only officials. Thereafter the number of unofficial members in the Council was gradually increased.[7] In the Chinese community, with the growth of entrepot trade, the native compradors and businessmen developed into a capitalist class, who were resentful of the discriminatory treatment they received. In their struggle to gain political power, the Chinese merchant class successfully ended the British merchant's monopoly of unofficial seats on the Legislative Council in 1888.[8] Despite the fight against racial discrimination, political struggles by the commercial elites had not been about equality among all the citizens. The fact was, the majority of the populace were denied the right to participate in the decision-making processes. They largely included the young, male immigrants who left their families in China to work in the colony as artisans, shopkeepers, manufacturing workers, coolies and servants.[9] Deprived of any means of direct access to the institutions of political power, the participation of the working class in the public arena often took the form of strikes, which were sporadic in nature.

The early commercial press had been a political weapon whereby the merchants openly expressed their opinions against unfavorable government policies. This 'mercantile' public sphere was strong in operation but remained sectional in nature, building upon a society of polarized class positions. Worse still, as the government later acquiesced to the demand of the merchants to be incorporated into the Executive Council and the Legislative Council, the merchants, in exchange, became less publicly critical of the government.[10] As such, the tinge of public criticism among the commercial elites began to fade as politicking took place primarily behind closed doors. It was not until the 1980s, with the growth of the economy and the increasing politicization of the society, that a general public sphere began to take shape.

The Undemocratic Colonial State and its Representation of the 'People'

For long the government in Hong Kong had been essentially of a closed, undemocratic structure under the executive leadership of a colonial governor who was ultimately answerable to the Secretary of State in London rather than the public in local community. It was an executive-led system of government wherein the bureaucracy of civil service became the sole repository of decision-making power advised and influenced by the non-elected Executive and Legislative Councils as well as a partially elected but powerless municipal council (Davies, 1997; Harris, 1978; Lau, 1982; Scott, 1989; Leung, 1990). The political structure as a whole exemplified a culture of paternalistic elitism prevalent within the government. Basically, as part of the governing strategy of the colonial government, the civil service and the councils provided for important sites for co-optation of the economic and social elites in society (King, 1975).

All along the government had not built up adequate institutional mechanisms to channel and respond to public opinion. In the early days, the kind of opinions expressed through the 'mercantile' public sphere had had great pressure on the government; however, this sphere of public criticisms was limited in accessibility and later faded into closed-door politicking with the merchants being incorporated into the Executive and the Legislative Councils. The majority of the people, being kept outside the political centre, had to resort to protests as a means of expressing their discontents with specific state policies. It was after the outbreak of social riots in 1966 and 1967 that the government became more conscientious of gathering and receiving responses from the ordinary people. (Indeed at the bar of global political climate against colonialism after the World War II, the British officials somehow felt obliged to show that the administration was run in the interests of the people.) Nevertheless, the government took the people to be a mass of subjects under its paternal rule rather than a public of autonomous citizens with equal political rights. As subjects, their opinions were channeled to the government by means of a system of consultation which aimed at minimizing open dissatisfaction with its policies. From the perspective of the government, politics meant the manipulation and display of public consent. Consensus politics was the name of the game.

In 1972, as part of its newly devised consultative scheme, the government began to publish Green Papers which outlined proposed new policies, and then invited the people to give comments through letters or in meetings held at the district and the central levels. The aim was to collate and assess public opinion from multiple sources before the Governor made the final decision. This practice of consultation by the government was nonetheless embedded within an authoritarian political structure. At the district level, the City District Offices, District Advisory Boards, City District Committees, Area Committees, Mutual Aid Committees and Heung Yee Kuk were not granted any formal power and played only an advisory role in the political system. In some instances changes were made in response to public criticism, but in most cases the changes made were slight. At the central level, Council membership was by appointment. The power of appointment, re-appointment and removal of members was solely in the hands of the Governor who was the head of the executive. This was to safeguard that the unofficial members − mainly the industrial-commercial elites − would take a pro-government stance.[11]

Under this system, when there arose public disputes over certain issues, say during the Sino-British negotiation in the early 1980s, the government would, typically, activate the political linkages with the Executive and Legislative Councils and the District Administration. The councilors usually pledged their allegiance to the government while the official line got echoed at district board meetings. The seeming unanimity of support from these leaders was then communicated to the press, which, coupled with the publicity campaigns, would create a climate of public opinion favorable to the government. It was on such grounds that the government claimed to be carrying public consent.

Full-fledged Development of Capitalism after World War II

After the Second World War, the economy has changed from a mercantile base to an industrial one, and later develops fully into one of the most important financial centres in the world. The growth of the economy not only lays a strong economic infrastructure for the development of the press industry but also gives rise to a bulk of middle class who are to play an increasingly conspicuous role in the political public sphere.

By the end of the nineteenth century, the city had already become a major port and established a nascent base for financial and manufacturing activities. In the first three decades of the 20th century, the manufacturing industry showed signs of growing strength; but due to the outbreak of the Second World War, which nearly paralyzed the economy, a strong industrial base did not develop until the second half of the century. After the War, the first impetus came in the 1950s when the communist victory in China unintentionally brought to Hong Kong a flow of capital, entrepreneurship and cheap labor. As Scott (1989) pointed out, '(t)he values of hard work, frugality, willingness to change and experiment and even to gamble, which the refugees and the new entrepreneurs embodied, were central to the process of industrialization and the establishment of a manufacturing base' (p.69). By 1959, the society had acquired a light industrial capacity and prospered on the export of manufactured goods. The result of this successful change from an entrepot before the War to a manufacturing base was sustained growth, despite occasional recessions, over the next thirty years. Between 1961 and 1981, the gross domestic product, in real terms, grew at an average rate of 9.9% annually, and at 7.4% per capita.[12] As a matter of fact, added impetuses to further development of the economy took place between 1977 and 1982 when funds flowed in from outside, due to both the changing global markets and the society's internal conditions.[13] This consolidated the society's basis as a financial centre. By 1988, Hong Kong was ranked as the world's eleventh-largest financial centre with 3.4% of the market.

With the continuing growth of the economy, the commercial papers have prospered and become the mainstay of the press in the society. The few commercial newspapers which were started between the two world wars managed to keep up good circulation for a few decades. They were founded by the big capitalists and most of them had strong connection with the commercial sector. For example, *Sing Tao Daily News* was started by Tiger Balm, Aw Boon Haw, who was a multi-millionaire who turned to newspaper publishing with an ideal to 'speak for the public'. The paper, which remained a popular paper in the early 1990s, was richly supported by advertisers.[14] In the meantime, as the economy brought about general improvement in the socio-economic situation of the workers, there appeared some papers which targeted at the lower stratum. (One example was *Success Daily*, which was established in 1939 and once ranked second in terms of readership in the early 1990s.) After the Second World War, the expansion of the Chinese-language newspapers has been remarkable. A few of the currently best-selling papers were founded in this period – *Ming Daily* (1959), *Express Daily* (1963), *Oriental Daily News* (1969) and *Economic Journal* (1973). By the mid 1970s, the proliferation of the commercial press amounted to what Chang (1982) called a 'veritable newspaper "explosion"'. The 'explosion' gave Hong Kong the highest density of newspapers in the world, averaging one daily to every 53,000 persons, as compared to one newspaper to every 600,000 in Japan and 110,000 in the United States.[15] As of 1980, Hong Kong had a daily consumption rate of 350 newspapers per 1,000 population – second to Japan in Asia, ahead of the United States and three times the world average.[16] Today the bulk of the circulation and advertising revenues continue to be claimed by these market-oriented papers, accounting for over 90% of the total readership.

Recently, with regard to these market-oriented newspapers, there have been some significant changes over ownership terms. Previously, most of the newspapers were owned solely by publishers and individual families. Ownership was essentially private. By the mid 1980s, as the press market became more and more competitive, the need to raise capital drove a few big newspapers such as *SCM Post*, *Sing Tao Daily News* and *Ming Daily* to re-organize their firms as public corporations and extend their investments in other related business areas. The result of this intense competition among the commercial press is a situation of oligopoly, with the top five papers grabbing hold of more than 80% of readership.[17] In this situation, while the relative autonomy of the commercial media is in doubts, it is nonetheless safeguarded, to some extent, by the presence of a competitive market versus monopoly, and the practice of press freedom by the state. The question of press freedom is an issue that I will discuss in the next section.

Finally, the economy has had some significant impact on the class structure. By the end of the 19th century, the society was divided mainly between a small capitalist class (6.7%) and a huge working class (84.2%).[18] The middle class did not make a marked presence in the society, in terms of both numbers and political significance. After the Second World War, the prosperous development of the economy together with the opening up of more and more educational opportunities facilitated upward social mobility from the working class to the middle class.[19] Employment in the major areas of the service sector rose substantially in the late 1970s and 1980s. These included the financial sector, utilities, and community, social and personal services. As we will see in section four, some of these young, middle-class professionals, strong in their political beliefs and aspirations, have played a most active role in the public sphere of politics since the late 1970s and the early 1980s.

Relative Political Autonomy of the Commercial Press vis-à-vis the State

In practice, state control over the press in Hong Kong had been one of the least direct and strict in Asia, second to if not equaled in Japan.[20] Yet rather paradoxically, strict legal restraints on press freedom had existed side by side with the practice of press freedom. From a legal perspective, the colonial state had immense coercive power over the press. Among the ordinances in Hong Kong, over thirty set very strict restraints on press freedom, for example, the Control of Publications Ordinance and the Public Order Ordinance.[21] Nevertheless, the law was one thing and practice was another. The reason for rare enforcement of the strict ordinances was two-fold. Firstly, the government could not afford to seriously offend China on whose good will only can Hong Kong survive. The initial intent of these ordinances was to stem the influence of Communist propaganda and to prevent the internal struggles in China from spilling into Hong Kong.[22] However, after an unsuccessful attempt to test China's might, the government had not been strict in their enforcement. Secondly, the government felt secure enough to let the media operate with little state intervention. It was not that the government did not fear public challenges – the fact was the government did have careful monitoring over public opinion so as to make sure the vital interests of British rule would not be jeopardized – it was rather because there were no indigenous political parties and no strong enough labor unions in the society to present any formidable challenge to the colonial power.[23] As a result, the law over the press was rarely enforced except in times of emergency, such as during the riots in 1951, 1956 and 1967.[24] On the whole, except for the few occasions when the government had taken action against newspapers to maintain public order, the press was allowed a high degree of press freedom. Moreover, after the Sino-British Joint Declaration was signed in 1984, many of these ordinances had been repealed, partly out of the fear that they might fall into the unrestrained hands of Communist China after 1997.[25]

As a matter of fact, the press were free to operate in the market with little requirement from the government.[26] In a situation where direct state control over the media was scant and where the economy developed quickly, the press system in Hong Kong had seen the coexistence of a pool of commercial newspapers competing intensely among themselves and a bunch of subsidized partisan newspapers serving as the mouthpieces of particular political parties or fractions in Mainland China and Taiwan.

While the commercial press owed no allegiance to any political group or party, they were not apolitical in its role but served as a political public sphere in the community in various ways. First, as agents of news-making, they provided an open discursive space for both state and non-state actors to comment on each other and speak to the public through press conferences, interviews, protests and other kinds of public campaign. The increase in social protests in the 1970s, the struggles over political reform in the 1980s, and the introduction of direct elections to the Legislative Council in the early 1990s had re-shaped the play of politics in a way that leaned more and more towards media publicity. (This is an issue I will discuss in greater depth in later sections.) Secondly, the editorial column in each paper was itself an expression of the opinions and positions of the paper, which belonged to the public of private citizens. Today the major newspapers all carried daily editorials, even though not all of them were of high quality. Previously, a small number of newspapers such as *Success Daily* had been too apolitical to bother publishing political commentaries of any kind. However, in the 1970s and the 1980s, with the formation of a 'pristine Hong Kong identity' and the emergence of the '1997' issue, a process of politicization in the society had its impact felt in the press. In mid 1983, for instance, *Success Daily* suddenly instituted a daily editorial and solicited articles from pro-China columnists. This revealed a change in the political stances of the paper. Thirdly, besides editorials, most of the newspapers had columns for political commentaries by free-lance writers and for letters from the readers, which formed an arena for debate of greater intellectual depth among the public, especially the academics, politicians and political activists. In this regard, *Economic Journal* is noted for its penetrating economic analysis and serious political commentaries, by both the editors and its outside contributors, and *Ming Daily* is noted for its 'juxtaposition of a reserved editorial stance on the front page ... with critical commentaries made by free-lance writers on inside pages'.[27]

For one thing, while the press industry flourished under a prosperous economy and the practice of press freedom, there had been limits to complete press freedom. In the first place, under British colonialism, the British Official Secrets Act prohibited media coverage of unauthorized official information. In a context where the Executive Council adhered to the principle of confidentiality, this curtailed the scope of publicness. In the second place, since the emergence of the '1997' issue, there grew a tendency of self-censorship among the press,[28] as inspired by anticipatory fear of the Chinese government taking offense at their criticisms and as a result of the gradually built-in media-state ties.[29] These constraining forces were indeed making partial inroads upon press freedom, but they were, at best, currently being offset by three major factors. The first one was the need for the press to take into account the market environment which was perpetually fearful of China impeding Hong Kong's interests. The second factor was the relative diversity that the press as a whole had shown, in terms of their political positions, their target readers, and their editorial policies. Third, as I will discuss in the following section, increasing political mobilization within the civil society helped keep alive a sphere of public criticism and expand the scope of publicness. In this connection, the strengthening of the link between the state and the society by means of elections, especially direct elections, to the Legislative Council instituted a new political culture that stresses the centrality of the 'public'. This will be discussed in the final section of the chapter.

Political Organizing within Civil Society by the Early 1990s

While the growth of the capitalist economy has given rise to a civil society relatively independent of state control, increasing political mobilization of the citizens, especially the middle class, has had a great impact on the development of the public sphere since the 1980s. Before the Second World War, Hong Kong was marked by the absence of a community of equal citizens. The society not only saw a deep division between a small capitalist class and a huge working class, but was also characterized as 'a society of transients and migrants' (Chan, 1989:1). In the early days, besides being a commercial haven for the foreign merchants, Hong Kong was a refuge for those Chinese trying to stay away from the turmoil in China. The several waves of immigration in the first half of the 20th century resulted in a population made up largely of China born. In particular, many of the anti-Communist Chinese had longed for returning to the Chinese homeland someday. As such, there was little sense of taking Hong Kong as a home-place or a political community of their own. After the War, demographic changes gave rise to an increase in the size of the local born Chinese who, unlike the preceding generations, had their 'roots' planted in Hong Kong. By the 1970s the proportion of local born grew so steadily that a Hong Kong identity began to emerge.[30] Among these local born, due to economic development and educational expansion, many of them have moved up the social ladder, swelling an otherwise small middle class in the society.

While structural changes resulted in the growth of a local-born middle class, in the 1980s, conjuncturally, a few events facilitated increasing organizational mobilization and public participation among the middle class, giving rise to a new form of politics which put increasing emphasis on the centrality of the public. These events included the Sino-British negotiations in the early 1980s, the discussion and introduction of political reform since 1985 (especially the introduction of direct elections to the Legislative Council in 1991), the drafting of the Basic Law in 1985-1990, and the Tiananmen Square incident in 1989. The society before then, of course, was not absent of political actions and political associations. Large-scale workers' strikes took place in the late nineteenth and the early twentieth centuries; a few political groups demanding constitutional reforms were formed in the late 1940s and the early 1950s; society-wide riots broke out in the 1960s and so on. However, these mobilization efforts showed to be infrequent and sporadic. Political action of more long-lasting impact nonetheless emerged in the 1970s. During that decade, in the context of a fast growing capitalist economy as well as an equally undemocratic colonial political system, politicization of local housing issues and a global current of student activism helped facilitate the formation of pressures groups by local activists and the mobilization of collective actions by student leaders who championed the cause of social reforms for the lower class. In particular, the People's Council on Public Housing Policy and Society for Community Organization were the most active instigators of social strikes on issues relating to general livelihood, especially housing.[31] At the same time, there existed a different kind of pressure groups, which were formed by the middle class professionals and which made criticisms against government policies not so much through strikes as through public writing and private lobbying. The Hong Kong Observers, which was founded in 1975, belonged to this category. According to Scott (1989), it was a group of young Chinese professionals who, in openly discussing current affairs, established a reputation as 'trenchant critics of the government' (p.209). In retrospect, it formed the forerunner of the type of middle-class pressure groups which was to emerge in the 1980s.

In 1982-84, as the Sino-British negotiations aroused uncertainty about the future of the society, numerous groups were formed among the middle-class businessmen, professionals and academics. The prominent ones included Meeting Point, Hong Kong Affairs Society, the Hong Kong People's Association, the New Hong Kong Society, the Society for Social Research, the Hong Kong Forum, Progressive Hong Kong Society and so on. Networking among these people was established upon three bases: (i) past participation in social movements, (ii) close friendship and common political concerns, and (iii) affiliation with some pre-existing groups in the society such as community groups, religious organizations, professional bodies or commercial organizations. During the Sino-British negotiations, their participation in politics mainly took the form of open discussion and debate through the media such as writing newspaper articles and speaking in mediatized forums. The reasons for adopting such publicist strategies were two-fold. First, they were loosely organized opinion and discussions groups, which intended to voice out their concerns and opinions in the public rather than seek for political power in any immediate way. Secondly, since the Hong Kong people had been denied the right to participate in the formal decision-making process, not only with regard to day-to-day operation of the local government but also vis-à-vis the Sino-British negotiation over the future of the society, it would be the media rather than the state that was more accessible to the people as a field of struggles. This consolidated the role of the media as the political public sphere in opposition to the state(s).

While the Sino-British negotiations ended with the signing of the Joint Declaration in 1984, political struggles continued among the people, out of which the current pattern of political alignments and divisions was to come into shape. In the two years after 1984, political alignments evolved alongside the debates on the 1985 elections and later on the 1988 elections in the context of the government's consultative exercise over its reform scheme. The society saw the gradual formation of two opposing camps – the democrats and the conservatives. By 1987, the democrats coalesced into a Joint Committee of 95 grassroots organization called the Committee for the Promotion of Democratic Self-government, which called for the introduction of direct elections to the Legislative Council in 1988, which up to then had had no elected members. In reaction, a group of 84 business organizations and 396 individuals formed to oppose the introduction of direct elections in 1988. (The government finally scheduled to introduce limited direct elections in 1991 rather than in 1988.) At the same time, starting in 1985, political alignments developed alongside the debate on the drafting of the Basic Law of the future government under Chinese sovereignty. 89 businessmen and professionals in the Basic Law drafting and consultative committees formed a bloc agitating for the preservation of the executive-oriented system of government whereas a coalition of 190 liberals, many of whom were not in the committees, formed to demand greater executive accountability to a directly-elected legislature.

In the summer of 1989, amidst the Basic Law drafting process, the thunderous Tiananmen Square event took place in Beijing, as a result of which political conflicts in the society were both deepened and re-configured, especially over the relationship with China. During the event, the Hong Kong people had demonstrated unprecedented unity and fervency in their condemnation of the Chinese government and in their demand for faster democratization in the society. While the democrats were quick to capitalize on this rising tide of public aspirations, the conservative groups and the pro-China forces were alarmed at the increasing influence of the democrats, especially in face of the scheduled introduction of direct election to the Legislative Council in 1991.

In December 1989, among the democrats, the United Democrats of Hong Kong (UDHK) was established, which was the first organization to proclaim itself to be a political party aiming at elections. UDHK was nonetheless labeled by Beijing as 'anti-China' because of the group's overlapping leadership role in the Hong Kong Alliance in Support of the Patriotic Democratic Movement in China. As a result, Meeting Point and the Association for Democracy and People's Livelihood remained independent of UDHK while at times acting as the group's strategic allies. Other liberal-oriented businessmen and professionals who did not identify with UDHK set up their own group in June 1990, known as the Hong Kong Democratic Foundation. By 1990-91, these different groups claimed to represent the pro-democracy camp.[32]

As regards the conservatives, they were split among themselves. Not only did the Democratic Foundation lean towards the democrats, the group of 89 businessmen and professionals in the Basic Law committees split into two organizations – the Business and Professional Federation (BPF), which actively lobbied the Chinese government for their own interests, and the Liberal Democratic Federation, which aimed at supporting candidates to run for elections to counteract the influence of the democrats.[33] As for the pro-China forces, the New Hong Kong Alliance was established in 1989 by some leading businessmen and professionals, who formulated a political model whereby the democrats might be prevented from dominating the future legislature. Other pro-China figures began to re-align among themselves in preparation for the 1991 elections. The Association for

Betterment of Hong Kong was set up in this context, which later developed into a political party in 1992.[34]

The introduction of direct elections to the Legislative Council in 1991 signified the beginning of a process of increasing societalization of the state, which resulted in increasing conflicts within the state institution. Political groups and individual activists who had been kept out of state power jockeyed for inclusion into the state through public elections. As it turned out, the democrats swept 12 of the 18 seats for directly elected members of the 60-member Legislative Council. Despite their landslide victory, the conservatives had a membership of 21 people in the new legislature and continued to play a dominate role there. By 1992, among the conservatives, 12 appointed members and 8 functional representative aligned themselves and formed the Cooperative Resource Centre, which evolved into the Liberal Party in 1993. On the part of the pro-China organizations, as Chinese officials openly claimed to support the development of party politics in Hong Kong by early 1992, the Democratic Alliance for the Betterment of Hong Kong (DABHK) aiming at the 1995 elections was formed in May 1992, with the blessing of China.

In a nutshell, with the increasing politicization of the society, the 1990s has seen the formation of political parties within the respective political camps, namely the democrats, the conservatives and the pro-China groups. Among the latter two, nevertheless, some prefer exercising their influence through private lobbying, especially with the Beijing officials, to participating in electoral politics. On the contrary, those who have formed into parties adopt a high profile in the public arena, taking every chance to enhance their own public credibility in the new political game – direct elections.

The Rise of a New Conception of the 'Public'

Since the 1970s, the system of political co-optation and channeled consultation by the government was designed to create an image of public consent while containing possible discontents against the administration. The system had worked for some time but later failed to accommodate increasing challenges from the periphery. The 1970s already saw a growth of incidents of strikes against state policies. In the 1980s, the system cracked up in the face of increasing political mobilization of the society. Conspicuously, the demand of public opinion went beyond the limits imposed on government by the colony's political and economic situation.

For instance, in 1984, the government organized the assessment of public opinion on the Sino-British Joint Declaration. An office was set up to monitor and receive public comments, but the government made clear that it could allow neither modifications of the terms of the Agreement nor alternatives to the document. As such, feelings of alienation and frustration set in for those who had been encouraged to speak up and then found that nothing came of it. More remarkably, in 1987, concomitant with the government's setting up of a Survey Office to assess public views on the 1988 elections, a mobilization of public opinion by non-governmental efforts reached an unprecedented scale in the society – plentiful public opinion surveys were commissioned, series of seminars were held, messages were continually broadcast on television and society-wide signature campaigns were launched.[35] In particular, the Committee for the Promotion of Democratic Self-government collected 230,000 signatures in favor of introducing direct elections to the Legislative Council in 1988. However, as it came out, the Survey Office report made it appear that the public did not want direct elections in 1988. The government was therefore suspected of unscrupulous manipulation of data due to oppositions from China and the conservative forces.

It was obvious to all that political system lacked the institutional resources to respond properly to public criticisms, as a result of which the public credibility of the government was severely undermined. In this context, especially in view of the '1997' issue, the people made increasing demand for political inclusion. In their struggles, a new conception of the 'public' is seen in the making, which poses a fundamental challenge to the one adhered to by the government. The new set of norms/ codes governing the public conduct of the actors in the public sphere, including state officials and citizens, are 'public accountability', 'representativeness' and 'transparency'. While these values get only partially institutionalized, they are becoming more and more important as the normative guides to the politics of public credibility.

Representativeness

Before the 1980s, the government bureaucracy was the sole repository of power with the appointment-based Executive and the Legislative Councils acting as its major advisory bodies. In the 1980s, the existing form of government, especially the appointment system within the two central Councils, began to be put into question. The confidential Sino-British negotiation over the 'sovereignty' question forced into being among the Hong Kong people the issue of whether they themselves would have any say in the determination of their future. While the two sovereign powers, in their competition for political control over Hong Kong after 1997, claimed to represent the interests of the people of Hong Kong, the OMELCO members (i.e. the Executive and the Legislative Councilors) went to London and Beijing to articulate the major concern of the Hong Kong people, as they understood it.[36] However, both London and Beijing refused to recognize the political status of the OMELCO members, which then raised questions in the public as to whether the appointed individuals could be considered as representing their opinions. Indeed for some time the Hong Kong people were at a loss about who represented their interests. What they were sure of was that neither the two sovereign powers nor the local elites did. In this context, the pro-democracy activists later came to provide for a more satisfactory answer, which was a system of direct elections based on equal political rights among the citizens. The years of political struggles for greater democracy since then have seen the budding of a new kind of political culture that gives high public regard for the directly elected members/ bodies and low public regard for those who hang onto a system of appointment. The Legislative Council and the two Basic Law Committees were two cases in point.

Public Accountability

Accountability is 'the liability to give an account to legitimate political authority about one's actions' (Lam and Lee, 1993:173). Despite the government's claim that it was run 'for the people', the civil service and the two major Councils were (and still are) by constitution held accountable to the Queen in London rather than the local people. In the struggle for representative democracy, the people have demanded public accountability, which requires the government to be appraised and monitored by the local citizens rather than the Queen in London or the officials in Beijing. It means, in other words, an affirmation of the importance of elections (especially direct elections), and the centrality of public opinion in politics. More concretely, with respect to the second emphasis, the government has to, in the least, respond to questions and criticisms being raised by the public including legislative members, political groups, interest groups, mass media and ordinary citizens. While the appointment of individuals to the Executive and the Legislative Councils may allow the administration to be exposed to a limited degree of publicness when answering questions and explaining policies to the Councilors, public accountability will be greatly enhanced by means of direct elections to the legislature and institutionalized executive accountability to the legislature.

Since 1991, when direct election was first introduced to the Legislative Council, the politics of public accountability begins to turn the Council into a form of adversarial legislature, which replaces the traditional style of politics of 'consent'.[37] As *SCM Post* put it,

> What will be new in the next session of the Legislative Council will be the sound of a voice unmistakably populist. Instead of being a chamber of patronage, and a rubber-stamping mechanism to approve the executive's will, it will take on the role of a public watchdog, albeit with too few teeth to inflict a real bite. (*SCM Post*, 9 September 1991)

In accordance with such changes, senior civil servants are required to act more frequently in public, to explain policies, to answer questions and to receive comments from the Legislative Council. The elected Councilors, in turn, ready themselves to be scrutinized by the public. In this context, on the one hand, the elected members begin exercising stronger supervisory role and legislative functions. On the other hand, public opinion surveys and public criticisms in the form of newspaper commentaries, television programmes, radio phone-ins have increased substantially, which thereby strengthen the role of the public in politics.

Transparency

One of the operative words today in Hong Kong politics is 'transparency', which means being open with the general public about the making as well as discharging of decisions. During the Sino-British negotiation, which denied the participation of the Hong Kong people, both the legislators and the public had called for the lifting of the veil of confidentiality. The idea of transparency or openness actually formed an essential element in the politics of public accountability. By 1991, not only did the politics of direct elections enhanced publicness through publicist campaigns, the newly-formed Legislative Council also instituted a practice of open in-house meetings which welcomed media coverage. As a result, 'the public can now see how some key decisions are taken, and how agenda items are discussed. The electorate can check whether or not their legislators are fulfilling their duties and honoring their campaign promises' (*SCM Post*, 30 November 1991). Concomitant with this was the administration's effort to re-organize its information channels with the declared aim of being more accessible to the general public. Consensus politics, which kept disputes out of the public eye, have become out of fashion.

In the political arena, while the culture of democratic publicness is in the making, there has not been a complete break with the tradition of consultative authoritarianism. China is alarmed at and unaccustomed to a system of democracy; the conservative elites has been resistant to changes and are now struggling to re-position themselves at the crossroads of two opposing sets of political values; the Hong Kong people in general, including the democrats, are just beginners in the new game of political democracy. In such a context, while the tide of change has been high, the remnants of the colonial legacy, which stresses political stability over and above democratic progress, may surface in public discourse from time to time.

Conclusion

The political history of Hong Kong started with Britain's occupation of the territory in 1842. Under British colonial rule, what appeared in the early days was not a civil society widely organized among a populace of equal citizens, but a mosaic of different sectional 'publics' within different communities of people. The early press did serve as an open arena for public discussion within the disparate communities, but due to the parochial character of these communities, the press did not develop into an inclusive public sphere. By the 1980s, the development of the commercial press has given birth to what I call a general public sphere within the wider community. This is the result of a number of interacting structural and conjunctural factors: (i) a growing private economic domain which has been financially viable enough to support the press industry, (ii) a state which is characterized by a relatively high degree of press freedom in practice, (iii) growing organizational mobilization among the citizens, especially the middle class, and (iv) the emergence of the '1997' issue as well as the related questions which has brought about a heightened political consciousness in the citizenry. At the same time, the gradual opening up of the Legislative Council as well as the lower-tier councils since the 1980s results in a process of increasing societalization of the state. This marks out a sphere of politics which increasingly stresses the role of the public. All these factors come to shape the political and discursive dynamics in the public sphere in recent years – in terms of both the kinds of actors that come to the forefront of the public stage and the conceptions of the 'public'.

Notes

1. For reference, see Lam (1977), Chang (1982).
2. Scott (1989), p.41.
3. According to Chan (1989), while the Opium War was the immediate event that brought about Britain's occupation of Hong Kong, the underlying cause was 'the conflict between British free traders and the Chinese Authorities, which had developed over a long period of Sino-British trade' (p.12).
4. Chan, 1989, p.32.
5. See Lam, p.6.
6. Chan, p.58.
7. Ibid., p.34.
8. Ibid., p.36.
9. Ibid., p.83 and p.188.
10. See Scott (1989), p.60.
11. Davies' study (1977) showed that in 1972, regarding the Executive and Legislative Councils, 45% of the members were representatives of the major business concerns, while 48% were top civil servants. It was also concluded that owing to common interests and strong social networking among them, the two categories of people together formed a cohesive elites group in the society.
12. See Miners (1986), p.35.
13. See Scott (1989), p.229.
14. Chang, 1982, pp.81-82.
15. Ibid. p.85. According to Chan and Lee (1991), of the 485 publications registered with the government, 57 were newspapers and half of these, appearing irregularly, were devoted to horse-racing tips and entertainment gossip. About 20 warranted government monitoring. See p.12.
16. See Chan and Lee, p.12; Hutcheon, 1983, p.129.
17. See Pui (1993), *Intraorganizational Power Distribution within the Newspaper Industry in Hong Kong*. According to Pui, among the numerous Chinese papers, only five were able to make profits – *Oriental Daily News, Ming Daily, Sing Tao Daily News, Success Daily and Economic Journal*, and the first three were then on the stock market. In fact, commercial competition was not the only reason for a change to corporatization. The year 1984 in which the Sino-British Joint Declaration was signed saw the forthcoming resumption of Chinese sovereignty over Hong Kong. Some newspaper firms responded to the power change with efforts to shelter themselves as public

corporations, hoping to use the public to fend off political pressure from China (*Economic Journal*, 2 March 1991). In this connection, there appeared some attempts to internationalize newspaper ownership in Hong Kong. On this issue, see Lee's analysis in *Economic Journal*, 18 December 1991.

18.   See Chan, p.86.

19.   Scott describes this new middle class as follows: 'it is more of a salariat than a traditional production-owning bourgeoisie. It owes its affluence to the expansion of private and public sector bureaucracies, to the economy's need for more professionals and to the new opportunities available in the financial sector. Its members are young, products of the educational progress of the MacLehose years. Often they come from poor families who emigrated from China in the 1950' (p.245).

20.   See Chang, p.82; Chan and Lee, p.7.

21.   Many of them were introduced after the Communist takeover of Mainland China in 1949 and after the 1967 local riots. Before the riots took place in 1966 and 1967, most of the legal suspensions of the newspapers were for publishing obscene rather than political matter. See Clayton, p.58.

22.   For reference, see Chan and Lee (1991), p.10; Chang (1982), p.83.

23.   This freedom was extended primarily with reference to the contending Chinese parties, not toward the colonial government itself. The Hong Kong press had always had considerable freedom to attack Chinese rulers, but it had never been allowed to jeopardize the vital interests of British rule.

24.   For example, in 1967, the publishers, editors and printers of three leftist newspapers were convicted of sedition under the Control of Publications Ordinance. The three newspapers were ordered suspended for six months and sentences of three years' imprisonment and fines amounting to US$2,000 were imposed on the executives.

25.   See Chan and Lee (1991), p.9.

26.   Before the mid 1980s, in principle, anyone could start a new publication so long as he/she was willing to pay a small amount as safety deposit or provide two guarantors approved by the government. In 1986 this safety deposit requirement was ended with the repeal of the Control of the Publication Ordinance.

27.   Chan and Lee, 1991, p.71.

28.   A survey with a systematic sample of jounralists from 25 news organizations conducted in 1990 revealed that self-censorship haunted the journalists in Hong Kong, who were very concerned about the condition of press freedom in the future. See Chan and Lee, p.145. '

29.   In Chan and Lee's book (1991:57), the authors list 21 prominent media proprietors and senior journalists who have been coopted by the colonial government, the Chinese government.

30.   A Hong Kong Observer poll taken in the early 1980s showed that 65% of the Hong Kong people considered their home-place to be in Hong Kong, and only 24% (mostly the elderly) in China. For reference, see Chan and Lee,

p.11.

31. The Reform Club and the Civic Association, which were founded in 1949 and 1954 respectively, had officially nominated candidates to run for the Urban Council elections since 1952 and were therefore sometimes considered as quasi-political parties. However, since the franchise of the Urban Council elections was limited to less than one percent of the population before 1981, they could not claim to have any mass support. They did not play any significant role at the local level and were gradually overshadowed by the emergence of some grassroots pressure groups in the late 1960s and the the 1970s. For reference, see Lam and Lee (1993), p.64.

32. See Lam and Lee, 1993, pp.65-71.

33. Ibid., p.72.

34. Ibid.

35. Ching, *SCM Post*, 9 February 1990.

36. See Lam and Lee (1993), p.89.

37. See Lam and Lee (1993), pp.154-160.

6 Political-Cultural Context in the Early 1990s

Power Relationships, Ideological Differences, and Contending Actors

Power Alliance between the Colonial State and the Socio-economic Elite

To reiterate, under British colonial rule, the political system in Hong Kong had been characterized as closed, authoritarian, elitist and consensus-oriented. Political power was highly concentrated in the hands of the central administration headed by the governor. As part of the governing strategy of the colonial government to establish legitimacy in the Chinese community, the civil service, the executive and the legislative councils provided for important sites for co-optation of the economic and social elite in society, especially the big capitalists (King 1975). In particular, the two central councils co-opted the elite by means of a system of appointment whereby the selected elite might build up a co-operative relationship with the government within the political institution (Lam and Lee 1993; Miners 1991).

Despite their pro-government stance, the socio-economic elite was not a group of loyalists who were ready to pay back the government at any cost. Rather they had their own interests to take care of. Partnership between the government and the socio-economic was based on a relationship of mutual interest within the context of capitalism. As we have discussed in chapter five, the early development of a vibrant economic sector of trading activity outside the state had nurtured the power of the mercantile community vis-à-vis the state. This laid the basis for the establishment of a strong political tie between the colonial state and the capitalists.

In large measure the state and the capitalists shared common interests, though history showed that there were not without conflicts between them in the early days. Economically, the government's concern for capital accumulation and economic growth struck consonance with the capitalists' self-interest in maximizing profits within their enterprises. Politically, both of them believed the time-honoured undemocratic political system could preserve their power while maintaining a politically stable environment conducive to economic growth. In other words, they believed in the ideology of economic prosperity and were resistant to political change, especially democratic reform. This partly explained why the colonial government's introduction of representative government in 1985 and 1998 was proved to be half-hearted attempts for democratic reform. For example, the political privilege of the socio-economic elite, capitalists and professionals alike, was being maintained under the guise of election by functional constituency after 1985 (Leung 1990).

As we can see, partnership between the state and the socio-economic elite was based on mutual interest. As such they formed into a strategic power alliance. Insofar as their relationship was dictated by the logic of pragmatic calculation as well as ideological affinity, the alliance between them would remain intact; however, as soon as their interests began to diverge, changes would take place in the relationship of alliance. This was the situation in the late 1980s and the early 1990s when the Chinese government began to consolidate its sovereign power in the local society in lieu of British colonial rule, and when the British government sought to introduce more democratic changes as part of its de-colonization scheme in the late-transitional phase (especially after the crackdown of the student movement in Beijing in 1989).

The Democrats' Struggles for Political Citizenship

The pro-democracy activists or the democrats were local-born, well-educated professionals, and belonged to the post-World War II baby boom cohort. They had been actively involved in the student movement and the community movement in the late 1970s just before the advent of the 1997 issue. These experiences of political mobilization to a large extent had nourished among them a critical stance toward the undemocratic colonial administration. More importantly, they had developed a strong sense about their role as citizens who were nonetheless denied the right to political participation under British colonialism.

The category of 'democrats' began to win its public recognition in the early 1980s when, with the emergence of the '1997' issue, this group of people asserted their citizenship rights vis-à-vis both British colonialism and the threat of Chinese autocracy, especially the right to democratic participation. Specifically, they aimed at a 'democratically-elected legislature (which) can be more trusted to speak for Hong Kong people and protect Hong Kong's interests' (*SCM Post*, 20 October 1992). In the second half of the 1980s, the introduction of Representative Government and the drafting of the Basic Law provided the major battlegrounds where the democrats played the role of democracy-fighter against the unholy alliance among the local socio-economic elite, the Chinese government and the British government. Their role as democracy-fighter was further transformed into a heroic image after the Tiananmen Square incident in 1989.

Before 1989, with their pro-national unification stance, the democrats managed to establish a dialogue with the Chinese officials at both Xinhua (the *de facto* embassy of China in Hong Kong) and Beijing. However, the incident in 1989 headed off any possibility for a closer relationship to be developed between the democrats and the Chinese officials. The conflict was basically one of democracy versus autocracy, which then developed into one of local autonomy versus central control, and also one of international community versus national sovereignty. The democrats acccused the Chinese government of suppressing the development of democracy and oppressing human rights. They also mobilized the Hong Kong people into open, large-scale protests against the Chinese government's crackdown on the student movement in China. In response, the Chinese government tightened its control over local politics, which was most marked in the early version of the Basic Law in 1990. In the face of political exclusion by the future sovereign state, instead of retreating from their political and moral roles, many democrats nonetheless stood up against the pressure with all the greater perseverance. It was probably this heroic image about their moral courage that led to their landslide victories in the direct elections to the legislature in 1991.

The pro-democracy activists had been struggling for inclusion into the power centre through the ideological appeal of political equality, public accountability and other democratic principles. The first introduction of direct election into the legislature in 1991 marked an important event of success in their struggles. However, since the power alliance had made strenuous efforts to restrict the pace and scope of democratic reform, the proportion of directly elected seats in the legislature was kept to a 'safe' number – 18 out of 60. The democrats, despite their landslide victory in the elections, had thus to continue with their pro-democracy struggle both within and outside the legislature.

Sino-British Competition for Dominance in Local Politics

The Chinese and the British governments had always been in an uneasy relationship over the 'Hong Kong' issue. Hong Kong was originally a part of China but was made a British colony in the 19th century under the force of some 'unequal treaties'. The numerous instances of the Hong Kong Chinese's popular mobilization between the 1830s and the 1920s had 'turned Hong Kong into a front line of Chinese nationalism vis-à-vis Western imperialism' (M. Chan, 1994). After World War Two, the British government's intent to maintain Hong Kong as part of the British Empire once came into conflict with the Chinese government's desire to reclaim Hong Kong in the context of growing anti-colonialism (J. Tang, 1994). Nevertheless, the new Communist government in China soon made clear that the recovery of Hong Kong would not be its aim in the immediate future while believing that continuation of British rule in Hong Kong might best serve China's interests for the time being. During British colonial rule, despite its proclaimed policy of making minimal intervention into the local way of life, the British had introduced western conceptions and models into the society such as rule of law and civil rights. At the same time, they guarded against any possible infiltration of Chinese Communist influence into the society. For in the shadow of the Cold War, the two countries were separated into the opposing camps of liberalism and communism. In other words, not only did the British enjoy sovereign rule in Hong Kong, it also ideologically set the society off from the Mainland. The first Sino-British negotiations on the 'Hong Kong' problem in 1982-84 were thus centred around the questions of sovereignty and governing ideology. Before the Sino-British Joint Declaration of 1984 was signed, the Chinese and the British governments had had disputes over the sovereignty issue. The British government would like to continue with their administrative rule in Hong Kong after 1997 whereas the Chinese government was adamant over the sovereignty principle. In their struggles, they had each sought to mobilize local public opinion to legitimize their positions. As it turned out, the British failed on the front of sovereignty and administrative rule but managed to secure the promise of having no change in the basic way of life in Hong Kong for fifty years after 1997.

The transitional years between 1984 and 1997 saw the two sovereign powers competing for influence and dominance in the local political setting. This was due partly to the geo-political reality of sovereignty change, partly to their ideological differences, and partly to their different national projects. On the part of the British, an important task in the de-colonization process was to introduce democratic reform as part and parcel of the national project of 'glorious retreat'. Democratic reform was their broad aim, but the specific contour of development would depend on the commitment of the British government at different historical conjunctures, the leadership styles of the different governors, and the struggles among the local elite, activists and the Chinese government. On the part of the Chinese government, its major national task vis-à-vis Hong Kong was to re-establish sovereign power and control in a lost territory where the people had shown great resistance to Chinese communism. In this connection, they kept a watchful eye on the development of political reform under the British during the transition so as to make sure things would not run off the desired track it had set in place for Hong Kong. More specifically, this would mean an opposition to drastic democratic reform. These different ideological positions of the two governments had their supporters and opponents among the local actors in one way or another. As a result, in the early transitional years, the introduction of the Representative Government by the British and the drafting of the Basic Law had provided for two major battlegrounds for struggles not only between the two sovereign powers but also among the local actors.

Shifting Political Relationships among the Contending Actors

For long the socio-economic elite had been close allies with the colonial government. They had had in common the concerns for capital accumulation and preservation of political power. At the other end of the scale, as we have discussed in the previous chapter, the pro-democracy activists had been fighting a hard struggle for democracy outside the power centre. Both the selfish orientations of the conservative elite and the lack of moral commitment to democracy in the British government had been their objects of criticism. However, the British's national project of a 'glorious retreat', which appeared to be all the more urgent after 1989, laid the basis for interest divergence between the colonial government and the socio-economic elite on the issue of political reform. (This did not present itself as an obvious change until the governorship of Chris Patten in 1992.) In the meantime, the conservative elite were drawn closer and closer to the Chinese government. The reason was two-fold. First, the two of them found much alignment between themselves on the matter of political reform. Simply put, both loathed democracy. Second, the geo-political reality of imminent Chinese sovereignty meant for both sides a political necessity to establish a relationship of strategic ally with the other. In short, in their pragmatic calculations, state power and economic power together made possible a good 'tango'. The late transitional years therefore saw the Chinese government seeking to assimilate the socio-economic elite and other influential categories of people (for example, media personnel) and the elite making every effort to secure favour with the future sovereign master. (The Patten controversy, which we shall discuss in the next few chapters, will see how the local elite were further mobilized into the pro-China camp through a process of narrative polarization.)

As we have discussed in chapter five, in the legislature in 1991, the democrats were represented mainly by members of the United Democrats of Hong Kong, Meeting Point, the Association for Democracy and People's Livelihood, and also a few individuals without party affiliations. The conservative elite were represented mainly by the members of the Co-operative Resource Centre (which later changed into the Liberal Party) and several legislators elected by functional constituency. In terms of size, the traditional pro-China forces, those from the leftist organizations, remained an insignificant force in the legislature. None the less, their presence made an innegligible presence in the political process in two ways. First, though they used to adopt a low profile in public discourse they became more vocal in the 1990s when they began to show a keen interest in direct elections. Second, as part of an expanding pro-China camp in society, their public discourses represented one of the important ideological forces shaping the cultural contour of politics in the late-transitional period. In particular, the leading members of the Democratic Alliance for the Betterment of Hong Kong had become the key spokespersons of the leftist pro-China forces over the Patten controversy.

Discursive Context at the Turn of the Decade

A culture is a web of meaningful codes that underlies the lived experiences of a collectivity. It is organized around a few central substantive value-themes put in specific narrative contexts whereby people understand their collective past, present and future as an integrated whole. Narratives, as a central mode of symbolic representation, reflect the concerns and passions of the people in a society in terms of the perceived limits and opportunities posed by their cultural and social environments. More specifically, as I have explained in chapter three, narrative form is meaning-laden in itself while allowing an intertwinement with different thematic structures to produce the meanings of a narrative in all its structural and thematic specificities. The frequent use of particular narrative forms in a society bespeaks the sedimentation of certain narrative cultures within it such as romanticism, comic realism, tragic defeatism and cynicism. In this section, I will delineate the narrative context – discursive formation – out of which the specific narratives were to develop in the event studied.

The Sino-British negotiations on the issue of sovereignty over Hong Kong started in 1982 and ended with the Joint Declaration in 1984. Despite the prevalent sense of anxiety and uncertainty among the people during the negotiation, the generally positive public responses to the Joint Declaration[1] helped institute a process of establishing the document as a sacred symbol which the Hong Kong people looked up to as the blueprint for their future. What the Joint Declaration laid out, however, was a set of abstract principles the specificities of which had taken an arduous process of struggles and negotiations to be worked out over the following few years. In particular, political conflicts developed around the government's attempt for political reforms up to 1997 and the drafting of the Basic Law, a mini-constitution of the Hong Kong under Chinese sovereignty. Notwithstanding these commonly agreed upon 'facts', the political history in this period had been narrated in different ways. In particular, the Basic Law was looked at as a symbolic configuration of very differently understood historical processes. The following will reconstruct three master narratives around three different sets of theme and lay out the variations within each of them.[2]

Narrative (I): Resumption of Chinese Sovereignty (A Mixture of Comedy and Irony)

Comic-sacredness	vs.	Profanity
Nationalism		colonialism/ imperialism
State control		local subversion
Convergence		divergence

Ironic Reality	vs.	Presupposed Ideal
State control		local autonomy

Hong Kong had been under British colonial rule for more than 150 years, and the signing of the Joint Declaration in 1984 marked the beginning of the process of China establishing its sovereign status in the society. In September 1982, the visit of the British Prime Minister, M. Thatcher, to

Beijing formally established that Britain and China would negotiate on the future of Hong Kong, which for the first time put into the public spotlight the question of Chinese sovereignty. In the Sino-British negotiation, Britain initially wished to retain an administrative presence in Hong Kong after 1997, but China insisted that they did not recognize the unequal treaties and their sole aim was to resume sovereignty over Hong Kong. To the Hong Kong people, the Chinese resumption of sovereignty not only meant a return to their long-separated 'motherland' but also an integration with a communist system. The fact was, most of the people are Chinese by blood but they have lived in a social system which is very different from that in Mainland China. Without any purposeful cultivation of a sense of nationalism by the colonial government, most of the people had not developed a strong emotional tie with the remote 'motherland'. However, as Chinese by race, neither do the people feel morally justifiable to be attached to British colonialism. Historically, the numerous instances of the Hong Kong Chinese' popular mobilization before World War Two had 'turned Hong Kong into a front line of Chinese nationalism vis-à-vis Western imperialism' (M. Chan, 1994); the late 1960s saw the storming out of anti-colonial sentiments among the more radical students and the workers of leftist trade-unions. Nevertheless, as the proportion of local born Chinese increased, the current of anti-colonialism was later pacified to a great extent through the government's public relations efforts, the system of consultation and the implementation of a number of welfare programmes in the 1970s. In this context, in view of the prospect of China's resumption of sovereignty, the Hong Kong people were torn between mild anti-colonialism and resistance to Chinese communism. On the one hand, it was generally recognized that Hong Kong was an inalienable Chinese possession which had been seized by British imperialists following the Sino-British Opium Wars in the Ching dynasty. From the perspective of nationalism, Britain had no moral base to rule over a population that is ethnically Chinese. As an academic put it,

> Hong Kong people could hardly be expected to accept the proposition that Britain had the right to rule the territory because of nineteenth-century gun-boat diplomacy conducted on behalf of drug-dealers; the advances of the 1970s had not sufficiently dispelled the image of decades of British colonialism to make that position tenable. (Scott, 1989:176)

Apparently, it was not so much out of strong nationalistic passions as out of a somewhat uneasy feeling about the continuation of British colonial rule that the people agreed to China's position. On the other hand, however, the people refused to be politically or economically associated with Communist China. The deficiencies of British colonialism were outweighed by the depth of suspicion over the Chinese government. The opinion of most of the people, as expressed in surveys and letters to the government, was that they preferred the status quo (Miners, 1986).

As it developed, the Joint Declaration signed in December 1984 saw the formulation of a resolution. It was stated that the Chinese government would regain sovereignty on 1 July 1997; yet in light of the enormous differences in the cultures and social systems of China and Hong Kong, China proposed the 'One Country, Two Systems' formula to allow Hong Kong to maintain a high degree of autonomy under Chinese sovereignty. Though the more concrete plans were yet to be devised to make the formula an actuality, the Joint Declaration was 'greeted with relief in Hong Kong and some temporary signs of confidence in the future' (Scott, 1989:189). In short, it was well-taken to be a comic advancement. However, depending on which part of the formula was stressed, some people (especially the conservative elite and the pro-China groups) were to find later development a logical fulfilment of their comic/ comic-realist expectation whereas others (especially the pro-democracy activists and critics) were disheartened at the rather ironic turn away from the once rosy promises.

The drafting of the Basic Law, which started soon after the Joint Declaration was signed, embodied the official process of political transition. The Basic Law was to be solely and ultimately a Chinese responsibility. From the perspective of sovereign control, the Chinese government insisted on the principle of 'convergence', which dictated that what was done now must not conflict with what was planned after the Chinese take-over. In concrete terms, it means that Hong Kong must be moved into alignment with the terms of the Basic Law. From the perspective of sovereign control, moreover, China sought to maintain a strong executive and a weak legislature in order to keep down the power of the challenging forces.

The Basic Law is a symbol of Chinese sovereignty. To China and the pro-China forces, the narrative development was one of comedy with China successfully resuming its lost sovereignty over the territory and then establishing its sovereign position in preparation for the formal take-over in 1997. To the conservatives, given the reality of Chinese sovereignty, the outcome was to be taken with a sense of comic realism. As a corollary, both the pro-China groups and the conservatives sought to look at the bright side of getting united with the quickly modernizing China. To the democrats, however, as the Basic Law was the result of a pressure for convergence and

China's interest in maintaining political control over the society, it meant the breaking of the promise of 'a high degree of autonomy' by the Chinese government and therefore symbolized an almost insurmountable obstruction to faster democratization than they had envisioned.

Narrative (II): The Society Struggling for Democracy (Romantic-Irony)

(a) Sub-plot I: China's opposition to faster democratic development

Ironic Reality	vs.	Presupposed Ideal
Authoritarianism		democracy
state control		local autonomy
selective consultation		equal representation
secrecy		openness

(b) Sub-plot II: Britain's moral retreat from the democratic cause

Ironic Reality	vs.	Presupposed Ideal
Submission		independent power
Retreat		responsibility
Concession		commitment
Secrecy		openness
Hypocrisy		honesty

Under British rule, no genuine democracy was developed before the 1980s, the political history in the past decade was marked by the Hong Kong people's struggles for democracy, which were a story about aspirations and continual frustrations. In the 1980s, in face of the prospect of China's resumption of sovereignty, the government began to install incremental measures of a more representative democracy in the society. Along with this, the Joint Declaration of 1984 promised a high degree of autonomy and democracy for Hong Kong, giving the people high hopes on their political future. In the meantime, the pro-democracy activists demanded an open and fully representative mode of government, both in place of the closed, consultative mode under British colonial rule and as a buffer against future communist control. However, the rather irresistible obstruction had come from the Chinese government (whom the self-seeking conservative elite allied themselves with) whereas the morally uncommitted Britain also played a part in undermining the democratic cause in the society.

To wit, the Chinese government would like to inherit the tradition under British colonialism that single-mindedly pursued economic growth and discouraged political activism. It therefore emulated the colonial status quo by absorbing into the Basic Law drafting and consultative committees largely the same conservative elite circle who would oppose comprehensive democratic reforms or drastic changes. As such, the bitter irony for the democrats to swallow was that the history of the Joint Declaration and the Basic Law represented 'a process of continuous erosion of the 1984 commitments' (Davis, *SCM Post*, 5 December 1992). In particular, in the wake of the Tiananmen Square event in 1989, the Chinese government was too alarmed to agree to the public's demand for faster democratization. In his account, Davies took China as the major obstructing power and put into context its positions on Hong Kong's political development at different political junctures:

> Back-pedalling on these commitments had its parallel in China's domestic political development during a period of crisis. When the Basic Law was signed China itself was considering political reform but this reform failed in late 1986, culminating in the demis of Hu Yaobang and the campaigning against bourgeois liberalism in 1987. The liberalising tendency was even further eroded in 1989 in the Tiananmen crisis by China's increased resistance to democracy. After June 4, intensified Chinese pressure aimed to insure that no autonomous self governing community emerged in Hong Kong. The Chinese feared Hong Kong serving as a "base for subversion". China's demands escalated moving further from the spirit of the 1984 agreement ... By the time the Basic Law was passed in early 1990, which was a few months after the June Fourth incident, China had developed extreme resistance to the democratization of Hong Kong. (Davies, *SCM Post*, 5 December 1992)

The Basic Law Drafting Committee's final version of Hong Kong's political model was much more restrictive than expected. In particular, in allowing for very limited direct elections beginning in 1991, the Basic Law fell short of the pace proposed in the model agreed upon among the society's major political groups, which had thus been regarded as a consensus of the people of Hong Kong. Moreover, the way it was hastily adopted made a mockery of first five-month consultation process. The Basic Law was therefore an index of China's opposition to more democracy in Hong Kong, and an index of China's assertion of its sovereignty at the expense of Hong Kong's autonomy. The pro-democracy camp regarded the drafting process as a farce while the community was described mostly as being disappointed:

The Basic Law is a Beijing-controlled farce ... Beijing's sole purpose seems to be to ensure as toothless and as pliant a legislative body as possible. (M. Lee of UDHK, *SCM Post*, 9 February 1990)

The final draft of the Basic Law is being greeted with a mixture of disillusionment, relief, anger, frustration and resignation. In the end ... it was secret diplomacy rather than open consultation that decided the shape of the Basic Law. (*SCM Post*, 18 February 1990)

The Basic Law is a celebration of stasis posing as progress, the preservation of privilege masquerading as a stable, 'non-radical' march towards democratic self-rule. (Lam, *SCM Post*, 28 October 1992)

At the same time, to the democrats, the Basic Law was an index of Britain's concessions in the face of China's opposition to faster democratization and a symbol of its lack of moral commitment to Hong Kong. In 1984 Britain announced a policy paper aimed to install measures of a more representative democracy in the society, partly to save face after losing battles to China and partly to forestall China's undue interference in the future. To the more cynical democrats, this reform effort by the government was a 'last-minute rush' to put institutions in order as soon as it learned of its scheduled demise, much like what a person being told of his/her terminal disease would do.[3] Still, better late than never, the democrats put their faith in the government and mobilized public support for democratic reforms. As later events showed, however, the reform plan was only a half-hearted commitment by the government.

Following the 1984 review, the government expanded the legislature with elections by functional constituency in 1985 and looked to the likelihood of introducing direct elections in 1988. The democrats called for the introduction of direct elections to the Legislative Council, and succeeded in mobilizing considerable public support through rallies and signature campaigns. However, owing to oppositions from China and the local conservative elite, the government finally decided to allow for a limited number of 10 directly elected seats to the Legislative Council in 1991 rather than in 1988. In 1989, a renewed attempt was made to press for democratic reform in the wake of Beijing's suppression of the pro-democracy movement in China. However, once again, Britain showed itself to be an untrustworthy ally who always conceded to China's will regardless of the interests and demands of the Hong Kong people. For the Basic Law was in fact a product of secret agreement between China and Britain. The narrative frame configured over the past events was one of cynical irony, which conveyed an element of distrust and a sense of betrayal:

> In the seven years since the Joint Declaration was signed, there has been the growing suspicion that Britain is retreating morally from the territory - a process of disengagement marked by compromise and concessions to the mainland authorities. Coupled with that is the impression that Britain and China are all too ready to make deals that affect Hong Kong's future without consultation and instead the territory is presented with a fait accompli on important matters... (T)rust is a quality Hong Kong people increasingly lack when they look upon the relationship between Britain and China. (*SCM Post*, 4 January 1992)

During the past decade, the Hong Kong people had met great obstacles in their fight for democracy. In this context, while the majority of the people were understood to have turned to ironic realism (or even mild cynicism), the democrats and some public critics showed romantic perseverance and/ or comic optimism about their cause. The leaders of democrats, staying on as romantic fighters for democracy, appealed to the public not to give up, saying that the day that hope was lost was the day when people finally ceased pressing for their rights. Disappointed though they were, the critics likewise painted a ray of hope out of darkness:

> If Hong Kong can demonstrate through next year's direct elections that its people are politically sensible, it will allay the Chinese Government's profound suspicion of democracy and prove to all that it can cope with 'a high degree of autonomy ... Should Hong Kong be prompted to act with more self-assurance and purposefulness by the Basic Law then this is the silver lining to the clouds shrouding an otherwise grimy situation. (*SCM Post* 18 February 1990)

In 1991, the victory of the democrats in the direct elections to the Legislative Council demonstrated that they had the support of the public for the yet-to-be-continued political battle. The weight of constraints under the Basic Law was heavy, but the public's aspirations for democracy were still there.

Narrative (III): Achievement of Prosperity and Stability (Comedy)

Comic-sacredness	vs.	Profanity
Stability		instability/ chaos
Prosperity		economic decline
Continuity		abrupt changes
co-operation		confrontation
Flexible pragmatism		naive idealism

To the British, the local government and the socio-economic elite, the success story of Hong Kong had been about its remarkable or even miraculous achievement of stability and prosperity in the few decades after the Second World War. In society, many Hong Kong people took pride in the success for it was achieved by means of hard work and other virtues rather than sheer luck. The success of the capitalist economy together with a stable polity thus created 'an aura of sacredness' around it (Lau 1988). In the early 1980s, with the emergence of the '1997' question, there were times of political uncertainty in the society giving rise to worries about possible changes in the status quo. As an act of pacification, both the Chinese and the British governments entered talks with an emphasis on 'the common aim of maintaining the stability and prosperity of Hong Kong'. This rhetorical appeal struck resonance among the people and since then became a focal point in public discourse. With these thematic concerns, some people, especially the conservatives, took the Basic Law to be symbolic pledges by China (and Britain) to ensure a stable and prosperous future for Hong Kong.

During the Sino-British negotiation in the 1980s, there were a few moments of apprehension in the society when the issue of Chinese sovereignty was raised, and when Britain agreed to retreat its administrative presence from Hong Kong after in 1997. Many people preferred the status quo of capitalism, for in their memories and imaginations Chinese communism was associated with chaos and turmoils.[4] Indeed the achievement of economic prosperity and political stability had made Hong Kong compare admirably well to China and therefore made British colonial rule tolerable or even desirable. The people, especially the businessmen, were worried that political uncertainty would lead to economic fluctuations or even decline in terms of capital inflow/ outflow. By 1984, when the 'One Country Two Systems' formula was made known to the Hong Kong society, the local businessmen felt reassured, for this made clear the message that China would not want to 'kill the goose that lays the golden eggs'. As the people had wished for, the existing socio-economic system was to remain unchanged in the near future. As such, the Joint Declaration marked a significant turn from the state of comic-ironic worries towards a comic resolution. This view was still affirmed after one year:

> In 1985, the greatest achievement of Hong Kong is its enhanced political stability. One year after the signing of the Sino-British Joint Declaration, the 'one country two systems' formula has come to impress more and more upon the people as a feasible proposal. (*Success Daily*, 7 January 1986)

Moreover, with the opening up of the economy in China since the late 1970s, the local businessmen who were most eager to start new economic ventures in the vast continent began to develop close economic ties with China. Apparently, in the economic arena, the two systems, despite their vast differences, were having a happy 'marriage' based on common interests. In a word, it was out of pragmatic considerations that the union with the 'motherland' turned into a comedy of reassurance and new opportunities.

During the 1980s, over the debates on political development, the conservatives businessmen, who had entrenched interests in the existing political system, opposed an early introduction of direct elections to the legislature for the reason that drastic changes and grassroots democracy might cost the society its stability and economic efficiency. Through their articulations, 'stability' and 'prosperity' became associated with orderly and gradual change as opposed to drastic reformation or democratization. Moreover, given that the Chinese government did not favor quick democratization in the society, the conservatives believed that co-operation with rather than confrontation against the Chinese government was desirable, for this was the only way to safeguard order, continuity and smooth transition. In the Basic Law drafting process, the conservative elite, many of whom were members of the Drafting or Consultative Committees, had proposed to slow down the pace of democratic reform, which was in alignment with the emphasis of the Chinese government. In this regard, the final version of the Basic Law was obviously skewed towards the positions of the Chinese government and the most conservative groups; to them, the Basic Law was a successful achievement after years of consultations, negotiations and compromises. In short, the narrative construction was one of comedy. The following two accounts were examples of a comic-realist mode of understanding which celebrated order, co-operation and pragmatic considerations:

The basic spirit of the Basic Law is to safeguard the preservation of the capitalist system and existing way of life in Hong Kong after 1997 ... After the political debate (over the Basic Law), the task of the Hong Kong people is to get united in their effort to strengthen the local economy and to contribute to China's modernization so as to create all the conditions conducive to smooth transition. (*Success Daily*, 17 February 1990)

The Business and Professional Federation of Hong Kong strongly believes a smooth transition in 1997 and convergence with the Basic Law is in the best interests of the territory ... Our future lies in a sound working relationship with China ... It is unrealistic to assume there could be major changes in China's overall policy towards Hong Kong. (BPF, *SCM Post*, 22 November 1992)

Concluding Remarks

As far as political culture is concerned, while the normative force of democracy was on the rise, there had not been a complete break with the tradition of consultative authoritarianism. The Chinese government was alarmed at and unaccustomed to a system of democracy; the conservative elite had been resistant to changes and were struggling to re-position themselves at the crossroads of two opposing sets of political values; the Hong Kong people in general, including the democrats, were just beginners in the new game of political democracy. In terms of narrative culture, comic realism and romanticism had co-existed as the major narrative currents in public discourses among, respectively the conservative elite and the pro-democracy activists. Comic realism celebrates flexible pragmatism and regards co-operation and compromises as the most desired attributes for an orderly existence whereas romanticism presents itself as a strong conviction in the spirit and conduct of combating for the democratic ideal vis-à-vis China. The Hong Kong people had showed their aspirations for more democracy and autonomy, but under the weight of the reality of Chinese sovereignty and of a deep-rooted fear for instability, they either learned to live with the two rather opposing narrative currents or turn to ironic realism. Among the major political actors, the democrats had stuck to the romantic-ironic frame of narration with the aim of continuing with the pro-democracy cause, but it was not quite clear how and how far they were able to break through the given constraints – the materiality of the Basic Law stipulations and the countervailing force of oppositions, reservations and indifference among the people. In this context, Governor Patten's reform proposals appeared to make an effective boost for the democratic cause.

Notes

1. The editorial in *Ming Daily* wrote, 'After a detailed reading of the agreement, we discovered the demands that we have raised in the past two years have all been incorporated. We may say that both China and Britain have accepted all – not just the basic ones but 100% – of the requests made by the majority of the Hong Kong people. We cannot really think of what else to add to such an agreement. The Hong Kong people have got what they wished, what else can they ask for?' (2 July 1984).
2. The master narratives are reconstructed by way of making a conceptual distinction between analytic autonomy and concrete autonomy of culture. For a more elaborate discussion of the distinction, see Alexander (1990), and Kane (1991).
3. See Ching's article in *SCM Post*, 25 Janunary 1991.
4. According to Chan and Lee (1991), 'Memories of China's tumults, bloodshed, and purges of the previous decades, especially during the Cultural Revolution, linger vividly in the minds of the Hong Kong people. China's reform decade of the 1980s was also interspersed with campaigns against "spiritual pollution" and "bourgeois liberation", each time making Hong Kong an easy target of attack'.

7   The Final Sino-British Battle over Democratic Reform (1992-94)

As we have seen from the last chapter, while the normative force of democracy was on the rise in public discourse, the conservative elites and the pro-China forces counteracted its growing prominence by stressing the value themes of nationalism versus colonialism, state sovereignty versus local subversion, smooth transition versus abrupt changes and stability versus chaos. In narrative terms, to the Chinese government, the existing order was a comedy of China successfully resuming sovereignty over the territory and embracing the Hong Kong Chinese into its nationalistic arms, and of the Chinese government establishing a more desirable order for the Hong Kong people than Britain. Among the Hong Kong people, the pro-China forces toed the same narrative line of that of the Chinese government the conservatives accepted the existing arrangement with a sense of comic realism, taking as its pragmatic concern the co-operation with the future sovereign power as a way to safeguard smooth transition; the democrats nonetheless adopted an ironic frame vis-à-vis their romantic ideal for democracy and autonomy. Accordingly, comic realism and romantic-irony co-existed as the major narrative currents in public discourse regarding the society's political future. While these two opposing forces deeply divided the political groups in the society, their co-existence bespoke some uneasy tensions between the idealistic aspirations, ironic doubts and pragmatic considerations (about the rather irresistible power of the Chinese state) among the people in general. In this context, while the political groups stuck to their respective narrative positions, the general public appeared to be susceptible to both narrative forces, pending on the mobilizational strategies of the political actors.

As we will see in this chapter, in the first few months after his arrival, Governor Patten had successfully capitalized on the new aspirations of the people, mobilized popular support for his reform proposals and established in public discourse a narrative of heroic romance for the cause of democracy. The 'heroic' aspect of the act hinged on a context where on the one hand, the Hong Kong people had been aspiring to more political democracy, and on the other, the all-powerful Chinese government was always frustrating their aspirations and attempts whereas the British government showed little commitment for the democratic cause in the society. Still, amidst the developing theme of romance, some undercurrents were also noticeable, which not only added complications to the heroic plot line but also pointed to different possible closures. These undercurrents were in part the result of the Chinese government's counter-response and in part the result of the pre-existing narrative-political currents. In this chapter, I will outline the development of the event in terms of the unfolding of Sino-British politics over Governor Patten's reform proposals. The discussion will focus on the political and discursive strategies of the Governor and the Chinese government's counter strategies. Their interplay with local politics and public responses will also be included but it will be analysed in greater details in the next four empirical chapters.

Stage I: Governor Patten as a Symbol of Change

Patten the Political Heavyweight versus Previous Governor-Diplomats

Chris Patten came to Hong Kong in July 1992 to be the last British governor of the colony. Unlike his predecessors, who were career colonial administrators from the Foreign Office and who proclaimed to be sinologists, Patten was a front-rank politician in Britain who assumed senior cabinet ranking and who was known to be unfamiliar with Chinese politics and culture. Moreover, as the chairman of the Conservative Party, he enjoyed a good relationship with the then Prime Minister, John Major, and the Foreign Secretary, Douglas Hurd. The question then arises as to why the British government should suddenly send a non-sinologist politician to the colony instead of a sinologist-diplomat? In part, Patten's loss in his own House of Commons seat in Bath earlier in the year left him with few promising political career options. In part, it signaled a possible change in Britain's foreign policy vis-a-vis Beijing on Hong Kong issues. The involuntary early retirement of the previous governor, David Wilson, was an indicator of Britain's determination for such a policy change. Britain's previous appeasement policy regarding democratic reform in Hong Kong became increasingly untenable after the Tiananmen Square incident of 1989. The difficulties involved in negotiations with Beijing over Hong

Kong's new airport project had led to the British Prime Minister's visit to Beijing, who became the first political leader in western democratic countries to have made such a diplomatic visit after the abhorable event in 1989. Against this background, Britain's sudden change in its appeasement policy with Beijing would become understandable.

Open Politics – A New Strategy with a New Culture

In several important ways, Patten's style of governing had departed from the colonial tradition. One of the most prominent features was his stress on openness. In his efforts to push forward political reform in the upcoming 1994-95 elections, he resorted to publicist and parliamentary strategies (Sum 1995) over and above the time-honored practice of secret diplomacy with the Chinese government. Upon his arrival, Patten immediately reorganized the government's public relations department, Government Information Service, and entrusted the task of publicity to the Press Secretary while himself orchestrating government promotion. His first fortnight in town as Governor showed maximum exposure to the public. Walkabout, shaking hands, outdoor press briefings and even minor commotion caused by him all contributed to prominent media coverage, creating an image of an energetic, accessible and caring Governor. The waves, the smiles, and the glad-handling of the welcoming crowds in the street all testified to the populist skills of a master politician. People were fond of him and, taking note of his chubby shape, immediately gave him the endearing nickname of 'Fat Pang.' In his publicist campaign, Patten succeeded in capturing favorable public attention, so much so that the media described his early presence in Hong Kong as the 'Pang (Patten) Tornado.' The following quotation came close to the meaning of the phrase: 'He is so good at getting the limelight that nobody even realizes that they have not been seeing much else' (Ng, *SCM Post*, 14 July 1992).

On 8 October 1992, the Governor released his proposals for political reform. In his efforts to muster sufficient popular support for the proposal, he introduced the Westminister-style of political campaigning to the society and practiced it to near-universal admiration. In a single day, starting from 7:30 in the morning to 11:20 at night, he kept industriously meeting with the public in numerous 'spectacular' consultation sessions to explain his blueprint. Not only did he speak directly to the public in various kinds of occasions, he also allowed himself to be questioned by his audience. Within the Legislative Council, he introduced a question time session.[1] The idea was modeled on the Prime Minister's question time in Britain's House of Commons, when members of parliament can ask the Premier about any aspect of the country's affairs. It was thought a special Governor's question time would enhance the Governor's accountability to the legislature and create a closer partnership with legislators. While enhancing the element of 'publicness' with the legislature, Patten always had in mind the general populace as his broader audience. He was the first Hong Kong Governor to take part in a live television forum debate on his maiden address.

By making himself available to questions from legislators and from the public, Patten intended to show that his proposed blueprint was what the people had told him they wanted. As a newspaper columnist put it,

> The point to all this show is that Mr Patten as Governor must establish his authority and demonstrate that he has the support of the people almost instantly if he wants to speak on their behalf - especially is he wants to speak strongly on their behalf to Beijing. (Ng, *SCM Post*, 14 July 1992)

In all these consultation sessions, Patten had presented himself as a smart, quick-witted, humorous, sophisticated yet approachable governor. Even though the press realized that such sessions would have no substantive effect insofar as the Governor was not to be accountable to the public through elections, they believed that the people would still find the experience impressively refreshing and uplifting. In part it was because Patten's performance was outstanding, but more fundamentally, these exercises brought about a new political culture of openness and accountability:

> It represents tremendous progress in Hong Kong's political culture that the Governor is willing to subject himself to the Legislative Council's public scrutiny. (*Ming Daily*, 14 October 1992)

> In his first ten days, he earned more and more public credits - the most outstanding performance being his unprecedented openness. (Chai, *Economic Journal*, 20 July 1992)

To many Hong Kong people, his open and populist style of governorship seemed to signify a change for something better. Opinion polls on his policy speeches were rife, which showed remarkably high popularity ratings in the first few months of his governorship. Nevertheless, there were at the same time those who, while recognizing his popularity, held a suspicious and cynical attitude and did not hesitate to voice their criticisms. Of all the controversies, the Governor's reform proposals had aroused the most heated debates in the society, putting on the public stage a drama of deep conflicts among Britain, China and the Hong Kong people. Inevitably, with Patten's populist strategy, the media became the arena where these actors got intensely involved in a politics of public credibility over both the reform proposals and the different personages.

The Reform Proposals: Stepping into the Gray Area and Sacred Terrain

As early as late May, it was made known to the people that the British foreign office minister responsible for Hong Kong, Alistair Goodlad, promised to place the issue of more directly elected seats to the legislature at the top of the agenda when the new governor arrived in July. In response, Lu Ping immediately raised opposition against any move to speed up democratic reforms in Hong Kong that would contravene the limit laid down in the Basic Law. According to the idea of 'through train', Legislative Council members returned in 1995 under the British administration might become members of the legislature in July 1997 under Chinese sovereignty, provided that the composition of the council was in accordance with the Basic Law. The Basic Law stipulates that in the first post-1997 the Legislative Council election in 1999, 20 members shall be returned through direct elections, 10 by the election committee, and 30 by functional constituencies. In categorically ruling out the possibility of adding more directly elected seats, the Chinese government reaffirmed the imposed boundary of the prohibited domain in local politics which none was allowed to cross. For the conservatives, to cross this boundary was to afflict the society with an impossible and dangerous undertaking; for the democrats, to stay chained within the confines of China's intent was to give up too much on an ideal. Apparently, there was not much room for the local politicians to manoeuvre.

It was against this background that tremendous courage and innovativeness were seen in Governor Patten's political blueprint for the 1995 elections. It was generally established that the proposals kept the letters of the Basic Law whilst making use of the gray area of non-specification to enhance democracy. Under the Basic Law, while the number of directly elected seats is fixed, there has been no detailed specification in the document as to how to define the functional constituencies and the election committee for the first legislature in 1997. The Preparatory Committee which was to decide on the concrete details on these matters would not be formed until 1996. In Patten's proposals, the number of seats allocated for each of the three voting methods remained the same; however, the more direct forms of election were strengthened by means of (i) broadening the franchise for the functional constituencies by extending it virtually to all eligible voters in Hong Kong's working population of 2.7 million,[2] and (ii) making the special election committee an institution made up of the directly elected members of the district boards, whose appointment system would be replaced by direct elections in 1994. Moreover, the proposals also defined the relationship between the Executive Council and the Legislative Council. In particular, they called for a complete separation of the membership of the two councils for the time being. The alleged merit was to allow both councils to play their different roles, enabling the Legislative Council members to freely debate their proposals without the confidentiality and collective responsibility constraints imposed by membership in The Executive Council, and at the same time ridding The Executive Council of party politics. (Nonetheless, it was noted by some that since neither the Hong Kong governor before 1997 nor the Chief Executive after 1997, would be directly elected by the people, a separation of a totally non-elected executive body from an elected the Legislative Council, without stronger guarantees of accountability, could do nothing to prevent the continuation of rule by oligarchy.)

By means of his reform package, Patten had ventured into the sacred terrain of democratic struggles in the society. Upon the immediate release the proposals, the public had shown very positive and enthusiastic responses. In most of the news media, the proposals were quickly established as a symbol of extended democracy carrying tremendous support from the public. Opinion polls were cited as showing that most of those who expressed their opinions were satisfied with the Governor's policy speech and believed that the Governor was giving the Hong Kong people more democracy. Among the newspapers, *Economic Journal* expressed the view that the proposals would bring about democratic progress; *SCM Post* described them as 'a bold and courageous package' to map out the route for Hong Kong's democratic development. Despite some criticisms,[3] there seemed to be little controversy in public discourse about whether they were really democratic or not. To many, that the Governor proposed to broaden the basis for popular participation in the forthcoming election was a significant enough indicator of a strong democratic element that could possibly be conceived within the confines of the prescribed course for the political development of Hong Kong:

While hopes for increasing the number of directly elected seats on the Legislative Council were dim because of China's refusal to amend the Basic Law to accommodate the change, Mr. Patten pledged to heed the demand of the community for as much democracy as possible in Hong Kong within the confines of the mini-constitution. (*SCM Post*, 8 October 1992)

A democrat and opinion columnist, Margaret Ng, believed that although it would be far more honest to press for more directly elected seats, the Governor was already making the best of a bad job. Drawing on the frame of 'local autonomy versus state control', she explained how, for the sake of a democratically-elected legislature, Patten's proposals were worth the support of the people under the given constraints:

> Hong Kong people believe that they will have greater confidence that a democratically-elected legislature formed before the PRC takes over will be more independent and can be more trusted to speak for Hong Kong people and protect Hong Kong's interests. That is why, believing that the election committee will be an instrument of Beijing and many of the indirectly-elected functional constituency members easily manipulated by Beijing, people place their hopes on the directly-elected members and concentrate their efforts in pressing for more. That is why, faced with the failure to secure more directly-elected seats, they support Mr. Patten's proposals. (*SCM Post*, 20 October, 1992)

The democrats placed their hopes on direct election not only because it was the way to achieve the ideal of political equality and popular participation, but also because it could guard against any easy manipulation by the Chinese government by means of the two methods of non-direct elections. Apparently, the Governor had worked out an ingenious way to introduce something more akin to direct elections from within the given frames of election committee and functional constituency.

The opinions polls conducted right after the Governor's policy address and throughout the forum broadcast showed solid support for him. Very remarkably, his personal rating of 72 points had shown a big 22-point upward jump within three months since his arrival. All in all, that he was able to top the list of overall public performance, overshadowing even the most popular local politician in the pro-democracy camp, gave added weight to a heroic image about him. Regarding his proposals, while a significant portion of the people felt satisfied with the Governor's policy speech (33.5% as compared with 3.9% who felt the opposite), almost half of them agreed (as compared to 14% who disagreed) that the Governor should proceed for more democracy even if the Chinese government opposed it. Taking out from calculation the 30-50% for the 'don't know' option, the press further raised the level of affirmative responses to something as high as 70-80%. Thus the overall image of public opinion as being imported back to media discourse was one of overwhelming support for the proposals as a democratic plan. As a corollary, those who supported the Governor maintained he had established a 'mandate' for political reform.

The Underside

Apparently, the Governor had successfully mobilized the public to an unusual state of exhilaration. Still, the picture of heroic strength and hope was not without an underside (even though the discrediting voices in this stage did not develop into a strong countervailing force). First, the Governor, despite his popularity, had his secret enemies. Specifically, the conservative elite were believed to be having some personal grudge against him, for the tough and arrogant Patten, in his tendency to play the 'strong man,' was slighting them. Not only had the Governor kept the councilors barely informed about his political plan concerning the 1995 elections, he also revamped the Executive Council and the Legislative Council by severing their established link[4] and by bringing in a few like-minded liberals and ousting some conservatives out. In the public, there were the criticisms that he might be weakening the Legislative Council while keeping power to himself as well as the cabinet, and that the ousting of some of the better conservatives from the Executive Council was an attempt to sideline the conservatives while boosting the liberal benches. In view of these changes, the press, including *SCM Post* and the *Economic Journal*, believed that the few leading conservatives, would feel slighted by the 'cruel' way they had been treated by the Governor:

> Outgoing Executive Councilors who have not been told of his plans for their future, and leaders of minority political groups who have not been invited to this morning's policy briefing, feel snubbed ... The whiff of sour grapes will be heavy in the air. (*SCM Post*, 7 October 1992)

As such, it was expected that the Governor could not count on them for firm support.

Secondly, there arose doubts as to the Governor's sincerity about reforms. Some held the belief that Patten was a shrewd politician who knew the way to make for himself a populist and democratic stamp even though he might not be a genuine populist or democrat:

> Yet despite the commitment to taking his cue from public opinion, Mr. Patten is unlikely to return to the drawing board. He will be firm in pursuit of what he feels is right for Hong Kong. (*SCM Post*, 7 October)

This portrayal was consistent with the image of him being a firm and tough governor, and it went further to suggest that he was not quite ready to entertain different or disagreeable opinions from others once he had his mind set. In a similar vein, some attacked him as displaying nothing but 'showmanship,' which in the context of Hong Kong seemed to carry the negative connotation that he aimed primarily at impression – to steal the show but not run it:

> It is a big invention that the Governor makes a showy fuss about his policy speech ... Yet juding his performance since his arrival, we find that while Patten the politician manages to keep up a high political profile about himself, he has not yet achieved much in solving concrete problems of various kinds. (*Success Daily*, 5 October 1992)

> Yesterday's speech proved how well Mr Patten performs on set-piece occasions. However, it is not so much by making speeches as by sensitively negotiated compromises that he will solve the territory's internal political problems, and break the deadlock over the financing of the airport, without either losing his own authority or harming relationships with Beijing. (*SCM Post*, 10 July 1992)

In any case, these remained mild reproaches to a title of glamour rather than hard evidences for wrong-doing, which raised doubts rather than seriously undermine the credibility of the Governor.

Nevertheless, on a deeper level, the lack of faith in the Governor revealed itself as distrust in colonialism. According to this line of thought, although Patten positioned himself as standing on the side of the public, ultimately he would take British interest as his prime concern. As *Express Daily* stated, 'From history, we learn that whenever there appeared conflicts between China, Britain and Hong Kong, the Hong Kong people were always the one whose interests would be sacrificed' (10 July 1992). It was therefore further speculated that the Governor had a hidden target at something else such as the new airport.[5]

In the meantime, quite a number of people, including the conservatives and the pro-China groups, stressed that the Governor's arrogance in his handling the relations with China would put Hong Kong on a collision course with the Chinese government, which raised the question as to whether Patten had produced a workable plan that would see Hong Kong through even beyond 1997. For this, we will turn to the Chinese government's reactions to the release of the proposals in terms of its counter narrative, and then look at how the Hong Kong people found themselves at the intersection of competing narrative frames.

China's Counter-narrative: A Villainous Attempt to Disrupt the Process of Smooth Transition

The Chinese government responded by defining the Governor as the villain rather than a hero. To do this, it put the events into a different narrative frame with a different thematic emphasis. While it criticized that the proposals were undemocratic on some counts, the major point of attack, nonetheless, was not so much that the proposals were not democratic as that it signified confrontation with China. Specifically, it put forward a counter-narrative of a villainous attempt by the Governor to disrupt the process of smooth transition of sovereignty (by violating their mutual agreement.) By re-interpreting the events as such, it might, on the one hand, discredit its opponents, and on the other, tone down the poignant relevance of the question of 'democracy' that had been the focal point of the more popular narrative.

Immediately after the Governor's policy speech, the Chinese government reacted within the two narrative frames of 'sovereignty challenged' and 'joint agreement violated and co-operation undermined'.[6] The central issues raised by the Chinese government were that there was no prior consultation with the Chinese government as the future sovereign power of the society and there was a violation of the joint agreements between Britain and China. An editorial in a Beijing-run newspaper, *Wen Wei Po*, stated that while consultation with the Chinese side would be conducive to a smooth transition, unilateral action by Britain would only make future co-operation between the two powers very difficult: 'Mutual trust can only be built on the sincerity to discuss. If the (British side) unilaterally carries out its own blueprint and then forces its partner to accept it, it will be difficult for future cooperation'.[7] Their concern, according to Zhang Junsheng, a Chinese official in Hong Kong, was that the arrangement for the 1995 elections should have taken convergence (with the Basic Law) into consideration. Moreover, the Chinese government insistently attacked the Governor as bringing very drastic changes to the electoral system, the relationship between the Executive Council and Legislative Council, and the system of electing members of district boards and municipal councils, which breached the Basic Law or did not fall in line with it. Specifically, it saw the changing electoral arrangements of the functional constituencies polls as de facto direct elections. All in all, by framing the Governor's act as 'extremely irresponsible and imprudent', it sought to excuse itself from the blame for any open arguments with him.

To further undermine the popular narrative, the Chinese government put into question the Governor's motivation and his character. It asserted that what went underneath the popular narrative of a heroic democratic fight was actually a 'conspiracy' plot of Britain as well as the Governor seeking self-interests or having some ulterior motives. This was, in short, a form of mock heroism. The underlying structure of codes that the Chinese government was drawing on would be one like this:

Colonialism	vs	Nationalism
the British		the Chinese
colonial interests		national interest
Dishonesty		Trustworthiness
Arrogance		Respectful
mock hero (enemy)		genuine hero (ally).

In proposing drastic changes in the political system, Governor Patten was trying to extend British influence in Hong Kong even beyond 1997 and was doing it in his own personal interest as well rather than for the interests of the Hong Kong people. Obviously, the Chinese government was trying to arouse a sense of distrust about him as both a British colonial governor and as a (self-seeking) politician. As a Briton, he would have British interests rather than Hong Kong interests as the prime concern. As a politician, he would think only about his political career back in Britain. In other words, for the sake of political fame, he was prepared to gamble with Hong Kong's future, putting into jeopardy what Hong Kong had been achieving such as stability as well as a good prospect of smooth transition in 1997. Not only was he selfish and dangerous, he also showed himself to be arrogant and dictatorial in his not adhering to the spirit of the signed agreements and his not being ready to accept different opinions. The sense of arrogance was most powerfully conveyed through the metaphor of him playing the role of 'savior' for the Hong Kong people. In the words of Zhang Junshen of New China News Agency,

> Somebody has masqueraded as a savior. It looks as if the new airport and democracy are gifts from the savior. But can we find democracy in Hong Kong throughout the past 150 years? Democracy in Hong Kong emerged because the territory has to be reverted to Chinese rule. The Basic Law has laid out democracy to its fullest extent. (*Success Daily*, 12 October 1992)

As an attempt to mock and unmask the 'savior' posture, Zhang explained that Britain had had no genuine attempts to build up a democratic system in Hong Kong in the past, and it was instead the resumption of Chinese sovereignty with the drafting of the Basic Law that brought about greater democracy in the society. Here, he was implicitly drawing on the code of colonialism which had the code of the lack of democracy to go with it, and he was characterizing Britain as the real enemy to the society in terms of democratic development. According to his reasoning, the present attempt by the Governor would look pretentious and even outrageous. In short, it was within a meta-narrative of 'colonial conspiracy' that Governor Patten was portrayed as a villain acting on selfish motives but disguised as a savior.

In the context of fierce opposition by the Chinese government and cynical doubts among some of the local critics, the challenge for the Governor was for him to engage the audience on the mimetic level sufficiently to make them care about his choice not only for what it meant thematically but also for himself.

The Governor Seeking Out Support

In view of the Chinese government's discrediting criticisms, Governor Patten was quick to put himself into a more favorable public light. On the one hand, he defended that his proposals were in line with the Basic Law. He even openly challenged the Chinese government to specifically point out which provisions in the Joint Declaration and the Basic Law were violated. Insisting that he did not violate any Sino-British agreements, he was trying to weaken the counter-narrative by the Chinese government. On the other hand, he sought to consolidate the popular narrative that he was genuine in his political reforms. First, he maintained that he would not sacrifice democracy for the sake of smooth transition or the airport project, implying 'democracy' was a matter of utmost importance which should not be traded with other things. Secondly, he explained that the proposals had to be unveiled first to the public based on the principle of openness. Defending, moreover, that his were only proposals rather than firm policies, he reiterated time and again that he would welcome criticisms from the local public and preferably specific counter-proposals from the Chinese government. Apparently, it signified a change in British policy with China and Hong Kong along the more democratic line. (In fact, he did have strong support back from Britain, as the British Prime Minister, John Major, soon made it known to the public that he fully endorsed the proposals, which he was certain represented the best way forward for Hong Kong.)

To go further along this line, the Governor reasoned that it would be up for the Legislative Council, rather than himself or the Chinese government, to make the final decision on his proposals, making it clear to the public that it would be the Hong Kong people themselves who were going to decide on their own political future at this critical juncture. This might strengthen the people's trust in him – for shrewd as he was, he was not going to control the situation as an authoritarian political leader would do, and neither was he trying to play the role of a savior, as its opponents had suggested. With the full awareness of the immense public support behind him, moreover, he further put himself on the moral high ground by portraying himself as a for-the-people Governor who respected the will of the people and whose success depended on their good will and support:

> The process would only succeed if Hong Kong's politicians displayed good sense and restraint and demonstrated the substantial contribution which greater democracy could make to the development of Hong Kong. His impression from consultations with the community since he arrived in July was that people wanted to see democracy taken forward but they wanted to see it taken forward in a 'sustainable' way so that it was in line with the mini-constitution. That's what I have tried to do.... (*SCM Post*, 8 October 1992)

Here, without weakening his position as the chief protagonist in the struggle, he was inviting the Hong Kong people, especially the legislators, to be his good and sensible allies in the fight.

As an attempt to mobilize the legislators, the Governor made an extraordinary ruling in the Legislative Council meeting over McGregor's motion that called on the legislators to endorse his proposal on the Election Committee.[8] The significance of this motion debate lay in its being a powerful indication of the level of support the Governor could muster within the Council when the going got tough and when he was just about to go on his Beijing visit on 22 October. As it turned out, the Council had the specific proposal endorsed, giving added weight to the public credibility of the Governor as well as his proposals. (Different political parties within the Legislative Council responded differently in the voting process. The next two chapters will analyse how these political groupings positioned themselves in the public and how they were positioned by the public.)

On one level, carrying the stamp of public credibility for his reform package, Patten was to advance the plot of heroic quest by putting together the legislation needed for the implementation of the package. On another level, interlaced as a sub-plot in the narrative of heroic romance, the deterioration of Sino-British relation was to have a profound bearing on the quest for democracy symbolized by the Patten package. Beginning with Patten's rather fruitless first meeting with his Chinese counterpart in Beijing on 23 October 1992,[9] the next two weeks stage saw the parallel development of Patten embarking on the legislative course on the one hand and the Chinese government seizing back the initiative and taking a series of revengeful actions on the other, which plunged the society into an anxiety-ridden state of escalating Sino-British hostility. From the perspective of the developing romance, the Chinese government's reactions had created an immensely huge obstacle for the Hong Kong people in their quest for democracy, reducing the people's confidence in the quest just at the time when it needed much firmer support than ever to carry the romance forward.

Public Discourse and Legislative Politics

How would the people find themselves as they were situated at the intersection of competing narratives? Undeniably, there had been great public support for the proposals as they were looked upon as a symbol of democratic progress, and there had been equally great support for the Governor as a strong charismatic leader in this struggle against the Chinese government's opposition. At the same time, there lurked some suspicions as to whether he was in fact an arrogant villain playing the role of a savior. Specifically, the counter-narrative challenges consisted in three open-ended sub-plots in the form of questions: *(1) Was Governor Patten doing what he was doing in the interests of Hong Kong, or was he doing it in the interests of Britain and himself? Was he carrying on a different game under the cover of his pose? (2) Had he really violated the mutual agreement between the two sovereign powers? (3) Would he be able to sustain his plans without resulting in unstable transition?* Within these broad narrative contexts, specific configurations varied among different political camps, different commentators and different newspapers. The next three chapters will delineate several kinds of position held in the public, ranging from an almost whole-hearted support for the proposals to cautious reservations about and even distrustful oppositions to them. Of particular interest will be the various ways the undercurrents made themselves felt in the specific accounts, which would have tremendous bearing on the ways the narratives would be unfolding in the later stages.

In the meantime, after the Beijing visit, Governor Patten prepared his next move of putting together the legislation that would be needed to implement his reform package. Once the legislative process was initiated, the Legislative Council was put in the firing line. On the one hand, there had been great public support for the Governor's proposals, which had been looked upon as a symbol of more democracy. On the other hand, the Chinese government kept warning the Hong Kong public not to support the proposals. Lu Ping pronounced in the press conference that the Chinese government would be ready in 1997 to unmesh the reforms introduced without its approval. In this connection, Beijing's mouth-piece, the overseas edition of the *People's Daily*, carried a signed commentary urging Patten to withdraw his constitutional reform package to pave the way for Sino-British negotiations on the territory's future political development. Furthermore, as it was circulated in the press, the Chinese government had warned the legislators that they would lose their council seats in 1997 if they supported the Governor's constitutional package. As a matter of fact, the Chinese government's constant warnings had neatly deflected the track of the argument away from the democratic implications of the Governor's blueprint, and the issue became one of whether or not to support the proposals in the face of the Chinese government's severe opposition. Within the Council as well as the wider public, there saw the beginning of a polarisation into two opposing blocs of two very different narrative responses to the situation they were facing. This will be discussed in detailed in the next three chapters.

Stage II: Beijing's Revengeful Actions

The 'Secret Deal' Controversy

The next critical episode was around the 'secret deal' controversy, which for a moment cast the counter-narrative of 'a breach of joint agreement and common understanding' onto the front stage. On 23 October, right after his meeting with Patten, Lu Ping, the Director of the China's Hong Kong and Macau Affairs Office, alleged in a press conference that some secret papers would prove the existence of a Sino-British deal concerning the composition of the Election Committee for the 1995 elections, which was now overturned by Patten's plans. In response, the Governor as well as the British Foreign Office spokesman confirmed the existence of diplomatic exchanges between the British and Chinese foreign ministers over the 1995 polls, but denied that the diplomatic exchanges amounted to a deal. Former Basic Law drafters came out to support the Chinese government's claim and maintain that in the process of drafting the Basic Law, drafters postponed their last round of meetings until a deal was reached by the governments.

In the society, most newspapers were concerned if there was any joint agreement and hence a breach. (Public discourse at this stage of the episode will be discussed in subsequent chapters.) The publication of the documents a few days later, however, failed to settle the 'deal' dispute. Among the seven secret exchanges between the two sides in January and February 1990, a crucial reference over the possible existence of an agreement was contained in the British Foreign Secretary's letter to the then Chinese Foreign Minister on 12 February in which he wrote: 'I agree in principle with the arrangements which you propose for an Election Committee, which could be established in 1995 ... The precise details of how this should be done can be discussed between our two sides in due course'. While the Chinese government considered this proof that an agreement had been struck, the Governor said this and other exchanges made it 'abundantly plain' that there had been no deal on the 1995 elections.[10] Apparently, both were right in its own terms. Legislators were divided on their judgement of whether the terminology of the correspondence constituted a deal. In terms of opinion polls, there was no majority formed in favour of either side – 35% of the respondents agreed with China whereas 30% disagreed, and 35% were unsure whether China or Britain was right.[11] Certainly, given that the dispute remained unresolved even with all the relevant evidence, it would be rather impossible for them to go forward in a narrative sense if they got stuck on this issue. As a matter of fact, public debate soon shifted its focus from the controversy itself to its wider or deeper implications. As we will see below, in order to *carry the sense-making process forward*, the public reconstructed their narratives in different ways, including an outright adoption of China's position, the suggestion that it was nothing but a detour from the developing romantic plot, and the construction of a new narrative (around the theme of 'autonomy') in conjunction with a discourse of distrust.

The Politics of Threat and Retaliation

Despite popular backing for the Governor's proposals, the Chinese government had remained entrenched in its opposing stance. On the one hand, following the earlier line of attack, very senior officials took their turn to criticize the Governor for breaking promises, for lying, and for sabotaging the peaceful transition, among other things. Its use of this narrative tended to be habituated and formulaic, the narrative being one of the chief instrument through which they maintained themselves separate from, hostile toward, and convinced of their moral and political superiority to the British. With this, the Chinese government therefore insisted that only the withdrawal of his proposals would permit the resumption of normal negotiations on Hong Kong's smooth transition to Chinese rule.[12] On the other hand, the Chinese government began a series of revengeful actions, threatening to paralyze the Hong Kong Governments' administrative power in the rest of the transition period and spelling out to the Hong Kong people the realities of the 1997 situation under Chinese sovereignty. The prime messages sent out were that it would start things afresh on all fronts in July 1997 and it would not co-operate with the current Hong Kong Government on any important matters.[13] To the first shock of the people, it called into question the Joint Declaration of 1984, resulting in the first serious plunge in the stock market. Indeed as the Hang Seng Index had been relatively impervious to the routine attacks from the Chinese government in the first few weeks, the 206-point drop immediately following the comments of the Chinese Vice Premier, Zhu Rongji, showed how much store was placed on his words. For the first time, the Chinese government cast doubt on the guarantees put down in the Joint Declaration when Zhu queried whether all the Sino-British agreements should 'go to the wind.' To the Hong Kong public, that his words carried a lot of weight was not only due to the fact that the Joint Declaration had been regarded as a sacred symbol of promise by the two sovereign powers, but also because Zhu as a 'character' had been thought to be more sympathetic for the liberal cause than the other Chinese officials.[14] Looked upon as a liberal reformer, the presence of Zhu in London at the same time as Patten had once raised hopes that the two men might meet to reconcile the recent differences. With this projected hope as the narrative background, it was certainly much to the disappointment and anxiety of the Hong Kong public that they suddenly found their hope completely ill-founded. Clearly, the Chinese leadership had already united itself on this particular issue.

Following this, there were reports in the press that read like 'a doomsday scenario' for Hong Kong if Patten's package was adopted. These included the threat of an early takeover of Hong Kong by the People's Liberation Army, plans to set up a shadow Government before 1997, and a reduction in mainland investment and economic dependence on the territory.[15] While some of these were quickly dismissed as groundless rumours, some had stayed as an alarming possibility, especially the setting up of a shadow government before 1997. These 'scare tactics' by the Chinese government, as the Hong Kong people understood it, had its intended effect. In a single week, the Hang Seng Index had dropped 488 points or 7.6 per cent, throwing the market into a wild state of panic and frenzy. Further still, the Chinese government warned that it would not honour contracts for developing Container Terminal Nine after June 1997. As if all these were not enough, on December 1, it declared that the validity of all contracts, leases and agreements signed or ratified by the British Hong Kong administration without the approval of Beijing would not be honoured after June 1997. This resulted in the biggest plunge in the recent few years since the Tiananmen Square incident in 1989.

Stage III: Back to Secret Diplomacy

Structurally, the beginning of stage three (February 1993) was marked with some significant development from both the romantic and the comic-ironic perspectives. On the one hand, it was supposed to see the furtherance and completion of the romantic-heroic action i.e. the legislation of Patten's reform proposals as scheduled. In fact, the legislative process was in the stage of The Executive Council's final scrutiny of the draft bills giving effect to the proposals before they were formally introduced to the Legislative Council in mid February. At the same time, on the other hand, a comic turn took shape when sudden and continued news reports about secret diplomatic contacts between London and Beijing, and softer rhetoric on both sides, fuelled the belief among the people that a breakthrough in the deadlock was imminent. Although the confidential negotiations were technically only talks about whether or not the two sides should talk, the possibility of talks became the focal concern of the public, and the process of 'talks about talks' was being foregrounded in public discourse. In terms of plot development, just as the reform proposals had been the crux of the problem in the current Sino-British relations, the prospect of talks between the sides would have an immediate bearing on the proposals. Indeed the two parallel processes – the Government's schedule to gazette the proposals and pass them into law (the local legislative process), and the continual diplomatic meetings between the two sovereign powers – got tightly intertwined in that the Chinese government demanded that the proposals be dropped altogether if Sino-British negotiations were to be resumed whereas the Governor insisted that the Legislative Council would have the final say over the proposals. These two processes underwent three intertwining phases of development as follows:

1) Talks about talks/ Delaying gazetting the reform bills
2) Talk Resumed/ Suspending the tabling of the reform bills to the Legislative Council
3) Talk Failure/ Tabling the reform bills to the Legislative Council.

In the first phase, as it was in the second phase as well, since the talks between the two sovereign powers were underway, in considering when to gazette the reform bills (and when to table the gazetted bills to the Legislative Council), the government was believed to be facing a fundamental dilemma:

> If it forces itself to put the package to the Legislative Council, it will aggravate its wrong of 'stubbornly persisting in having its own way', however, if it sits on it rather than put it to the Legislative Council, it will be regarded as 'bowing to pressure', and the Patten package will be likened to a 'dead fetus'. (*Ming Daily*, 12 February 1993)

Among the legislators, opinions were divided as to whether the government should table the bills containing Patten's package while the talks were still underway. The conservatives, whose most important goal was to allow more time for the talks to come to fruition, favored a delay in the legislative process. In contrast, the democrats as well as a few other members were against any delay for the sake of 'legislative autonomy.' For them, while the ironic memories with the 'secret deal' controversy was still fresh, the Chinese government's insistence that 'any agreement reached between the British and Chinese governments should not be overturned by the

Legislative Council' further added to their worry that a Sino-British negotiation might mean a possible sell-out by Britain.[16]

At this juncture, as the Hong Kong people were struggling with conflicting worries and hopes among themselves, Patten's public credibility would rest on its ability to show that he was both genuine about his reforms and willing to have negotiation with the Chinese government. Apparently, Patten did try to strike a delicate balance between the two demands, yet as the story developed in this final stage, the people, be they the realists or the romanticists, experienced a disheartening time of disillusionment in one way or another. Changes in the narrative contour of the 'public' in the process of political struggles will be discussed in details in chapter ten.

Notes

1.   Before 1920, governors did not take part in the Legislative Council debates; in recent years, the governor has acted only as president of the Legislative Council and made an annual policy address.
2.   In the 1991 elections, 21 the Legislative Council seats were returned via the so-called functional constituencies. These represent the various industrial, commercial, financial and professional sectors. The number of votes cast for many of these seats were very small, limited to a few corporations. In Patten's proposals, the number of functional constituency seats will be increased to 30 in the 1995 elections, the 9 new constituencies are defined in a much broader than the existing ones, and the franchise of the existing constituencies will be expanded in such a way that voting that was limited to corporate entities will be done instead by individuals who own or control the management of the corporations. (However, eligible voters who are not working, such as housewives, students, senior citizens, the unemployed, are in fact deprived of one vote.)
3.   The democrats regarded the proposals as a move in the right direction but not going far enough. In particular, they criticized that cutting off the link between the Executive Council and the Legislative Council was a regressive act from the perspective of democratic development. While this latter point had not been taken up as the major line of criticism, for some reasons not quite clear to the writer, it did serve, as I will explain later in the text, as a basis for the development of other sub-plots.
4.   The separation was effected by the Governor not appointing anyone to the Executive Council who was on the Legislative Council. As an alternative, he proposed a 10-member Government-Legislative Council Committee to ensure that the Government's legislative and financial programmes would still be conducted efficiently.
5.   See *Express Daily*, 29 May 1992.

6. In a strongly worded statement soon after the Governor's speech, the NCNA said, 'According to the Sino-British Joint Declaration, the British Government will be responsible for the administration of Hong Kong, with the objective of maintaining and preserving Hong Kong's economic prosperity and social stability; and the Chinese Government will give its co-operation in this connection... During the transitional period, any major changes to Hong Kong's political system which migh result in th weakening of the executive-led administrative capability will be a violation to the spirit of the Joing Declaration ... As far as the question of the 1995 elections is concerned, it is only reasonable to make a formal announcement after a consensus is reached by both sides through negotiation ... Now that the British side unilaterally released the so-caleed proposals, disregarding the views put forward by the Chinese side in a solemn manner, this is extremely irresponsible and imprudent' (*SCM Post*, 8 October 1992).
7. The quotation was cited in *SCM Post*, 7 October 1992.
8. Supposedly, the Standing Orders would prohibit discussion of the Governor's policy address within 14 days; however, the Governor, as the President of the Legislative Council, exercised his right to overrule the Standing Orders, provided the Council members agreed.
9. Upon returning to Hong Kong, Patten admitted to the media that during his visit to Beijing he was unable to make any progress in the airport talks or convert the Chinese to his proposals. The result, according to him, was not unexpected.
10. British and Hong Kong government statements accompanying the letters said Britain had made clear repeatedly its dissatisfaction at the Chinese proposals for the number of directly elected seats in the Legislative Council, and '(a)t the end of these exchanges, the question of electoral arrangements in Hong Kong up to 1997 remained open ... The final version of the Basic Law was not satisfactory on this point because it did not spell out, as we had asked, the five principles agreed between the two sides as a framework for an Election Committee system.'
11. See *SCM Post*, 22 November 1992.
12. For example, Beijing's mouth-piece, the overseas edition of the *People's Daily*, carried a signed commentary on 7 November urging Patten to withdraw his constitutional reform package to pave the way for Sino-British negotiations on the territory's future political development.
13. Lu Ping had already hammered home China's plan to unmesh the reforms proposed by Governor Patten and to set up a new 'stove' when it resumed sovereignty over Hong Kong in July 1997. On 13 November, the New China News Agency issued a stern warning to the Hong Kong Government against what China believed to be a unilateral move by the Government to build the airport alone. Without first securing an overall financial agreement with Beijing, it said, the franchises for handling air cargo and fuel at the new airport would not be honoured beyond 1 July 1997.

14.   An editorial in *SCM Post* explained succinctly the force of this narrative component of characterisation: 'China's Vice-Premier is the acceptable face of communism for many people in the territory, with a reputation as a standard-bearer for the post-1989 breed of liberal reformers ... It was always a spurious assumption that, as a prominent economic reformer, Mr. Zhu would also be sympathetic towards Hong Kong's demcoracy trend. By making his remarks in London, he gave added sting to the sense of disappointment felt by the many Zhu fans here' (18 November 1992).

15.   See *SCM Post*, 21 November 1992.

16.   There was a fierce tug-of-war between the conservative CRC motioning to freeze the bills for three months, who also won the support of pro-China legislator Tam and independent legislator Chim, and the UDHK, together with a few others, rejecting the motion. (A few of them such as pro-China Wong Yu-hong opposed the delay on the grounds that Patten simply had to withdraw his package.) Taking the middle path, the others including a number of independents as well as the democrats from Meeting Point agreed to a one-month deferment if talks resumed.

8 Discursive Formation (I): Democracy, Romanticism, and Cynicism

A thematic discourse is constituted in an intertwinement between cultural codes and narrative modes. It has both a relatively stable structure and an element of instability subjectable to conflict and change in the process of narrative progression. This chapter will examine, with reference to the early stages of the Patten controversy, the structure as well as tensions in the discourse of democracy in the public sphere and also the process of alliance formation and political differentiation that was generated through the discourse .

As we will see, on the one hand, as a result of the interplay between the Governor's strategy and the politico-cultural context, the discourse of democracy was crystallized in a heroic-romantic form in a number of newspapers, mapping out the different roles of the political actors in a discursively constructed order of moral relationships. In particular, the Governor was identified as a romantic hero in a quest for democracy in a situation where the Chinese government had been seen as playing the role of an oppressor against and the local democrats as desperate fighters for democratic development in the society. In the event of a heroic-romantic construction, the discursive juxtapositions between hero and villain, and between hero and coward would become all the more necessary for the romance to sustain itself. In other words, once the heroic romance was set in place, the narrative exerted itself as a relatively autonomous discursive force which inclined to represent the political actors as morally related and contrasted types. Such narrative constructions, in terms of characterization, helped mediated the process of alliance formation and political differentiation.   .

On the other hand, however, a cynical counter-narrative on democracy by a few critics posed challenges to the romantic discourse out of a critique of colonial authoritarianism. They challenged it not so much by reversing the moral order in the latter's narrative constructions, as the direct opponents did, as by exposing some of the contradictions and inadequacies in the then prevalent romantic discourse. Specifically, the set of codes of autonomy versus colonialism embedded within the cynical discourse, and also the different interpretation of democracy in it, raised the question of what a true hero was, as opposed to a mock hero. The cynical discourse, albeit constituting a peripheral position in the public sphere, helped conjure up a higher vision of democracy and therefore served to keep up certain tensions within the discourse of democracy throughout the event.

This chapter is divided into four sections. The first two sections will present the prevalent heroic-romantic form of the discourse on democracy and some variations within it as they appeared in the newspaper editorials and commentaries. The purpose is to explain both the cultural codes (with regard to the value theme of democracy) and the part agency played in constructing different specific narratives within the same mode. The third section will discuss the self-positioning strategies of the democrats vis-à-vis the Governor's reform proposals. It will show how, under the sway of the heroic-romantic construction in public discourse and as a result of the Governor pushing on with the legislative process, the democrats changed their attitude of reservation to one of unreserved support for the proposals whereas the conservatives were identified first as a coward and later as an enemy in the struggle for democracy. In this context, the democrats, in supporting the Governor's proposals, took up a decidedly confrontational role vis-à-vis China as well as its allies in a renewed struggle for democracy. Finally, the fourth section will focus on the cynical discourse on democracy as well as the tension it generated within the pro-democracy camp. It will be noted that the democrats, while playing the role of a courageous fighter, were nonetheless at the same time being caricatured as 'official fire-fighter' from a cynical perspective. They found themselves having to face a moral dilemma in their alliance with a colonial governor. For a short time, the romantic discourse helped put together the aspirations of different fragments in the pro-democracy camp; but in the midst of competing discourses on democracy, a split within the camp was gradually in the making.

The Construction of Heroic Romance on 'Democratic Autonomy'

In public discourse, with the general conception of the proposals being a symbol of democracy, there developed a plot, with the Governor being the protagonist, of a heroic fight for more democracy for the Hong Kong people. The 'heroic' sense was imparted through various practices of narrative construction in the mass media. Firstly, in terms of (thematic) plot development, public discourse developed itself as a romantic projection of a new order around the twin themes of *democratic autonomy* and *Britain's moral responsibility*. On the one hand, there was a conception that the Governor was reversing the previous British policy of passive submission and moral retreat to one of active engagement in political reforms. Unlike the previous governors who always made compromises with the Chinese government behind the back of the Hong Kong people, Mr. Patten did not have any prior consultation with the Chinese government at all until the very last few days, and he remained adamant about the Chinese government's request not to publicize the proposals. On the other hand, the event meant a bold and much longed-for introduction of more democratic changes despite opposition from the Chinese government. *Economic Journal*, for instance, strongly believed that in standing up against the Chinese government's opposition to greater democracy, the proposals showed the principle of 'two systems' in operation. This assertion of Hong Kong's autonomy against China was a welcome reversal of the previous mode of succumbing to the Chinese government's whims by the Governor's predecessors. It thus regarded the proposals as signifying a strong voice after a long period of government inertia. In a nutshell, the event signified *a romantic turn from the weak state of moral retreat, political stagnancy and gloomy political prospects to an active pursuit of a higher noble cause as propelled by moral courage and vision.*

In terms of mood, secondly, the event had increased the confidence of both the administration and the general public, giving them hope for a better political future. The strongest rhetorical depiction of such a hopeful mood within the administration was found in an *SCM Post* editorial a few days before the release of the proposals:

> There were talks before his arrival of creeping 'Government inertia'. There is no such talk now inside Mr. Patten's 'go for it' Government House, a place brimming with confidence and a new-found feeling that what was once impossible is now achievable. (4 October 1992)

In fact the change in mood became all the more poignant when it was understood against the background that the removal of the previous governor, Lord Wilson, was announced long before a new person was identified (and an election in Britain was to intervene) – this had left the government with a lame duck image. The re-vitalization of the government under Patten projected instead an image of strength in the eyes of the public: 'The smack of firm government resounded around Hong Kong yesterday as Chris Patten delivered his first speech as Governor' (*SCM Post*, 10 July 1992). With this, the press highlighted the findings from opinion polls that more than half of the people had increased their confidence in the governorship of Mr. Patten.[1] In particular, that almost 70% of the people agreed to his way of handling the relation with China i.e. having no prior consultation with it on the proposals, showed their faith in his open and strong Posture. Indeed this new-found feeling of hope and confidence must be understood also in relation to the third narrative practice of character portrayal.

Characterization about Patten had been the crux of public concern long before he arrived. Soon after the announcement of the name of the new governor, the media already hazarded guesses about his way of governing the society. On the bright side, he was portrayed as having the kind of qualities that would provide exceptionally strong leadership for the society – something which the local leaders were found wanting in. First and foremost, in terms of political status, the media all highlighted the fact that he was a front-rank politician who enjoyed a good relationship with the Prime Minister and the Foreign Secretary. An *SCM Post* editor described him as 'a rising Tory Star, temporarily disabled by defeat in the April 1992 British election, with close allies in the highest political places' (3 July 1993). Whether one found it an agreeable arrangement or not, it was no denying that his appointment signified a break from the tradition of putting Foreign Office diplomats into Government House. To some, it meant specifically that the society would have as its governor a strong politician who was used to fighting tough political battles and masterminding vote-catching campaigns:

> After the dry, professionally diplomatic style of Lord Wilson, Hong Kong is rather relishing the prospect of a change of leadership that promises to inject some drive, humor and street-credibility into Government House. (*SCM Post*, 26 April 1992)

As far as his character was concerned, Patten had had a reputation for being his own man. There were quotations in the press of his self-description as an aggressive and tough person: 'I fight aggressively when necessary. I'm quite bad at knowing when to stop. I don' like being cornered' (*SCM Post* 26 April 1992). Upon arrival, he immediately stamped his personality on the place by distancing himself from the formalities of the past which required him to wear the colonial uniform. In a nutshell, the kind of political profile he showed, the type of personality he had impressed upon the others, and the way he sought to break from the colonial tradition all helped arouse among the Hong Kong public a high expectation on this paramount political figure.

Building on his already impressive political background, the Governor's reform proposals for Hong Kong further established for him an image of an exceptionally strong leader. His reform proposals, which were released during his first policy speech, were looked upon as a bold and creative attempt at political reforms. In most of the press, he was described as a tough, confident, ambitious, sophisticated and forward-looking politician:

> Mr. Patten, no matter what his detractors or admirers may have to say about him, is a man of determination. (*SCM Post*, 20 October 1992)

> (It) shows the self-confidence and bravery of this ambitious and far-sighted politician in his taking up the challenge to make an upturn in local politics. (*Economic Journal*, 8 October 1992.)

> Governor Patten was deliberately making the *Pos*ture of an open and frank governor while showing himself to be brave enough to take progressive steps rather than abiding rigidly by the conventional rules. (*Ming Daily*, 8 October 1992)

In short, the Governor was seen to be the symbolic embodiment of strength, skillfulness and vision. With these qualities, it was no wonder that he was believed to be able to seize back the initiative and propel the situation forward:

> (W)hen one abandons the high ground, one can, in certain circumstances, get bogged down in the marshland. That is where Hong Kong is now - unable to move forward. That is, until now. Mr. Patten is left with essentially no way to go but forward. (*SCM Post*, 20 October)

Nonetheless, for Patten to become a romantic hero in the society, it was not enough that he appeared to be bold and tough; as a matter of truth, he must be perceived as bold and tough enough to override the Chinese government's opposition:

> It is to his advantage to be able to show that things do not come to a standstill in Hong Kong merely because China disapproves. In going ahead, he will be emphatically denying that Hong Kong is at China's mercy. (Ng, *SCM Post*, 20 October)

Indeed within a romantic frame, the moral force of the 'public' requires the identification of an antagonist who would be associated with profanity, as representing the nicked forces in society. In this early stage, although the Chinese government had not yet taken any revengeful action, it was imagined to be a villain who would pose the greatest obstacle to the Governor's pursuit. Thus it was relevant that Patten had built up his credibility as an unyielding, no-nonsense leader 'who will not be cowed by bullying or blackmail from China' (*SCM Post*, 20 October 1992).This aspect about characterization helped hammer loud his role as a crusader, who sought to bring in a new order vis-à-vis the overbearing the Chinese government.

Variations within the Heroic-Romantic Construction in Public Discourse

Undeniably, there had been great public support for the proposals as they were looked upon as a symbol of democratic progress, and there had been equally great support for the Governor as a strong charismatic leader in this struggle against the Chinese government's opposition. At the same time, however, there lurked some suspicions as to whether he was in fact an arrogant villain playing the role of a savior. (The counter-narratives will be discussed in greater details in the final section and in the next chapter.) Specifically, the challenges consisted in three open-ended sub-plots in the form of questions: (1) Was Governor Patten doing what he was doing in the interests of Hong Kong, or was he doing it in the interests of Britain and himself? Was he carrying on a different game under the cover of his pose? (2) Had he violated the mutual agreement between the two sovereign powers, as the Chinese government claimed? (3) Would he be able to sustain his plans without resulting in unstable transition? Within these broad narrative contexts, specific configurations varied among different political camps, different commentators and different newspapers. The following will delineate two major kinds of position held among those newspapers which basically supported the Governor's reform proposals. Of particular interest in this section will be the various ways the undercurrents made themselves felt in the specific accounts, which would have tremendous bearing on the ways the narratives would be unfolding in the later stages.

A Romantic Projection with an Undertone of Disquiet

There were a very articulate portion of the media public, represented by the pro-democracy critics like Ng in *SCM Post* and Chai in *Economic Journal*, who seriously took the Governor as the protagonist in whom the public could place their trust in the fight for democracy. Indeed the sense of combat was very strong, making public support all the more urgent and indispensable for a victory:

> In his negotiations with Beijing, the only weapon with which he can hope to win is clear and overwhelming popular support ... The thing to do is to support Mr Patten because he is doing what we want ... (Our) case is being put to the test. (We) should do all (we) can to help him to win. (Ng, *SCM Post*, 13 October 1992)

In this narrative of combat or heroic quest, the Hong Kong people would play a secondary yet important role in giving the Governor the kind of support that he needed in order to succeed. This was in part a matter of expediency, and in part a question of sharing the same goal and the same spirit. In spite of what one might disagree to, Ng insisted, the public should support Chris Patten because his speech did put together a number of aspirations of many liberal-minded people in the community: (i) he had proposed what they wanted, (ii) he supported democracy openly, (iii) he took his argument to Beijing, and more importantly, (iv) he had stood for what the people wanted regardless of what Beijing might think and thereby asserted the autonomy of Hong Kong. In particular, the democrats of the United Democrats, led by Martin Lee, were urged to assure the Governor of their partnership and backing within the Legislative Council to ensure a strong and effective combat team. In the same article, she wrote:

> Martin Lee's credibility with the public together with Chris Patten's power should make every joint proposal the strongest possible on behalf of Hong Kong.

> The thing to do is not to oppose Patten now on suspicion. Or on reflex, or because he is a rival in popularity. The thing to do is to support Mr Patten because he is doing what we want ... Any differences can be sorted out later.

> For the moment, Mr Patten needs Hong Kong's support. Let it not be said by a future historian that Mr Patten failed for want of it.

While there was a slight suggestion that Patten might not be regarded as one of 'us' who shared a common dream or who had the same interests, the more important message was that the people should put aside all their differences, suspicion or even jealousy (regarding his popularity) at this critical time and join the fight. For the big enemy was not anyone else but the dictatorial Chinese government to whom political control was always of overriding concern:

> ... should not be harbouring hopes that economic considerations would deter Beijing from extreme measures – As it was in 1982, to the Communist Government in Beijing, political control is always paramount, for which economic interest will be sacrificed without hesitation. (Ng, *SCM Post*, 27 October 1992)

The understanding of the Chinese government being such a ruthless and crazy villain, instead of weakening their determination to fight the battle, had on the contrary hardened their position to go ahead and not to concede based on certain ill-founded hopes. In this narrative context, the people were certainly thinking less about resolutions of the conflicts than about the ways to carry the proposals through in the context of the Chinese government's opposition. A romantic projection was most vividly articulated as follows with the belief that one might take a big step forward to reach a point of no return. In the same article, she put:

> While (Mr Patten) cannot prevent China from reversing the reforms after 1997 if it chooses to do so, he can hope that, once these reforms are in place, their value will become so clear that the public will resist attempts to change them. More importantly, Beijing will not be inclined to change them.

Obviously, the question of sustainability had been taken into account, except that instead of showing reservations and retreatism, the writer was optimistic that a win in a small battle in the short run might mean a good start for the bigger battle to come later.

Nevertheless, even with all the support for the Governor, Ng was a bit anxious that he might be too self-confident or even arrogant in his way of handling the question of political reform:

Mr Patten must add humility to his many virtues. He must recognize the advantage in winning over political leaders, not just the public. He may think that with his political acumen he can easily do this without their help, but this will not be good for Hong Kong in the long run.

This showed a tinge of worry that with the overly strong political leadership by the Governor, he might be bypassing the local political leaders. While the idea of autonomy was not emphatically spelled out in this stage of narrative construction, the advice for the Governor to be more humble with the local political leaders bespoke a sense of unease about him tending to be an all-powerful leader standing over and above the community. As we will see in the following chapters, as the events developed with all the twists and turns, it was this sense of unease that drew the Governor slightly away from the public.

Among the press, in a similar and yet slightly different fashion, *SCM Post* both applauded the Governor's reform proposals and showed persistent faith in him as a respectable leader whose leadership was characterized by strength, integrity and mandate. Little reservation was shown about his character. Nevertheless, regarding the question of sustainability of the project, an undertone of disquiet was shown in the paper in that (i) it was keenly alert to the fundamental point of divergence between China and Britain and at the same time (ii) it placed lesser optimistic hope on the people than political critic Ng and indicated instead an awareness of the force of ironic realism that might be at work among them in the event of Sino-British confrontation:

Mr Patten's determination to prevent China rigging the system to put its placemen in the Legislative Council before 1997 is evident from his proposals. Yet it is precisely the desire to ensure pro-China elements hold the upper hand that shaped the Basic Law in the first place. Without compromise, convergence is a remote hope indeed. (*SCM Post*, 20 October 1992)

In the special circumstances of Hong Kong, however, a referendum would be ill-advised. The electorate is inexperienced and vulnerable to intimidation by pro-China forces promising instability and confrontation. Hong Kong cannot afford a lame-duck Governor unable to lead it convincingly for the final years of British rule, should the population turn him down even in a non-binding plebiscite. Matters of principle are also stake. (*SCM Post*, 23 October 1992)

In such a context, the paper, firm in its position vis-à-vis the Patten proposals, summoned the legislators to call forth their determined support for the Governor:

> Mr Patten has put his cards on the table. It is now up to legislators to get off the fence and offer the Governor their full support in steering the territory through the next five years.

A Sense of Guarded Hope – Keeping a Distance with the 'Hero'

Among the press, *Economic Journal* showed an attitude of guarded hope about the quest. On the one hand, it had its position firmly rooted in the narrative of asserting autonomy and increasing democracy. It celebrated the democratic cause the proposals embodied and welcomed the change in Britain's policy. This was believed to be a rightful assertion of the autonomy of the system in Hong Kong vis-à-vis that in China; otherwise, succumbing to the Chinese government's whims, as the previous governors did, would only lead to the loss of freedom of the Hong Kong people. Moreover, it argued that although the Chinese government might not be without reasons in its attack of the Governor, it failed to specify in a concrete and convincing manner how his proposals violated the legal document. The problem was therefore not with the proposals. Making reference to the various expressions of public opinion such as opinion polls, the radio audience and the consultative sessions, the paper further claimed that the Governor as well as his proposals was able to garner exceedingly favorable and enthusiastic public responses. From a retrospective perspective, it explained how such public applause must be the result of the Chinese government's having all along been too uncompromising and harsh on the Hong Kong issue. Indeed in a romantic quest, there would not be a hero without an identifiable villain. In its narrative account, the paper helped buttress the larger romantic plot in its supporting the Governor's cause and de-validating the Chinese government's counter-narrative of a violation of agreement.

On the other hand, however, regarding the question of Britain's moral position, it had shown a kind of bitter feeling of suspicion and reservation about Britain the state. At the very least, past records showed that Britain had never fought for the best interests of the Hong Kong people on matters relating to world trading. In a more sarcastic tone, the paper stated that it would be too luxurious a hope on the part of the Hong Kong people to expect Britain to come out and fight for Hong Kong's justice and human rights after 1997. Obviously, the paper was implicitly drawing on the code of colonial untrustworthiness. The question here was, how far would the Governor being a British take on a thematic significance of colonialism that would alienate him from public support? In this stage, the paper did not say much about the Governor's motivations; instead, it deliberately bracketed this question and looked at the proposals as they were. It regarded the proposals as basically just and righteous, and was on the whole a good one given the great political constraints. It called upon the people to rid themselves of any kind of self-restraining fear for the Chinese communist state and to support what they believed to be right and just.

At the same time, the paper was aware of the possibility of a Sino-British confrontation. It realized that the attempts to push through the proposals would be fragile without the backing of the Chinese government and therefore, it resisted taking the western media's view of Chris Patten being the fearless hero. The postulations were that it would be no good for the first Special Administrative Region (SAR) government to be created in the midst of Sino-British hostility, and that those who had expressed their support for the Governor might be taking the risk of a revenge by the Chinese government after 1997. However, in a rather inconsistent way, the paper also projected that the Chinese government might not be so irrational as to take any action to have harm done on Hong Kong for what was at stake was also its own economic interest in the society and its international reputation. As a narrative, it was a bit self-incoherent, and the major source of incoherence, I would say, came from the tensions in its attitude about the Governor. There were expressed on the one hand a sense of appreciation for Patten's daring and open leadership, and on the other hand a sense of distaste about his arrogance and also his confrontational style which would be 'fatal' to the Hong Kong people. As such, the paper seemed to be taking Patten neither as the romantic hero in a pure sense nor as the villain in the Chinese government's sense, but as some kind of mixed hero – a hero with the underside of an arrogant trouble-maker – whose cause should be supported independent of his approach. In other words, it was with an ironic distance that the paper was taking the Governor as the central hero in a narrative of asserting democratic autonomy against the Chinese government. Without discrediting his proposals, this characterization might serve to put the people on guard against a total trust in him and subject him to continual lampooning.

Counter-narrative: Cynical Mockery of the Popular Romance

While the romantic discourse had become prevalent, diffused in the public sphere was also a sense of distrust in British colonialism which cast a haze over the Governor's sincerity about reform. The suspicion was that, although Patten positioned himself as standing on the side of the public, ultimately he would take British interests as well as his personal interests as his prime concern. This sense of distrust could be found in different thematic discourses held by different groups and people. The following will focus on the cynical counter-part of the discourse of democracy while leaving another thematic counter-discourse to be explored in the next chapter.

The Pro-democracy Cynics: A Higher Vision of Democracy

Ironic Reality	vs.	Presupposed Ideal
authoritarianism		democracy
colonialism		autonomy
ingenuineness		genuineness
hero-worship		self-leadership.

A cynical mode of narration underlines a discrepancy between ideals and reality, with respect not so much to the constraints of reality as to the will, commitment and sincerity in those who have made a claim to the ideal. In the Patten controversy, alongside the romantic construction, there existed a tiny minority of pro-democracy critics who had shown faith in neither the Chinese government nor the colonial government. To them, real democracy was built upon a solid basis for autonomous development within the society, which must be kept free from external interference and rely instead on the participation of the people rather than single individuals. However, the truth was, the colonial state had never been sincere about democratic reform in the society. The gradual introduction of representative government in the early 1980s was a sham which filled the new bottle with the old wine of political elitism and favouritism. Such a colonial legacy, however, turned on the head of the British when the self-interested political elites, in view of the hand-over of sovereignty, began to switch their allegiance to the future sovereign state. The release of Governor Patten's reform proposals signified an attempt to drum up popular support for the British side in its final governing years rather than a genuine attempt at democratic reform.

In the eyes of a critic, On[2], Patten was skillful enough to provoke the anti-communist feelings widespread among the Hong Kong people in order to mobilize public opinion in his favour; however, his ideological orientation was actually rooted in the British conservative brand of 'authoritarian populism' or 'Thatcherism,' which relied on strong person politics as well as mass mobilization rather than democracy. Thatcherism consisted in three components: first, charismatic leadership which carried in it an ideology; second, ideological predomination over proceduralism; and third, populism. Holding an attitude of cynical distrust about the Governor's reform proposals, the critic, as well as other critics in this category, did not hide his feeling of contempt for the political leaders and the general public alike (who needed someone to be their hero). The counter-narrative, in a word, was one of cynical mockery of the popular romance out of a higher vision of democracy.

China: Patten as a Symbol of Colonial Vices

As we have seen in the previous chapter, in its attempt to undermine the popular narrative, the Chinese government put into question the Governor's motivation and his character. It asserted that what went underneath the popular narrative of a heroic democratic fight was actually a 'conspiracy' plot of Britain as well as the Governor seeking self-interests or having some ulterior motives. This was also a form of mock heroism, but the set of codes that the Chinese government was implicitly drawing on was one of British colonialism versus Chinese sovereignty rather than that of colonialism versus democracy.

It was propagated that the Governor, in proposing drastic changes in the political system, was trying to extend British influence in Hong Kong even beyond 1997 and was doing it in his own personal interest as well rather than for the interests of the Hong Kong people. Obviously, the Chinese government was trying to arouse a sense of distrust about him as both a British colonial governor and as a (self-seeking) politician. As a British, he would have British interests rather than Hong Kong interests as the prime concern. As a politician, he would think only about his political career back in Britain. In other words, for the sake of political fame, he was prepared to gamble with Hong Kong's future, putting into jeopardy what Hong Kong had been achieving such as stability as well as a good prospect of smooth transition in 1997. Not only was he selfish and dangerous, he also showed himself to be arrogant and dictatorial in his not adhering to the spirit of the signed agreements and his not being ready to accept different opinions. The sense of arrogance was most powerfully conveyed through the metaphor of him playing the role of 'savior' for the Hong Kong people. As an attempt to mock and unmask the 'savior' posture, Zhang explained that Britain had had no genuine attempts to build up a democratic system in Hong Kong in the past, and it was instead the resumption of Chinese sovereignty with the drafting of the Basic Law that brought about greater democracy in the society. Here, he was drawing on the code of colonialism which had the code of the lack of democracy to go with it while associating democracy with Chinese sovereignty, and he was characterizing Britain as the real enemy to the society in terms of democratic development. According to his reasoning, the present attempt by the Governor would look pretentious and even outrageous. In short, it was within a narrative of colonial conspiracy that Governor Patten was portrayed as a villain acting on selfish motives but disguised as a saviour. For instance, the 'secret deal' controversy was aroused precisely because the Chinese government wanted to prove Patten 'polluted' in doing dishonest politics.

The Democrats' Self-positioning Strategies

The democrats at first expressed mild criticisms about the Governor's reform proposals, but once the legislative process was initiated, they showed their unreserved support for the proposals, taking them as a symbol of an assertion of democratic autonomy against the Chinese government. Under the moral force of the heroic romance, those who supported the proposals in the face of the Chinese government's opposition would be looked at a courageous fighter as opposed to an 'cowardly other' who hesitated to commit himself/ herself to the righteous cause. With this, the initiation of the legislative process marked the beginning of a process of political differentiation between the democrat-legislators and the conservative-legislators with regard to the reform proposals. The legislative process, moreover, marked the beginning of a subtle shift in the role of the democrats – from a supporter to the Governor at the sidelines to a major protagonist at the centre of the stage. In supporting the reform proposals, they drew on the codes of legislative autonomy versus the Chinese government's intervention. With this shift in both their role and the thematic concern, the more villainy the Chinese government was seen to be doing in threatening local autonomy, the more ready the democrats were to assume a heroic posture for themselves.

Acting as an Ally-Fighter

The democrats started their latest political campaign in May 1992 – almost two months before the new Governor arrived. The leaders of the United Democrats went to London and urged the British Prime Minister to speed up the pace of democracy in the society before it was handed back to China. They expressed their discontents about the 'Foreign Office line of appeasement and kowtowing (to China)' that the British government had been adhering to. More specifically, they demanded that at least half of the legislature to be directly elected by 1995 and three quarters by 1999, a plan implacably opposed by the Chinese government. Immediately after the Governor's reform proposals were made known, the United Democrats showed general support while maintaining some distance from him on specific issues:

> There is much to welcome in Mr Patten's speech. He has grasped the twin themes on which the democrats campaigned so successfully last year ... He has brought a gust of fresh air into the Government, and the people of Hong Kong greatly appreciate his willingness to face the public and answer questions on his policy speech. While we appreciate he has accepted a number of important elements of our election platform, there are several major flaws in Mr Patten's blueprint.[3]

The major flaws included the severing of the link between the Executive Council and the Legislative Council, and his lack of commitment to increase the number of democratically elected seats in the Legislative Council. On the whole, the United Democrats did not so much raise sustained criticisms against the proposals as expressing the worry that the government's commitment to political reform would once again crumble under pressure from the Chinese government. Thus when asked to vote on McGregor's motion in the Legislative Council, they showed no reservations. This gave rise to a conception in the public that the United Democrats were on the side of the Governor, playing the role of a primary supporter.

Discursive Forces over the McGregor Motion Debate – Non-supporter as Coward

Within less than two weeks after the release of the reform proposals, the Governor, as an attempt to mobilize support from the legislators, made an extraordinary ruling in the Legislative Council meeting over McGregor's motion that called on the legislators to endorse his proposal on the composition of the Election Committee. Supposedly, the Standing Orders would prohibit discussion of the Governor's policy address within fourteen days; however, the Governor, as the President of the Legislative Council, exercised his right to overrule the Standing Orders, provided that the Council members agreed. The significance of this motion debate lay in its being a powerful indication of the level of support the Governor could muster within the Council when the going got tough and when he was just about to go on his Beijing visit on 22 October:

> The public had already shown a high degree of support. That must be maintained and increased before Mr Patten sets foot in Beijing ... In his negotiations with Beijing, the only weapon with which he can hope to win is clear and overwhelming popular support. (Ng, *SCM Post*, 13 October 1992)

Urging the leader of the democrats and legislator to back up the Governor in the Legislative Council, the same critic continued,

> Martin Lee should have welcomed Mr Patten's stance, telling him that he will take him on as the government's leader in Legco and assuring him that the Governor will get the effective checks he looked forward to in his inaugural speech.

While there were these democrats committing themselves to the democratic cause symbolized by the Patten package, there were the conservatives appearing undecided as to how to react. The latter were worried that the Legislative Council would be put into a dilemma if they were asked to vote before Britain and China reached a consensus. In terms of public credibility, they had fared poorly. For example, *SCM Post*, referring to the 'public' as a great sanctioning force, suggested that those legislators being unable to make clear their stand would be seen as failing to take up the challenge expected of them, which would cost them public respect:

If, when coming to the vote, many members sat on the fence or absent themselves to avoid declaring a position, they would be accused of flunking their examination, and would be widely ridiculed in the community and abroad. (9 November 1992)

Amidst the narrative force of a heroic fight for democracy by the Hong Kong people, those who hesitated or refused to join the fight were inevitably considered by the public as cowards and turncoats who did not stand on principles but had their allegiance changed with the change of the source of power. As a result of their non-support, they were characterized by the press as 'the less fully committed to democracy who were pressed to make a choice they may have wanted to put off until they see which way the political winds are blowing' (*SCM Post*, 14 October 1992). Since the value of democracy carried the force of public credibility of the day, the conservatives were negatively regarded as having no firm principles on the question of democracy. This was an instance to show the public force of the prevalent narrative of heroic romance which worked as much on plot as on characterization.

Under the force of heroic romance, public discourse did not so much explicitly take the democrats as the heroic fighter as presupposing them to be so in contrast to the cowardly image of the conservatives. (It is often the case that the image of coward does not stand on its own but is meaningfully coded in opposition to the image of a courageous character.) At this stage, the public image of the democrats appeared to be more one of a committed supporter of the Governor's reform proposals rather than a leading hero. Nonetheless, as the legislative process proceeded, they began to assume a more central role in the struggle.

Taking up the Role of Protagonist — Autonomy vs. (China's) Intimidation

After the Beijing visit, Governor Patten prepared his next move of putting together the legislation that would be needed to implement his reform package. Once the legislative process was initiated, the Legislative Council was put in the firing line. On the one hand, there had been great public support for the Governor's proposals, which had been looked upon as a symbol of more democracy. On the other hand, the Chinese government kept warning the Hong Kong people not to support the proposals. Lu Ping pronounced in the press conference that the Chinese government would be ready in 1997 to unmesh the reforms introduced without its approval. In this connection, Beijing's mouth-piece, the overseas edition of the *People's Daily*, carried a signed commentary urging Patten to withdraw his constitutional reform package to pave the way for Sino-British negotiations on the territory's future political development. Furthermore, as it was circulated in the press, the Chinese government had warned the legislators that they would lose their council seats in 1997 if they supported the Governor's constitutional package. As a matter of fact, the Chinese government's constant warnings had neatly deflected the track of the argument away from the democratic implications of the Governor's blueprint, and the issue became one of whether or not to support the proposals in the face of the Chinese government's severe opposition.

The Governor had kept saying that the fate of his vision of reform ultimately rest with the Legislative Council. Indeed in the legislative process, it would be the legislators rather than the Governor who were expected to take up the challenge and come up with a decision on the blueprint. Some even realized that as the Governor was passing the ball to the Council, he would be excusing himself from the responsibility for a defeat:

> If Mr Patten's proposals are defeated in the Legco, it would be cold comfort to be able to say that it is Legco's and not his responsibility that Hong Kong loses its chance for greater democracy. (Ng, *SCM Post*, 3 November 1992)

While generating a sense of ironic distance with the Governor, this realization also strengthened the notion of autonomy in the sense of self-determination. It was conceived that the legislators had to make the decision themselves rather than count on a foreigner who would not stay beyond 1997:

> After all, Mr Patten is only a foreigner from London. However able to well-meaning he is, he will be gone in 1997. It is the local leaders that count. Legco will stand between the public and Beijing. (Ng, *SCM Post*, 27 October 1992)

In a situation where the legislators were shouldered with the responsibility for self-determination and yet threatened with the Chinese government's warnings, some of them, especially the democrats, felt all the more urgent to assert their autonomy against any external interference from the Chinese government. For instance, angered about the warning, legislator Cheung of the United Democrats responded as follows:

> To ask legislators to vote against what the people want, by saying whose who vote otherwise will get off the through train, is tantamount to moulding us into a rubber-stamp.

Clearly, a new understanding dawned on the public that the issue had become one of autonomy versus external interference, if not outright control. As one of the pro-democracy critic put it,

> The attacks by Beijing officials are not just attacks on the substance of Mr Patten's proposals. They are about the right to put forward proposals and the right to determine issues. (Ng, *SCM Post*, 11 November 1992)

Likewise another political commentator in *Economic Journal*, Hung, made the point that the issue to think about was not so much whether or not the people should support the Governor's proposals as to whether or not the people would have the right to choose and decide on this question. Within this narrative frame, the articulate pro-democracy legislators expressed their anger and their determination not to be bullied:

> If I can be intimidated, I should have resigned. Let them do it. Let's show them our real colours. This shows how disgraceful they are. (Lau, *SCM Post*, 6 November 1992)

> I am ashamed to change in the face of that bullying... In the past few years, China resort to bullying tactics rather than normal diplomacy in the event of disputes and that was deplorable. (McGregor, *SCM Post*, 6 November 1992)

In characterizing the deeds of the Chinese government as shameful, disgraceful and deplorable, they were posing themselves as righteous and honourable – In their standing firm even in the face of intimidations. Indeed the higher the possible risks and costs were seen to be incurred on them by the Chinese government, the stronger the sense of martyrdom would be conveyed. With a shift in the theme from democracy to autonomy, the democrats were making themselves the new fearless hero and the Chinese government the same or even more abhorrent villain in the new narrative construction.

In view of the Chinese government's escalating threats, while many found a cause to feel scared, there were the democrats who insisted it was morally relevant that the Chinese government's retaliations were 'drastic beyond all bounds of reason or necessity'. Instead of feeling intimidated or resigned, they expressed their anger about the Chinese government:

China's hysterical reactions to Chris Patten's modest political reforms underlines its determination to exert total political control over the colony ... No doubt it wants a prosperous and stable Hong Kong, but it wants it on its own terms. If ever it feels that its control of Hong Kong is threatened, it will do anything to get its way whatever the price. (Lau, *SCM Post*, 5 December 1992)

It is highly relevant that Mr Patten's iniquities (if such they be) are small, and Beijing's retaliations drastic beyond all bounds of reason or necessity. If Mr Patten goes ahead with putting the proposals to Legco, all Beijing has to do is to declare that in that case China refused to uphold them after 1997 should they go through Legco to implementation, and then it would be up to Legco to decide. Where is the need to start a program to wreck the stabilizing effects of the Joint Declaration and Basic Law on private enterprise? (Ng, *SCM Post*, 8 December, 1992)

Seen as an oppressor who abused power over weaker subjects, the Chinese government was condemned for irrationally harming innocent parties in Hong Kong. While their anger was directed at the Chinese government, they were also concerned that some were succumbing to the Chinese government's threats, and hence blurring the line between what was right and what was wrong:

As the Beijing-London row deepens, more and more people are trying to sidestep the issue of who is right or wrong ... (I)f Beijing is in the wrong, then people are being urged to condone a wrong simply because it is accompanied by threat of force. So might is right ....

Thus instead of retreating from the cause they had supported, they stood firm on their principles. The major issue at stake was not about democracy, but autonomy. In particular, they were angry that the Hong Kong people had been turned into helpless innocent victims of other people's disputes:

The people of Hong Kong are faced yet again with paying the price for a dispute which is not of their making. Once again, we endure the frustration of standing by helplessly while our affairs are discussed by others ... This row is not about who has the biggest political muscle. The lives, the hopes, the plans, the families of six million people are at stake, not those who participate in the present tug-of-war ... Hong Kong is rightly indignant that China should be harming Hong Kong in its fight with Britain. (Dunn, *SCM Post*, 10 December 1992)

The decision might be difficult to make, but because it was a matter of dignity and autonomy, the decision had to be made 'by Hong Kong people themselves without pressure from either Britain or China' (Dunn). Among the press, *Economic Journal* persisted with the 'autonomy' theme. It was concerned about the preservation of the present way of living i.e. freedom. For this, it urged the Hong Kong people to come out to express their views and to fight for their own interests rather than showing themselves to be at the mercy of the two sovereign powers. To make the idea of 'one country, two systems' work after 1997, the society must work together on it before 1997 rather than leave the task to the Chinese government in 1997 because the latter did not really understand the differences between the two systems. Disappointed at the businessmen who did not support Patten's proposals, the paper characterized their action as selfish and timid.[4] Holding such a strong belief in the principle of autonomy, as we shall see in later chapters, some of them also expressed a cynical attitude of disbelief and ridicule about those 'well-meaning' conservatives and 'mild' democrats who sought to pave way for the backdown of the Governor at the end of stage two. In their view, these people not only side-stepped the issue of what was right and what was wrong, but also failed to see the futility in their acts. Only 'fools' would ask for a backdown whereas clear-sighted people would uphold the position of strength.

The Moral Burden of the Label of 'Official Fire-Fighters'

On the part of the democrats, the situation had been complicated with the added meaning of nationalism versus colonialism, which helped put into doubts the sincerity of the Governor's reform plan. To the Chinese government, as it appeared, the issue at stake was not only a matter of sovereign control versus local challenge, but also one of national dignity versus foreign or international intervention. In view of the sudden change in Britain's policy towards China as well as the expressed support for Patten's proposals by Australia, Canada and the United States, the Chinese government found itself in a position to promulgate a hideous plot of an international conspiracy of the Western powers joining hands to push for some kind of 'peaceful transformation' in China.[5] More insistently, it accused Britain of playing the colonial tricks of polarizing the society; in this connection, it attacked those who supported Patten's proposals as democracy-fighters directed by Britain:

> Looking back at the 'dirty history' of British-colonized countries, it was not difficult to find cases where their rulers meticulously directed local people into polarization through the so-called 'democracy fighters', resulting in riots and bloody confrontation.[6]

In labeling them as the pawns of Britain, it was suggesting that Patten was holding up the heroic ideal so that the democrats would be 'taken'. As such, not only were the democrats regarded as unable to see through the cover of his pose, they were also seen as being dangerous or disloyal to the nation.

No matter whether the Chinese government's accusations were valid or not, the truth of the matter was that in a culture of an underlying distrust of the British government, the code of anti-colonialism did carry certain public force. In the society, without embracing nationalism in the Chinese government's sense, the more cynical critics had sniffed at the paltry offer of democracy in the Governor's proposals and saw in the democrats' support an indication of naivete and passiveness.[7] The democrats began to find themselves in a very tough dilemma where they could trust neither China nor Britain. Ng's retrospective account of the dilemma was worthquoting in length:

> Because Beijing has been so entrenched in its anti-democratic stance, insisting that democracy is the converse of loyalty to China, democrats often look to Britain as the only possible ally.
>
> But even at the best of times that alliance is extremely uneasy. It also carries a not insignificant price. Because of the underlying anti-colonial sentiments among local people, anyone close to the British becomes suspect.
>
> In recent memory, the only occasion after 1967 when there was some sort of alliance was during the crisis of the Sino-British talks, when a great many Hong Kong people committed themselves to seeking to retain some kind of British administration for as long as possible.
>
> That alliance ended in great disappointment, though it was accepted as almost inevitable. Perhaps the feeling was not exactly one of treachery, but the sense of betrayal came close enough later when the promise of autonomy and democracy held out by Governor Sir Edward Youde in his famous 1984 green paper first waned and then was rescinded altogether after dishonourable 1987 political review.
>
> The present alliance between the democrats and Mr Patten is the closest. Should the democrats be suspicious and so lose the advantage of an alliance, or should they be trusting, and risk the humiliation of yet another betrayal? (*SCM Post*, January 5, 1993)

Thus while the democrats defined the Chinese government as the villain and the conservatives as the fool, they did not see Patten as an unflawed hero. Rather, their emotional responses about him ran the gamut from unease to distrust. This was in part due to their own sense of growing distrust about a colonialist and in part due to the force of the public which was associating them with a symbol of ridicule and disrespect — the 'pro-British' label. Among the press, *Economic Journal*, which had all along been supporting Patten on his proposals, discredited him as 'too self-confident and too arrogant' (8 December 1992). It understood him, the ex-chair of the Conservative Party in Britain, to be feeling somewhat belittled in being asked to be the governor of a colony, and hence wanting to get things done in an unusual and daring manner once he assumed governorship. In so doing, he was able to increase his fame in the international arena, yet at the cost of doing harm on the relationship with the Chinese government, polarizing the Hong Kong society, and alienating the conservative forces from the government. Although the paper continued to support his proposals, it did not believe his confrontational approach was the right way to push through political reforms. In other words, the paper advocated separating the democratic cause from Patten the actor.

For the more radical democrats, while they were having a grudge against the Chinese government, somehow their anger was also directed at Britain. There was a projected feeling, probably based on a fear, that Britain would be giving in as it had been in the past:

> China's hysterical reactions ... underlines its determination to exert total control over the colony. It has been aided and abetted by Britain, which has repeatedly succumbed to China's unreasonable and dictatorial demands ... The Chinese have blatantly ripped apart the Joint Declaration and Britain has been able to do little apart from wringing its hands in despair. Developments in the coming weeks will determine whether the final chapter of the history of the British Empire is going to end in a shabby way. (Lau, *SCM Post*, 5 December 1992)

Towards the end of the year, rumours were rife that the British had softened, and that secret talks would be held with the Chinese. This gave rise to the concern that Hong Kong democrats would be betrayed once again by the British. Ng explained this as a peculiar way of thinking among the Hong Kong people — 'a strange blend of wishful thinking and fearing the worst':

> The voices urging the Governor to climb down have been loud. People are

anxious for relief, and so they will believe it will come in the way they want it to. But they also think it's bad for London to capitulate. They would despise London for it. And because they fear it is just what London might do, they begin to believe it. (*SCM Post*, 5 January 1992)

According to this logic of reasoning, underlying the fear of the people was in fact a self-conflicting mixture of a wishful belief in Britain's backing down and a projected feeling of contempt for it. While the former was understandable in the light of their desire for a relief, the latter bespoke a sense of distrust about Britain's sincerity and conviction for political reforms in Hong Kong. According to Ng, fear of betrayal was a symptom of helplessness, and the way out of the trap was independence – to be independent by gathering strength:

> Once they know their own strength, they will never be caught making unnecessary concessions for untrustworthy promises. Above all, the moment they are alerted to the possibility of betrayal, they know they will only have to take the battle into their own hands and carry on.

The democrats were certainly at the same time struggling with the 'pro-British' label. From the perspective of 'autonomy,' the challenge for them was one of disassociating themselves from the British side without nonetheless forsaking the democratic cause:

> They (the liberals) have taken neither Mr Patten nor the British government on trust. Prominent in the many advertisements which appeared in support of the proposals is the statement: 'Although these proposals are not perfect, we think their general direction is right.' It is not that they lack reservations or even suspicion about Britain's motives. They fight for democracy because it is vital to Hong Kong's future. (Ng, *SCM Post*, 24 November 1992)

While some of them wanted to break loose from the apparent grip of Britain by making their own more radical proposals, Ng still suggested the democrats remain as cautious allies with the Governor:

> From the liberals' point of view, there is certainly much to be cautious about in any alliance with the Government. They certainly do not want their electorate to suffer under the misapprehension that they are in Mr Patten's pocket or have become official fire-fighters ... But they should know ... though democracy for Hong Kong has never had much of a chance this is the best. They must seize the reins and take advantage of Mr Patten's pledged position. (Ng, *SCM Post*, 24 November 1992)

Conclusion

In the first stage of the event, a heroic-romance was constructed alongside some reservations and cynical responses within the pro-democracy camp. With the support of public opinion, the heroic-romance nonetheless remained predominant in public discourse. In this context, the democrats played the role of supporter for Patten the protagonist, not so much for him as for the cause that he symbolized. Their moral presumption of the Chinese government as the villain as well as their characterization of the conservatives first as timid cowards and later as stupid fools was a logical product of such a narrative construction. In the second stage, the Chinese government's threats further ignited a response of romantic persistence among some of the democrats. At the same time, with the growing force of the discourse of autonomy versus colonialism, it appeared that the democrats were having an uneasy public relationship with the Governor as a colonial figure and bordering on a split between two heroic romances. The dilemma was, should the democrats continued to support the governor as a strategic ally or should they take up the role of heroic fighters themselves against both Chinese autocracy and British colonialism? Stage three of the event would see the democrats split among themselves in the final legislative process as well as subtle changes in the narrative construction of the whole event.

Notes

1. *Ming Daily*, 12 October 1992.
2. On To, *Economic Journal*, 18 October 1992.
3. Published in *SCM Post*, 10 November 1992.
4. *Economic Journal*, 16 November 1992.
5. This view had been taken up by other commentators as well, and it was given the widest attention when Lee Kuan Yew from Singapore made a similar suggestion in December. See *SCM Post*, 17 December 1992. On 17 December, China singled out a well-established British company, the Jardine Group, for attack, accusing it of prospering unscrupulously under British imperialism and condemning it for supporting the Governor's proposals.
6. Hong Kong China News Service, 21 November 1992.
7. See Wong's articles in *Economic Journal*, 30 November and 11 December.

9 Discursive Formation (II): Stability and Comic-Realism

In the last chapter, we have discussed the discourse of democracy in its different narrative forms as well as ways of specification. In concrete practices, the discourse of democracy, of course, did not stand alone but had to constantly assert itself against alternative discourses in a field of competition. This chapter will focus on the thematic discourse on stability which gradually emerged as a strong competing force vis-à-vis the prevalent romantic discourse on democracy. Three specific questions will be tackled. First, how was the discourse of stability being articulated in a comic-realist frame which helped project a different line of action from that of a quest which in turn mediated the process of political differentiation and alliance formation? Second, how could a comic-realist discourse on stability gain ground amidst the heroic-romantic construction as a competing narrative? Third, how did comic-realist discourse on stability exert itself as a discursive force in politics, especially regarding Governor Patten's reform proposals?

As we shall see, the Chinese government's revengeful action had its intended effect of mobilizing local oppositions against the heroic-romantic cause, and among the latter, the conservatives changed its role from uncommitted waverer to mediator (comic hero) through the construction of a comic plot of action. It was through these changes that the conservatives made a clear-cut move to differentiate themselves from the democrats with regard to the reform proposals while clinging more and more to the ever expanding pro-China camp. The narrative was articulated primarily through the successful construction of two moral metaphors in public discourse – the Governor as a trouble-maker and the Hong Kong people as victims. With the parallel construction of a comic irony in opposition to the heroic romance, public discourse put the event in a different light which thereby created new demands on the Governor.

In the first section, I will briefly delineate the discursive structure of comic-realism in general, and with regard to the value theme of stability in the local context in particular. This will then be followed by elaborate discussions in the second and the third sections on China's reaction in conjunction with the process of narrative formation in public discourse on the theme of stability. Special attention will be given to the narrative form of the counter-thematic discourse, the changing role of the conservatives, and the also the discursive force the narrative generated in the political process. Finally, as an attempt to explore the points of divergence and convergence within the discourse of stability, this chapter will end with a section on the variations within the thematic discourse as they appeared in the final stages – at a time when the event developed towards the ironic pole within the comic frame of narration.

The Comic-Realist Mode of Discourse

It is contended that in Hong Kong the pragmatic discourse on stability is most congenial to a comic-realist mode of narration. As a kind of narrative culture, comic realism celebrates flexible pragmatism and regards compromise and co-operation as the most desired attributes that will bring about a result of reconciliation or restoration of order. In comedy, the essential element of plot is reconciliation or the restoration of order involving a hero/ heroine seeking to achieve this end and an obstructing character standing in the way of the action. The obstacles to the hero/ heroine's will form the action and the overcoming of them the comic resolution. In such a frame, the primary form of villainy is embodied in the symbolic character of a trouble-maker which disturbs an orderly existence rather than an oppressor which maintains or seeks to maintain an unjust order.

In the context of Hong Kong, pragmatism indicates a readiness to adapt oneself to the situation in such a way that one could both take advantage of it and stay on the safe side. To the conservatives, in their pragmatic mode of reasoning, given the reality of the resumption of the Chinese sovereignty in 1997, the wise way of going about the situation was to co-operate with the future sovereign power on transitional matters so as to maintain stability and prosperity. The conservatives, with their pragmatic concern, had been most ready to trade democracy and autonomy for peace with the Chinese government. In the public sphere, drawing on a discourse of stability, they expressed their concerns with order, harmony and smooth transition as opposed to disorder, conflict and unstable change. It is through such discursive terms that they fought hard to maintain the existing order which privileged the interests of the conservative elites, to oppose democratic reforms that might jeopardize their established interests and/ or fall outside the orbit of China's intent. In their mode of narration, people who attempted to introduce changes against the will of the Chinese government would be conceived as trouble-makers who brought in an ironic situation of conflict and instability.

The conservatives' prime concern was with stability, and the kind of stability they aspired to was tied in with a peaceful relationship with China. It was at this juncture of discursive articulation that the conservatives were found to be more and more prone to a pro-China stance. A pro-China stance was a position which tended to take for granted the Chinese government's authority as well its prescribed order of things. Such a position was usually couched in terms of the codes of sovereignty, nationalism and stability which, through discursive practices, often went together. As we shall see, towards the final stages of the Patten controversy, the conservatives did bring in an idea of nationalism in their discourse on prosperity and stability and re-interpret their role accordingly as a mediator for a modernized China. In the final legislative process, the conservatives were able to form a strategic alliance with the pro-China groups in making a concerted attempt to beat down the Governor's reform proposals.

As we may see, the discourse of stability, in the way it was being articulated, had become a common discursive field whereby the Chinese government, the pro-China groups and the conservatives could join together as a strategic power bloc in opposition to the democrats. Within the thematic discourse, different actors nonetheless made their own specific articulations which might vary among themselves. The differences could lie in the ways the different codes were related among one another and also the poles – the comic versus the comic-ironic – which the narratives inclined towards at particular political moments.

The Narrative of Trouble and Disorder

Immediately after the release of the Governor's reform proposals, the Chinese government responded by defining the Governor as a villain rather than a hero. Putting the events into a different narrative frame with a different thematic emphasis, it put forward a specific counter-narrative of a villainous attempt by the Governor to disrupt the process of smooth transition of sovereignty by violating their mutual agreement. Following suit, the pro-China forces, represented by the Democratic Alliance for Betterment of Hong Kong, warned the Governor of taking the risk of provoking a protracted war of words with the Chinese government. Among the newspapers, while most of them did not make a direct opposition to the proposals, a few of them were concerned, to different degrees, about the question that the row might not be conducive to a smooth transition. Here they were all drawing on the code of stability and, framing the event in a comic-ironic narrative, they characterized the Governor as a potential trouble-maker. On the part of the conservatives, for a short moment, trapped between the discursive force of the popular heroic romance and its own pragmatic concern with a stable relationship with the Chinese government, they appeared undecided in their position with regard to the Governor's reform proposals. Nonetheless, later, it was with their pragmatic concern that they began to formulate a counter-narrative on the theme of stability in the midst of changing political climate in the society.

Comic-Realist Response in Public Discourse – The Governor as a Nuisance

The pro-China forces, represented by the Democratic Alliance for Betterment of Hong Kong, equated the Governor's style with showmanship and saw in it an element of impudence. They warned the Governor of taking the risk of provoking a protracted war of words with the Chinese government: 'In all likelihood Mr Patten's constitutional package will be regarded by the Chinese Government as a deliberate attempt to undermine the intentions of the Basic Law, if not a blatant contravention of its provisions'.[1] Many of them expressed the worry that the Governor's act of arrogance towards Beijing would put Hong Kong on a collision course with the latter, which then raised the question as to whether smooth transition would be secured. Out of this concern, they therefore looked on his open and populist posture with disdain and suspicion. On the question of democracy, they reiterated that they did not want political reform to cost the society its social stability and economic prosperity, but favored democratization at the pace of 'gradual and orderly progress'. In their characterization, the Governor approximated to a trouble-maker rather than a romantic hero.

> Trouble-maker = Those who bring about instability
> = Those who ignite confrontation with China.

The image of a trouble-maker embodied vices of lesser moral severity than that of a villain, but it also clearly delineated the boundary of what was regarded as morally good as opposed to the undesirable. Likewise among the newspapers, a few of them were concerned, to different degrees, about the question that the row might not be conducive to a smooth transition. In their editorial accounts, as shown below, the Governor was conceived as carrying an element of potential danger and a quality of self-interestedness. While some newspapers like *Express Daily* pinned the characterization on a personal level, *Ming Daily*, in particular, did it on a state level, seeing in the Governor a trait common to the British politicians and dismissing it as a short-term political as well as colonial thing.

In *Express Daily*, the editorial position seemed to be swinging between the two value themes of democracy and smooth transition. It saw both as important and the two as not necessarily mutually conflicting. Its position was that Patten's proposals themselves were good because they brought in a significant portion of democratic elements and thereby satisfying the people's aspirations for democracy. However, if this led to the Chinese government's opposition and therefore resulted in very hostile Sino-British relations, it was no good for smooth transition. Probably, it assumed, most of the people wanted both, and it would not be their wish to see smooth transition sacrificed for democracy. Thus on the one hand, in supporting the democratic cause, the paper would not and did not advise Patten to withdraw his plan, and believed instead that the Chinese government was over-sensitive about a British conspiracy. Yet on the other hand, for fear of instability, it disagreed to Patten's dangerous approach. It characterized him as a bull in a China shop i.e. a person who was rough and rash where skill and care were needed to handle the relationship with China.

In a more straightforward way, *Ming Daily* published an editorial entitled ' 'Stability' and 'Prosperity'?' in which it expressed its concern with smooth transition. In the first place, it raised doubts about Patten's motivation, saying that he, being no different from other British politicians, was bent on winning 'a standing ovation from the public so (that) he can return to Britain in glory and continue his illustrious political career after leaving ... Of course, as far as Hong Kong affairs are concerned, the British no longer have to take a long-term view'. In the second place, claiming that the question of motives was of lesser concern, it argued that the more important question was about consequences:

> The question is whether Mr Patten's new deal is conducive or detrimental to Hong Kong's 'smooth transition', 'stability' and 'prosperity'. What Hong Kongers really want is no more than 'stability' and 'prosperity'. (9 October 1992)

Strangely, while it seemed to indicate a negative response to the Governor's reform from the perspective of 'stability' and 'prosperity', it also showed that it did not care much about what the Governor was doing. It reasoned that the controversy was no big deal and was unlikely to be furious because the Chinese government would restrain itself, 'Even if the Governor adamantly insists on having his way, the Chinese will probably avoid going to extremes or resorting to antagonism or retaliation.' Believing that the Chinese government would have its plan to simply undo any unwarranted changes introduced by the British in 1997, the paper quoted a source saying that 'If the British want to change anything, they can go ahead and have fun'. In other words, the paper was adopting a rather detached attitude towards the Governor's reform plan, showing neither any firm support nor very strong criticisms. Yet, that the paper had expressed its primary concern with the maintenance of 'stability' and 'prosperity' might indicate how it would likely respond to the situation when it became less sure of whether the Chinese government would resort to extreme measures of retaliation.

Similarly, *Success Daily* had not made a clear stand as to whether to support or to oppose the Governor's reform proposals, but in various places it dropped hints about its reservation. First, while admitting that the development of democracy was an inevitable trend that the Chinese government should not hinder, political reform had to proceed in an orderly and gradual manner. Secondly, it was supposed to be the Governor's main task, as he himself had emphasized upon arrival, to maintain co-operation with the society's future sovereign power in order to safeguard smooth transition. Although Patten had made cautious compliance to the letters of the Joint Declaration and the Basic Law, he erred in overlooking the spirit of co-operation and mutual concession that underlay the drafting processes.

The Conservatives Metamorphosing Out of the Role of Uncommitted Waverer

In the early stage of the event, the conservative group, represented by the fourteen legislators from the Co-operative Resource Centre, had not committed themselves to a clear public stand as to whether or not to support the Governor's proposals. On the one hand, they called for a referendum, leaving the matter for the public to decide. On the other hand, in their public statement, they both paid tribute to the Governor's policy of democratic government and expressed the hope that the Governor and the Chinese government could work out an agreement to safeguard smooth transition.

Apparently, they were trying out for a middle path and adopting a kind of wait-and-see attitude. This gave the public an impression of them being pragmatic waverers, which was further reinforced in the Legislative Council voting over the McGregor motion.

It was believed that the group as well as its conservative allies were likely to 'make their support conditional on some sort of deal struck with China, rather than a unilateral decision to go ahead, which would risk confrontation with China' (*SCM Post*, 14 October 1992). Thus when pressed to give a show of hands with regard to the McGregor motion in October, they withheld their support. To them, the Governor's exercise of special right in the Legislative Council was a bit inappropriately high-handed, for it seemed to be giving unwarranted pressure on the Chinese government. This created for them a public image of having weak commitment to the cause of democracy. In this connection, earlier on, the Co-operative Resources Centre had been publicly blasted with thinly-veiled criticisms from the Bank of East Asia chairman and independent legislator, David Li Kwok-po, who described the group, without naming it, as 'once being pro-British, but switching allegiances to being pro-China to protect their own interests'. This image of pragmatic waverers, despite their defenses, had decreased their already low public credibility.

However, within the Legislative Council, the dividing line between the conservative group and the few pro-democracy groups became unmistakably clear when it came to voting on the proposals on November 11. Abandoning their earlier strategy of non-commitment, the conservative group as well as a few other legislators voted against the proposals. What explained such a decided change in position among the conservatives? Both political and cultural forces were at work in facilitating the change. Politically, the legislative process precipitated by the Governor put the legislators in a situation where they were hard pressed to declare their stance in a clear-cut manner even though they might not be completely ready for it. The conservatives hesitated to join the game over the McGregor motion, but as legislators they simply could not withhold themselves from showing a clear position for long. At the same time, the Governor's visit to Beijing, which was scheduled a few days after the McGregor motion debate, brought back a hidden message that the Chinese government was determined to stand firm on its position to oppose the reform proposals.

On the cultural level, the conservatives, with a tinge of pragmatism, reasoned that it would not be in Hong Kong's interest to adopt a package of reforms that could not survive 1997. In public discourse, such a concern with discontinuation had been expressed in narrative terms with the Governor being characterized as a trouble-maker. Such a counter-narrative was given a boost when there emerged in the society more and more calls for prudence against a foolhardy pursuit with the heroic romance. The most remarkable ones, as we shall see below, came from an organized attempt by a large number of business groups and also a newspaper which had supported the Governor's reform proposals. It was in the midst of changing political-cultural climate that the conservative legislators made their opposition to the reform proposals, probably without having to worry about losing much public credibility. In standing clear of their pro-democracy counterparts, they were in a way mocking the heroic posture by the democrats by making the latter's romantic narrative look rather impractical and imprudent. This paved the way for their taking alternative moral roles in a different thematic plot of action. Within such a short time span, the changing political stance among the conservatives illustrated very well the ways narratives exerted themselves as a discursive force while being shaped and consolidated through political action.

Public Discourse: An Appeal to Prudence

While the democrats insisted on the principles of democracy and autonomy even at the expense of their relationship with China, there was in public discourse an increasing concern with the problem of unstable transition. In particular, the Business and Professionals Federation, a group which claimed 159 members representing many of the territory's biggest companies and leading professional organizations, came out in favour of convergence, arguing that Patten's attempts were not worth the risk of creating conflicts with the Chinese government. Among the newspapers which supported the Governor's reform proposals, *SCM Post* advised the legislators not to overlook the Chinese government's will when deciding on the reform proposals:

> Asking Hongkong people to judge the package without taking account of the views of a sovereign power which promises to unmesh the plans as soon as it regains control would produce a debate of little relevance. (8 November 1992)

This was in essence a practical concern with the question of smooth transition versus abrupt changes. In this context of changing concern, *SCM*

Post began to show some sympathetic understanding towards the conservative legislators who had been ridiculed for their hesitations. Specifically, it saw them as getting lost in the sweep of a new way of politicking introduced by the new Governor:

> Mr Patten's expectation that they should be ready to stand up and be counted pays no heed to their history and track record. Hong Kong has only recently been introduced to direct elections, and legislators have never been exposed to Mr Patten's type of politicking before. They are trapped between his persuasive skills and power, and the clear message from an increasingly large and vocal section of the business community not to create confrontation with China over an extension of democracy at this late stage of Britain's sovereignty over Hong Kong. (9 November 1992)

The underlying sub-plot was one of the Hong Kong politicians, or more specifically the appointed and conservative councilors, having long been adapted to the old mode of consultative politics which stressed consensus and concession, and therefore being unused to the mode of democratic politics which allowed for open discussion, insistence and even confrontation. As such, they were understood as some public figures who were still too much tied to the past way of doing politics and whose 'good will' was being out of touch with public aspirations. While this aroused a little sense of pathos, there was, as the paper saw it, actually a cause for worry — the Legislative Council might not be able to take up the great challenge suddenly thrown upon them. Thus, instead of whole-heartedly celebrating the cause of democracy and autonomy, as it had been in the previous stage, the paper began to show some reservations and called for prudence:

> Mr Patten should consider very carefully whether or not he is taking a risk that in trying to extend democracy, he is not actually posing a threat to the viability of the most senior semi-elected body in the territory. (Ibid.)

Indeed it had been realized that the legislators would be facing a tough dilemma over the political future of the society. A pro-democracy critic, for instance, analysed the pros and cons of taking either position in terms of what were being valued in the short run and in the long run:

> To vote down Mr Patten's proposals may buy peace in Hongkong-China relations in the short run, and may look the easy way out ... But in the long run this option will actually make it increasingly difficult to defend Hong

Kong's interests and way of life against Beijing's encroachment, and ultimately to protect the success that Hong Kong is, from being eroded away ... To vote in favour of Mr Patten's proposals is to risk success ... (I)f they win ... they will have to face the consequence of their success, which is an immediate and lasting difficult relationship with Beijing, and the real possibility that what they set up will be dismantled after 1997. (Ng, *SCM Post*, 3 November 1992)

Given this understanding, the choice to make was not as easy as it had seemed before.

At this point of time, the two opposing counter-narrative positions had taken quite good shape. It was in this context that the conservatives, in voting against the Governor's reform proposals, had made their position clear. With this, later when the Chinese government embarked on a series of revengeful action, they were more than ready to take a further step in asserting their political position with a better-organized counter-narrative, taking up the role of a mediator in a comic plot of reconciliation and smooth transition.

Turning Point: China Generating a Comic-Ironic Situation of Chaos and Anxiety

After the votes in the Legislative Council, which gave a strong backing to the Governor's reform proposals in terms of their broad principles, the Chinese government took a series of revengeful action by means of threats and warnings which touched on the nerve of the people. Emotionally, there was great anguish among the people, who were left to wonder what had happened to all those oft-repeated pledges by the governments to preserve prosperity and stability. In the course of such an ironic construction of the plight of the people, discourse on public opinion showed a significant decrease in support for the Governor's reform proposals. In such a context, the comic-realist mode of narration began to gain ground whereby the conservatives took up the role of comic hero in a plot of restoration of order. Within the comic-realist frame, the Chinese government's reaction was taken as given whereas the Governor was demanded to concede.

China's Action – The Politics of Threat and Retaliation

As we have discussed in chapter seven, the prime messages sent out by the Chinese government's threats of retaliation were that it would start things afresh on all fronts in July 1997 and it would not co-operate with the current Hong Kong Government on any important matters.[2] To the people, the Chinese government had meant its words and actions to be 'a petulant wrecking operation' to hurt the local economy and throw investors into disarray. It showed on a deeper level that the Chinese government was prepared to sacrifice even its short-term economic interests in Hong Kong for the sake of political interests.[3] With this realization, the question of smooth and stable transition got catapulted to the public foreground in an overbearing fashion. The people became more and more aware of the collective dilemma they were then forced into:

> Are we to retreat in the face of China's objection and allow the 'high degree of autonomy' promised to Hong Kong to be devalued? Are we to proceed with the Governor's proposals and risk the dismantling of our political systems after 1997? (Dunn, *SCM Post*, 10 December 1992)

Looking from the point of view of the democrats, the issue was about autonomy versus submission to China's power. Looking from a realist perspective, however, some realized that the choice laid in front of them was between convergence and Beijing-inspired instability and economic uncertainty. In the first stage, amidst the mood of hopes and strength for a better political future initiated by the Governor, there had already been some undercurrents of reservations. In particular, there was the question about whether the Governor would be able to sustain his plans without resulting in unstable transition. Now that the confidence of the people was greatly shaken as a result of the Chinese government's threats and warnings, it came to a critical time at which the public had to decide whether they could continue to support the Governor's cause.

An Ironic Realization: The Hong Kong People as Victim

Emotionally, there was great anguish among the people. In numerous accounts, the Hong Kong people were likened to helpless pawns in other people's power games. What characterized the mood of the ordinary people was a strong feeling of helplessness about their own fate:

> It is beginning to look like trench warfare with both sides dug in for a long battle, but in that situation it is the poor foot-soldier who suffer most - in other words, the ordinary people of Hong Kong. (*SCM Post*, 1 December 1 1992)

Apparently, the force of realism had become so strong as to overcome the sense of heroic romance. The imagery of themselves being a victim signified a sizable ironic turn from the romantic mood of hope to an attitude of 'resignation'[4] regarding the romantic pursuit.

In this context of fear, helplessness and uncertainty, the discourse on public opinion showed a primary concern with the decreasing support for the Governor's proposals. Notably, the discourse largely took on a realist tinge, highlighting the costs and risks involved in the romantic action. In *SCM Post*, for instance, the news headlines on 22 November read: 'Governor faces loss of support' and 'slippage in reform backing', despite the facts that much more people were in support of the proposals (57%) than those against them (17%), and that support for the Governor himself appearing to be holding up well. The major highlights were to underline the idea that more people felt it was not worth the confrontation with the Chinese government.[5] For example, on the one hand, 40% believed the Governor should push ahead even if through train was impossible, down from a previous figure of 49%, with 14% undecided. On the other hand, only 34% believed the Governor should push ahead at the price of sacrificing convergence, sharply down from 56% in the last survey. Moreover, almost half were unwilling to sacrifice the new airport for the sake of political reforms, with 46% saying the Governor should not go ahead if it meant more delays on the airport project, up from 31% in the October 8 poll. Picking on these findings, the editorial suggested that the possible price of opposing the Chinese government over the reform proposals, which began to sink in, was higher than many were prepared to pay. *Economic Journal* likewise stated on November 16 that the Hong Kong people did have aspirations for more democracy, but they were not prepared to fight for it at whatever cost. Published letters to the editors showed a similar reading of 'public opinion':

> On the one hand, we hear public calls for a faster pace of democracy at all costs to safeguard Hong Kong's autonomy. On the other hand, the call for a smooth transition for the long-term good is gathering momentum, culminating in the recent stock market slump that illustrates the decline of public confidence in Hong Kong.[6]

Even democrats acknowledged the waning support for Patten's proposals in the recent polls, though they insisted that it showed a lack of confidence rather than a change in aspirations.[7] Jumping on the bandwagon, the pro-China forces went further to say that the trend of public opinion spoke loud and clear the idea that 'Mr Patten will soon lose majority support from the public if the present impasse continues'.[8]

The Comic-Realist Discourse: Turning to a Plot of Restoration of Order

On the part of the conservative groups, it was in this situation of hopes turned sour among the general public that they forged a narrative of comic versus ironic action whereby they defined not only the locus of blame, but also the desired order as well as the course of action to be taken for resolution. Within the frame of 'prosperity and stability', a few newspapers such as *Express Daily* and *Ming Daily* had expressed their concern about the danger of spreading the conflicts between China and Britain into the community or even polarizing it, hence putting into jeopardy the achievement of prosperity in Hong Kong. Understood as such, the situation became one of undesirable disruption of an orderly and prosperous existence, as it was in an ironic comedy, rather than one of hard struggle for a romantic end. From the comic-realist perspective, *Express Daily* and *Ming Daily* hoped that the two sides could continue negotiation in consideration of general interest rather than resorting to extreme measures. Amidst this general desire for reconciliation, prominently, the conservatives were anxiously looking for ways to enable Patten to 'climb down' from his uncompromising stance with Beijing. Playing the role of *mediator* or go-between (comic hero/ heroine), the conservative legislators tried to negotiate with the Chinese government while attempting at moderate reform proposals which they thought would be both a 'ladder' for the Governor to climb down and a chip to get the Chinese government's approval. (Likewise the moderate democrats, albeit having some sympathy for the British, were keen to retreat into defeatism, seeking for resolutions instead of pressing ahead with the Governor's reform.) This started a process of local struggles in which the conservative groups sought to replace the Governor's proposals with their more conservative models.

The Conservatives and the Pro-stability Press: Comic Projection

Holding onto a comic-realist frame, the conservatives were anxious to see the restoration of Sino-British co-operation through their mediation. In February 1993, from the perspective of the conservatives, a comic turn took shape within the comic-realist frame when sudden and continued news report about secret diplomatic contacts between Britain and China, and softer rhetoric on both sides, filled the belief among the people that a breakthrough in the deadlock was imminent. At this time, the legislative process was in the stage of the Executive Council's final scrutiny of the draft bills giving effect to the proposals before they were formally introduced to the Legislative Council in mid February. Among the legislators, opinions were divided as to whether the government should table the bills containing Patten's package while the talks were still underway. The conservatives, whose most important goal was to allow more time for the talks to come to fruition, favoured a delay in the legislative process. As a result, the government delayed the introduction of his proposals, which was generally taken as an amiable gesture made in the hope that Sino-British talks might resume and help break the impasse over plans for Hong Kong's constitutional reforms.

Among the press, *Ming Daily*, *Express Daily* and *Success Daily* shared the position of comic projection. In terms of plot and characterization, they believed Patten to be an arrogant trouble-maker who disrupted the order of smooth transition. What they instead wanted to see was a comic resolution – the restoration of Sino-British co-operation in the transitional period so that prosperity and stability could be well preserved. Comic realism celebrated flexible pragmatism and regarded compromise and co-operation as the most desired attributes. In judging the credibility of Patten's action, they believed the deferrals 'did not so much damage his reputation or authority as exemplify his cool-headedness and prudence' (*Ming Daily*, 13 March 1993). More specifically, *Ming Daily* applauded that the Governor, who had been very arrogant, was beginning to take a more flexible and realistic attitude with the Chinese government, because this marked a probable comic turn towards the resumption of Sino-British negotiation:

> Mr Patten has switched to a flexible attitude, which is a far cry from his arrogance over the past five months. If one can mend one's ways upon realizing one's mistakes, one may still be successful. It is only right for any politician to look reality in the face and adopt a realistic attitude. (*Ming Daily*, 7 March 1993)

The idea of conversion, which was clearly spelt out in the above quotation, was a distinctive structural principle in comedy, for it constituted a significant turn making possible the final scene of reconciliation. In terms of affect and mood, having delivered themselves from the state of anxiety, these papers were therefore optimistic about a final resolution. Further to this, they made reference to the Hang Seng Index as an indicator of public optimism:

> Every time the government delayed gazetting Governor Chris Patten's constitutional package, the stock market climbed sharply ... Stock buyers use their hard-earned money to voice their wishes about Hong Kong's future, and this is a far more serious decision than choosing between 'yes' and 'no' when asked to do so by pollsters ... Hong Kong's future virtually hinges on its economy ... Therefore, sentiment in Hong Kong's economic sector is of overriding importance. (*Ming Daily*, 8 March 1993)

In this account, almost everyone must be feeling happy about the delay. The highlights on the rising stock market were meant to convey a mood of festivity as would prevail in a comic ending.

In making a comic ending of reconciliation an eventuality, this category of newspapers would want to see another major obstacle removed, which was the scheduled legislative process. In their comic projections, these papers stressed that the legislative process should not and would not pose as an obstacle to the diplomatic negotiations between China and Britain:

> (U)nder Britain's constitution, The Legislative Council, being part of the British Hong Kong government (which is inferior to the British government) rather than a supreme legislature, is not competent to reverse its superior government's decisions. This is indeed the case. The Chinese need not be over-anxious about this. Therefore, there are no foreseeable obstacles to diplomatic negotiations between China and Britain. (*Ming Daily*, 7 March 1993)

> If both China and Britain concede a bit in the interest of all, then there will be hope for the political row to come to an end ... In fact, it is not really very difficult for each side to find a face-saving ladder to climb down. On the part of Britain, the Patten package is just a proposal and therefore, the British team could be flexible about it. On the part of China, so long as the Patten package does not get gazetted, it would mean the package has been withdrawn .... (*Express Daily*, 6 March 1993)

It is right to delay gazetting the bills, especially because the two sides seem to be coming closer and closer to an agreement .... We hope that they do come up with an agreement before The Legislative Council start discussing the bills ... In fact, in the transitional period, political reform should be co-decided by the two sovereign powers rather than by Britain alone or by the local government. (*Success Daily*, 13 February 1993; 1 March 1993)

The resumption of Sino-British talks leading to the maintenance of prosperity and stability was what they were praying for. With such a comic hope, focal concern in these papers had been about how to provide Patten with a ladder to climb down in terms of giving up his reform proposals.

Narrative Variations and Changes among the Pro-stability Press

On 12 March, the Governor together with the Executive Council nonetheless decided to gazette the proposals. In gazetting the reform bills, the Governor was able to assert its administrative autonomy, yet at the risk of alienating those who had been waiting anxiously for the resumption of talks. The Chinese government had reacted ferociously with anger, showing its determination not to co-operate with Britain on any front. On March 16, condemning Patten as 'a man of guilt', Lu Ping announced that the Chinese government was ready to set up a new 'stove' to institute the territory's post-1997 political structure. A freeze on meetings of the Joint Liaison Group and hold-ups on major infrastructure-related projects threatened progress on several fronts. Among those newspapers in the comic-realist category, positions differed between those who were still hopeful about the resumption of talks and those who turned more pessimistic about the deterioration in Sino-British relations.

Ming Daily: *The Discourse of Comic Optimism*

Interestingly, *Ming Daily*, while favoring the resumption of talks, did not discredit the government's action at all, but just expressed the same comic hope in earnest, showing a consistent attitude of comic optimism. Making reference to the 'general public', it repeated its persistent hope for the comic development of reconciliation:

Hong Kongers approve of any efforts to bring about Sino-British reconciliation. This is because their real concern is stable life, good business,

and social harmony and tranquillity. We hate to be perturbed by such rows
and quarrels. Probably few Hong Kongers can see what the Chinese and the
British are quarrelling about. (13 March 1993)

It was true that for a short while, its initial response had been ironic in that
it believed it to be difficult to see what could be done to end the Sino-
British deadlock in the foreseeable future, because 'the Chinese will
certainly try even harder to make the situation difficult for Patten' (ibid.).
Thus rather helplessly, it concluded with a suppliant attitude, 'We can only
hope that (Beijing) will try to be considerate towards the Hong Kongers'
(ibid.). These few dissonant notes, however, did not mean any significant
change in its narrative, for after a few days, the familiar comic themes re-
emerged:

> The fact that Lu Ping made Patten the target of his attack seems to lend force
> to the injecture that the Chinese will be more than happy to talk with the
> British once they dump 'Pawn Patten' ... This being the case, we maintain
> that the two sides should adhere to the principle of mutual understanding and
> accommodation and return to the conference table ... Hong Kongers should
> remain optimistic about the territory's political-economic future and avoid
> being so affected by imaginary troubles. (18 March 1993)

Its account was persistently comic in structure, ready to absorb a signal or
event as a comic sign. Reconciliation could be achieved at the expense of
Patten, whose being 'dumped' would seem to cause no regret. The key
mood conveyed remained strongly optimistic.

Express Daily: *A Turn to Ironic Realism*

Regarding the deterioration in Sino-British relations, *Express Daily*
configured a decisively ironic turn of the events within its narrative frame.
The paper showed decreasing faith in the two governments in their efforts
to restore co-operation. By October 1993, it was the first among the comic-
realist group to give up hope on the talks. In its several retrospective
accounts published in October and November, it spoke of the experience of
a double irony of hopes turned into despairs. Such a discursive turn helped
facilitate an overall shift in the narrative progression of the 'public' toward
the end of the event, which will be discussed in the next chapter.

Political Actions of the Legislators toward the End

The Conservative Legislators Taking up the Role of Mediator

Among the political parties, the Liberal Party (the former Co-operative Resource Centre) had always adopted a comic mode of understanding and assumed the role of a mediator. In mid October 1993, as the talks showed little progress, the Party sent a delegation to Beijing whereby they portrayed themselves as acting as a courageous mediator required to bring about a comic turn in the ironic stage of a desired comedy. On 11 October 1993, the day the Party headed for Beijing, the Party chair wrote in *SCM Post*, 'We are heading into a storm in Beijing because we know that British and Chinese relations are turbulent. But we will be there to speak for what we believe are the worries and aspirations of the people of Hong Kong, and ask the Chinese government to resolve its differences with the British Government'. However, for a while in early December, as the talks came to a breakdown point, it was to their bitter disappointment that they found their comic hopes and efforts betrayed. In a retrospective account, the Party chair explained how the news of the resumption as well as progress of the Sino-British negotiation bred a mood of optimism, and how, after eight months, such optimism was replaced by a regretful feeling that the Party had been too optimistic to realize the 'deep mutual distrust' between the two powers:

> Now the people of Hong Kong know that the eight months of wrangling have been in vain and that the embittered sides are more wary of each other now than at any time since they began deliberating our future -without our participation ... What they we did not calculate was the deep mutual distrust that would frustrate all the efforts we made in Hong Kong to broker peace. (A. Lee, *SCM Post*, 9 December 1993)

What this ironic realization brought about were not only a feeling of disappointment but a sense of betrayal:

> Evidence from the failed talks shows that Hong Kong has been the least of Britain and China's concerns, and therefore the first to be betrayed ... Hong kong should not be asked to take sides in a quarrel we did not initiate and cannot appreciate. (9 December 1993)

In view of the problem of political discontinuity in 1997, and realizing that Hong Kong could not rely on the two powers for its own well-being, A. Lee appealed to the public for self-help:

> While we plead and pray for Britain and China to resume negotiations, we have to keep our composure, continue with our jobs, families and lives. We have no choice than to rely on ourselves to minimize the damage inflicted on us by two powers that have promised in earnest to anchor our stability. (9 December 1993)

Persisting with their cherished hope for smooth transition, they played a more active role in the legislative process, trying to bring about what they believed to be a semi-comic ending of something close to political convergence even in the absence of Sino-British agreement.

In the Legislative Council voting on the partial reform bill on 24 February 1994, the Liberal Party, assuming the role of a comic mediator, had attempted to block the bill by first supporting veteran Tu's motion to delay the bill, and failing on that, they tried to stall the more controversial part concerning the single-seat, single-vote system for the 1995 election of the legislature.

The Pro-China Alliance

On the part of the legislators, the first partial bill was but a small part in the larger struggle yet to come. Immediately after the first partial bill was approved, they quickly prepared to put forward amendments to the remaining items of the Patten package. The '1994 package' by the Liberal Party, containing fewer democratic elements than the Patten package, was devised to the Chinese government's (implicit) blessings so as to secure some kind of unofficial convergence.

Indeed in trying to cultivate a more amiable relationship with the Chinese government, the Liberal Party had been injecting a nationalistic element in its account of comic hopes and worries. Earlier on, in a piece of commentary on the Preliminary Working Committee, the Party chair advised the Chinese government on the way nationalism might be 'channeled towards a positive cause' (*SCM Post*, 25 July 1993). In the October 11 article, he constructed more or less the same narrative line based on the idea of 'nationalism', with an added emphasis on the role of Hong Kong could play in China's modernization. In a most persistent way, the

Party hoped for a more heartening scenario wherein China and Hong Kong would work, willingly and proudly, in the mutual interests of each other – the preservation of prosperity and stability in Hong Kong, and successful economic modernization in China.

The pro-China groups opposed the Governor's proposals but they did not yet have a strong power base within the Legislative Council. By late June, after much lobbying, the chances of the Liberal Party holding sway in the Legislative Council took a sharp turn for the better on the eve of the voting, when seven pro-China legislators indicated they would lend their support to the '1994 package'. Of the seven legislators, Tam Yiu Chung from the pro-China organization, Democratic Alliance for the Betterment of Hong Kong, had kept its voting decision secret until two days before the voting when Chinese officials signaled approval. (In the public, however, officials from China still said the three-tier government would be disbanded no matter which electoral package was passed.) Tam supported the '1994 package' in the name of convergence and stability, along the same line that the conservative Liberal Party explained itself.

Conclusion

This chapter has shown how the pragmatic discourse on stability in Hong Kong was given a particular form within a comic-realist mode of narration. Comic realism stresses flexibility, pragmatism, compromise, and co-operation for the sake of order and stability as opposed to disruption of order. For very pragmatic reasons, the conservative elites could ill afford to put their economic and political interests at stake in a situation of political instability and confrontation with the Chinese government. Their hesitation in supporting the Governor's reform proposals in the early stage was an index of such pragmatic concerns. However, it was only through a clear articulation of a comic-ironic narrative, in the midst of China's threats, that they later became determined to take up an active role – mediator –to bring about the restoration of political stability. The ideological equation between political stability and a co-operative relationship with the Chinese government laid the basis for the development of a pro-China stance among the conservative elites. It is at this juncture of discursive articulation that a strategic alliance was made possible and necessary between the conservative elites and the pro-China leftists in the final legislative process in the Patten controversy.

Notes

1. Quoted in *SCM Post*, 11 October 1992.
2. Lu Ping had already hammered home China's plan to unmesh the reforms proposed by Governor Patten and to set up a new 'stove' when it resumed sovereignty over Hong Kong in July 1997. On 13 November, the New China News Agency issued a stern warning to the Hong Kong Government against what China believed to be a unilateral move by the Government to build the airport alone. Without first securing an overall financial agreement with Beijing, it said, the franchises for handling air cargo and fuel at the new airport would not be honoured beyond 1 July 1997.
3. In fact, China's salvo had helped wipe several billion dollars off the value of its own shares in Hong Kong companies. See *SCM Post*, 2 December 1992.
4. *SCM Post*, 17 December 1992.
5. *SCM Post*, 22 November 1992.
6. This is from the 'Letters to the Editor' section in *SCM Post* on 15 December 1992.
7. See M. Ng, *SCM Post*, 24 November 1992.
8. Y.S. Tsang, *SCM Post*, 27 December 1992.

10 The Changing 'Public' in the Political Process

The event under study started on 7 October 1992 when Governor Patten released a blueprint for political reform, and then developed through a number of episodes involving intense social conflicts over the legislation of the reform package, and finally ended with its successful legislation on 30 June 1994. In narrative terms, the release of the reform proposals developed instantly into a popular heroic romance, with Patten the protagonist seen as embarking on a quest for democratic autonomy vis-à-vis China. Apparently, the final legislation of the reform proposals would signify a victorious ending as a fulfillment of the promises of the heroic-romantic beginning. However, the fact was, as the event developed over time, the public meanings of 'Patten' and his reform proposals changed in the process so much so that the story of heroic romance lost much of its initial colour and emotional charge. The question is, what explained the rather paradoxical development of the event – a victory without a sense of victory – at the end?

In this chapter, I am going to show how a symbolic force of the 'public' was at work in the public sphere which, through the initial construction of heroic romance, informed, guided and constrained political practices in the process of endowing cultural meanings upon the latter. Upon the release of the reform proposals, despite certain places of incoherence in the narrative construction of the event, the structure of heroic-romance, once consolidated in public discourse, persevered as a discursive force which 'demanded' Patten, his supporters and also the British side to stick to the initial line of action, or they would make a public mockery of themselves. In a significant way, the final legislation of the reform proposals, despite continual delay and attempts for diplomatic concession, testified to the discursive power of the narrative.

At the same time, there took place a process of narrative progression which changed the public meanings of the event in terms of the public's experiences with it. The narrative process could be conceived as one of de-heroization and de-romanticization, taking place through the interplay between the discursive force of the heroic-romantic structure, counter-narrative challenges made out of pragmatism and cynicism, and also a number of contingent episodes involving Sino-British politics.

Stage I: Some Open-ended Projections Alongside the Heroic Romance

Public Discourse

At the outset of the event, as chapters seven and eight have shown, there had been great public support for the proposals as they were looked upon as a symbol of democratic progress, and there had been equally great support for the Governor as a strong charismatic leader in this struggle against China's opposition. In public discourse, the prevalent narrative was basically one of heroic romance. Still, amidst the narrative construction, some undercurrents were also noticeable, which not only added complications to the heroic plot line but also pointed to different possible closures. As it stood, the counter-narrative challenges consisted in three open-ended sub-plots in the form of questions. The three questions were about whether (i) Mr Patten was acting in the interests of Hong Kong, or Britain and himself, (ii) he had violated any agreement with China, and (iii) he would be able to push through his reforms without disrupting the process of transition. This section will analyse how far the counter narrative questions were challenging the prevalent narrative of heroic quest.

Let us summarize how and how far the counter narrative questions might challenge the prevalent narrative of heroic quest. The first question was a difficult one, for there was no one definition of what the interests of the Hong Kong people were. There might be at least two ways to look at the issue – (i) whether his plan was congruent with the wishes of the people and (ii) whether he had some ulterior motives. Regarding public opinion at this stage, despite some criticisms, the overall imagery was one of popular support for the Governor as well as his proposals as shown in the media, the opinion polls and also within the Legislative Council. Nevertheless, as public opinion would change in the course of narrative development of the events, it still remained to be seen how far and how strong the existing undercurrents would carry the public into alternative narrative paths. In this light, the second way of looking at the issue would make more substantive sense. On the question of whether the Governor had other interest considerations or bad intentions, most of the press found it quite understandable that the Governor might want to show the world and especially the British electorate that the British government had done its best to get as much democracy as possible before Hong Kong was handed back – if it succeeded, it would be able to retreat with honor. It seemed that to the people back in his home country and to the democrats in the local community, insofar as it was about introducing more democracy in Hong Kong, the Governor was doing an honorable task. This, as it appeared, would not constitute a problem unless he was doing it at the expense of the Hong Kong people or he had some other hideous concerns. At this stage, it was not widely discussed (or it could not be clearly articulated) in the public as to what the other interests he was probably thinking about in private. Within the top business community, nonetheless, there was some sneak speculation (which was only indirectly mentioned in the press) that the Governor might have introduced the proposals as a bargaining chip to be sacrificed if concessions were needed to win China's acquiescence on the rest of the constitutional package. However, as there was no way to get at what was really in his plan, the logic of the sub-plot would require some kind of progressive revelation of his real intentions and calculations. As such, this question remained to be a major underlying concern and later became one of the foregrounded sub-plots as the event unfolded.

The second question was more straightforward but there was also no easy answer. The main difficulty lay in the fact that even a document written in black and white could be open to different interpretations, for there were not only gray areas but also some tacit understanding or what China called the 'spirit' of an agreement. This could be further complicated by the problem of secret documents which had been barred from the eyes of the public but were later made known to them. With these complications, the logic of this question would call forth some kind of retrospective interpretation and revelation, which required the actors as well as the audience to look closely at the past documents as evidence. As we will see in the 'secret deal' controversy, a significant discovery would likely make a remarkable turn whereby the major characters would be differently perceived and judged and the events differently narrated.

Finally, the answer to the third question of sustainability and stability would require some kind of projective anticipation of what might happen in the future given certain conditions at this point of time. It was not just a simple prediction of what followed what, but involved a great deal of anticipation and anticipation of anticipation – of desires, worries, beliefs, actions and calculations. In fact, most of the press realized that the two plots were very much intertwined in that the struggle for more democracy in the society would only result in confrontation and tensions with China. It was not because the Governor was unmistakably seen as violating the joint agreements. In fact, there seemed to be a kind of consensual view among the media that the Governor was maximizing the space for democratic election by appropriating the gray areas in the Basic Law in a very clever and daring way so such so that its opponents had not yet been able to point out which specific provisions his proposals had violated. The problem was nonetheless that the kind of 'sweeping' changes proposed were very much against the will of China. In a most explicit way, *SCM Post* and *Ming Daily* respectively pointed out the crux of the problem that suggested an almost head-on clash between the desires and plans of the two sides:

> Mr. Patten's determination to prevent China rigging the system to put its placemen in the Legislative Council before 1997 is evident from his proposals. Yet it is precisely the desire to ensure pro-China elements hold the upper hand that shaped the Basic Law in the first place. Without compromise, convergence is a remote hope indeed. (*SCM Post*, 20 October 1992)

> The Chinese Communists believe it is absolutely important for them to have political power firmly in their hands ... Hongkongers who want to speed up Western type democratization will contravene this fundamental Chinese Communist doctrine. (*Ming Daily*, 20 October 1992)

In terms of consequences, with the conflicts on political reforms, it was believed that Sino-British co-operation on other matters such as the airport question would be made all the more difficult. Already locked in a disagreement over whether the future SAR Land Fund should be used to fund the airport plan, the Governor's plans to democratize Hong Kong were expected to pull the two sides further apart. As it turned out, the collapse of the talks over the controversial airport project on 15 October dashed hopes that the Governor might bring about a settlement to the row when he visited Beijing.

Nonetheless, although the public were not unaware of the bad consequences in the event of non-cooperation with China, this was not their major concern at that time. Firstly, they were largely in the midst of an ecstasy as they had been very much carried away by the Governor's personal charm and the hopes he had generated for their political future. Secondly, as neither China nor Britain had taken any concrete action to put the future of Hong Kong into jeopardy, the idea of having a possibly smooth transition disrupted had not yet occurred to the people as immediately threatening. For instance, it appeared that the 'market' had decided that Hong Kong could absorb a little confrontation with China. The Hang Seng Index, which would have plunged on such news a year ago, soared to record heights on the two days of the Governor's visit to Beijing.[1] In this context, it was understandable why the first suggestion (by a Chinese official in Hong Kong) of China overthrowing all the changes introduced by the Governor was not seriously taken up in public discourse.[2] For this was probably viewed as empty threats rather than a hint of the concrete action China would really take; or in the view of a newspaper, the implications of a confrontational relationship with China had not yet become apparent.

As far as the polls are concerned, we may conclude that on the one hand, the dominant narrative frame guiding public opinion was that of 'increasing democracy against China's undue interference'. On the other hand, since some people expressed an opinion on the more specific question but not the general 'satisfaction' question, it showed that they were having reservations. Specifically, that a total of 15.2% of the people did not think the Governor was giving more democracy to Hong Kong and that a total of 14.4% would be against the proposals if China objected, suggested that more than 10% of the people did not trust the Governor, suspected a possible violation of agreements and/ or feared about China's objections. On the whole, the polls showed quite solid support (for democracy) and some reservations for various possible reasons.

In sum, from the perspectives of romanticism and realism, respectively, there were on one side the narrative of the strong and unyielding governor venturing into the sacred terrain of democratic struggles against China's opposition, and on the other side the undercurrent of the arrogant and self-seeking politician dashing into the prohibited terrain of confrontation with China. By so doing, according to the conservatives who held the latter view, the Governor would be creating some kind of troubles for the society the magnitude of which was yet to be known. In another, more satirical form, the cynical critics in the pro-democracy camp, raised doubts as to whether the Governor was genuine about democracy, in terms of both his reform proposals and his character. These undercurrents notwithstanding, at this stage, the collective image of popular opinion was largely one of solid support for the Governor's proposals, which served to put a stamp of high public credibility on them. This paved way for the second stage of the conflicts in which the legislature endorsed the proposals on the one hand and China started a series of attacks and threats to undermine the public's confidence in the proposals on the other.

Interplay between Legislative Politics and Sovereign Politics

Within the Legislative Council, the dividing line between the conservative group, Co-operative Resource Centre, and the few pro-democracy groups became unmistakably clear when it came to voting on the proposals on November 11. The latter supported the proposals whereas the former, as well as a few other legislators, voted against them. As it turned out, the Legislative Council votes gave a strong backing – 32 to 21 votes – to the Governor's reform proposals in terms of their broad principles. For those supporting the proposals such as *Economic Journal*, the voting result was a sign of public support for democracy. Patten was quick to enhance his own public credibility by making a reference to the 'community' and relating it to the Council votes: 'the government's judgement about the community seemed to be very strongly endorsed by the Legislative Council as recently as 11 November'. In terms of legislative procedures, the endorsement meant that the proposals, whether modified or not, would be presented by the Executive Council in their legislative form before the Legislative Council by the next spring, when the latter would have to make a final decision on their fate and shape. At this point of time, the story had ended with the first victory of the Governor as well as those who supported his proposals. Nevertheless, as the event continued to develop, in a context where China was very unhappy with the Council votes, this was but the beginning of a longer story yet to unfold itself.

The problem was that to China, the Council votes signified escalating confrontation against China by Patten, for the Council debate was conducted under pressure from the Hong Kong British authorities. Immediately on the next day, the New China News Agency proclaimed that the Legislative Council was just a consultative body with no right to approve a resolution to overthrow the agreements and understanding reached by the Chinese and British Governments. Here, it was drawing on the frame of 'sovereign power versus local autonomy', weaving the event of the votes into a counter sub-plot of the Hong Kong people over-asserting their local autonomy and hence challenging the power of its sovereign state(s). Indeed in the midst of increasing open conflicts with China, there developed among the Hong Kong people a growing realization of a failed promise of 'Hong Kong people ruling Hong Kong' by China. It was suggested that China was having some more profound fear beneath the surge of anger, which was a fear that if Britain was transferring power to the Hong Kong people instead of China, Hong Kong would be turned into a semi-independent state rather than coming under its firm control.[3]

Following this line of reasoning, *SCM Post* believed that Beijing feared a Patten Plan passed by the Legislative Council and endorsed by the people much more than a package of ideas promoted by a new governor from London.[4] In this way, by means of a projected understanding of China's side of the story, the public was alerted to the meaning of confrontation implicated in the Legislative Council conscious disregard for China's opposition to the reform package.

In the society, on the one hand, given that some people were already having reservations, it was likely that they would be mobilized into disapproval when China stepped up its retaliatory efforts. On the other hand, however, given that some democrats were persistent with the democratic cause, it was unlikely that they would yield to China's pressures. The question then was, was Governor Patten still able to show himself to be the trustworthy hero for their struggles?

Stage II: The Governor on the First Test of Public Credibility

The 'Secret Deal' Controversy

The first critical event was around the 'secret deal' controversy, which for a moment cast the counter-narrative of 'a breach of joint agreement and common understanding' onto the front stage. On 23 October, right after his meeting with Patten, Lu Ping, the Director of the China's Hong Kong and Macau Affairs Office, alleged in a press conference that some secret papers would prove the existence of a Sino-British deal concerning the composition of the Election Committee for the 1995 elections, which was now overturned by Patten's plans. In response, the Governor as well as the British Foreign Office spokesman confirmed the existence of diplomatic exchanges between the British and Chinese foreign ministers over the 1995 polls, but denied that the diplomatic exchanges amounted to a deal. Former Basic Law drafters came out to support China's claim and maintain that in the process of drafting the Basic Law, drafters postponed their last round of meetings until a deal was reached by the governments.

In the society, most newspapers were concerned if there was any joint agreement and hence a breach. For the first time the good faith of Patten was seriously in question:

> He is not entitled to continued trust and support if he cannot give a satisfactory explanation and dispel the suspicion engendered by Lu Ping. (Ng, *SCM Post*, 27 October 1992)

Among the legislators, a growing number said they would withhold support for the Governor's political reform blueprint until the matter was cleared up. 'Before Hong Kong people can lend their whole-hearted support to Mr Patten's plan, we must first clarify who is lying and who is hiding the facts', said Li of Meeting Point. Many legislators, democrats and conservatives alike, and quite a number of newspapers urged for the release of the letters in order that the Hong Kong people could judge for themselves. Clearly, this demand by the public was driven by their strong urge to know if the 'romantic hero' Patten could come out clean and thereby earn their continued trust. Equally strong, moreover, was their desire to be the master of their own fate:

> The publication of these letters is a good thing because it makes the present Sino-British relations more 'transparent'. By referring to the letters, Hong Kongers can see for themselves what the present dispute is about, judge how serious it actually is and express their own views. (*Ming Daily*, 29 October 1992)

> For the first time the people of Hong Kong will be in possession of all the facts that bind their future, for the first time able to make sensible decisions about their future. Without the facts no one can be master of their fate. (Ng, *SCM Post*, 27 October 1992)

> After all, it is all about the future of the Hong Kong people and therefore, the matter should be made known to them. It should be up to the people to make a judgment about whether there had been any trading going on under the table which betrayed their interests. (*Express Daily*, 27 October 1992)

In essence, the above three quotations were drawing on the common democratic code of transparency versus secrecy. From these commentaries, we can see how the frame of 'a breach of the agreement', in the context of the people having been put in the dark and then having to demand the release of the diplomatic documents as evidence, began to land itself on a new narrative theme of 'autonomy' – asserting the people's right to know and to judge for themselves.

On the part of the government, the voices of the public were so strong and united that it had to answer their demand in order to clear itself of any suspicion by them. The publication of the documents a few days later, however, failed to settle the 'deal' dispute. Among the seven secret exchanges between the two sides in January and February 1990, a crucial reference over the possible existence of an agreement was contained in the British Foreign Secretary's letter to the then Chinese Foreign Minister on 12 February in which he wrote: 'I agree in principle with the arrangements which you propose for an Election Committee, which could be established in 1995 ... The precise details of how this should be done can be discussed between our two sides in due course'. While China considered this proof that an agreement had been struck, the Governor said this and other exchanges made it 'abundantly plain' that there had been no deal on the 1995 elections.[5] Apparently, both were right in its own terms. Legislators were divided on their judgement of whether the terminology of the correspondence constituted a deal. In terms of opinion polls, there was no majority formed in favour of either side - 35% of the respondents agreed with China whereas 30% disagreed, and 35% were unsure whether China or Britain was right.[6] Certainly, given that the dispute remained unresolved even with all the relevant evidence, it would be rather impossible for them to go forward in a narrative sense if they got stuck on this issue. As a matter of fact, public debate soon shifted its focus from the controversy itself to its wider or deeper implications. As we will see below, in order to carry the sense-making process forward, the public reconstructed their narratives in different ways, including an outright adoption of China's position, the suggestion that it was nothing but a detour from the developing romantic plot, and the construction of a new narrative (around the theme of 'autonomy') in conjunction with a discourse of distrust.

A Romantic Response among the Critics: A Detour from the 'Democracy' Plot

Among the press, except for *Success Daily* which toed China's line in stating that the issue was about a breach of promise and that Patten had wronged China in this regard, there seemed to be a consensus in the other newspapers that some kind of common understanding, but not a deal, had been reached between China and Britain. The following was a succinct example of such an account:

> Through the exchanges, both sides made concessions on small points in dispute and managed to narrow the gap between them. In this sense, they

208 Narratives, Politics, and the Public Sphere

> may be regarded as having reached some sort of understanding or
> agreement. They, however, have not come to any consensus on the whole
> issue, nor have they signed any binding documents, nor has either side
> promised not to take issue with the other about relevant matters. (*Ming
> Daily*, 29 October 1992)

This, while generating more sympathetic understanding for China, did not
discredit the Governor's proposals in any significant way. *SCM Post*
believed that the correspondence itself proved less conclusive than Lu Ping
had claimed; what the publication instead highlighted was that 'Mr Patten
has interpreted the correspondence and the Basic Law as liberally as the
sharpest legal advice would allow' (29 October 1992). Similarly, Ng, the
democrat-critic who had compared Patten's plan to a romantic combat,
considered it a case of overstating the position by China:

> The community, on the whole, does not think that the messages vindicate
> Mr Lu Ping's assertions. People do not see in them the question of how the
> 1995 election committee should be formed was all settled. Even more
> clearly, despite Mr Lu's claim, there is little said about functional
> constituencies. People do feel, however, that there is 'something in it,'
> such that it is understandable that Beijing should have come to the view
> that Mr Lu put forward. It is more a case of overstating the position than
> downright fabrication. And they are prepared to leave matters at that. The
> thing to do, the community clearly urges, is for both sides to go back to the
> negotiation table, and see if they can't achieve something.

In the above text, the writer was not only expressing her views, but was
trying very insistently, with all the references to the 'community' and the
'people', to speak in the name of the 'public'. The main idea was that while
there seemed to have been some kind of mutual understanding between
China and Britain, it did not constitute a deal as the Chinese side had
claimed it to be. This reference to the 'public', as we have just seen,
appeared to be consonant with most of the views expressed in the media,
and it also served to reinforce the sense that the expressed views were
widely shared in the public. In so doing, the writer would be in a position to
give *closure* to the counter-plot of Britain breaching the promise and
violating the agreement, and then claim that the people were prepared to
'leave matters at that'. Similarly, Martin Lee of the United Democrats
stated that the point was not whether there was an agreement but whether
the Governor's proposals, which gave more democracy to the Hong Kong
people, should be supported. The narrative implication was that the people

should leave behind this whole 'secret deal' controversy for it was nothing more than a detour from the developing plot of a romantic fight for more democracy vis-à-vis the Governor's proposals.

In this connection, there was a portion of the public who cared little about what the 'secret deal' issue implicated. *Ming Daily*, for instance, had its focus instead on the question of stability and prosperity, and therefore showed lesser concern about the problem of divergence from the Basic Law than about continued Sino-British discussion in the spirit of the Joint Declaration:

> It is not serious and certainly not 'disastrous' even if Hong Kong's political system does not converge on that provided in the Basic Law ... (I)t is more important for the two sides to maintain Hong Kong's stability and prosperity through the implementation of the Joint Declaration. Therefore ... China and Britain must seek to continue discussion ... (29 October 1992)

Although its concern with stability and prosperity did not add any weight to the romantic account, the sense of indifference shown about the 'breach' issue helped put a closure to China's counter-narrative of a breach of agreement.

A Cynical Response in the Press: The Discourse of Distrust and Autonomy

For one thing, despite their unwavered support for the romantic project, the democrat-critics also realized that the British government had not emerged from the published messages all innocent: 'The position it adopted over directly elected seats truly hurts, though no one really wants to refer to it'. While it was not picked on as an issue, probably for fear of a backlash for the democratic cause that the Governor's reform proposals signified, it did sow the seeds of distrust of the British government, which would lend force to the development of a new narrative around 'autonomy'.

Indeed among the public, there was a heightened sense of distrust of both governments, especially Britain. Drawing on the democratic code of participation versus exclusion, political groups such as Meeting Point and the Association for Democracy and the People's Livelihood expressed their disappointment that the Hong Kong people had been deprived of their right to decide on their own future and that their will had not been respected by the British and the Chinese governments during their negotiation. Likewise among the press, *Express Daily* pinpointed the 'secrecy' problem instead of the 'deal' issue. No matter whether it was a deal or just mutual understanding, it proclaimed in its October 31 editorial, the problem was that there had been no participation of the Hong Kong people in the negotiation process. The sense of distrust against Britain was shown in its raising the time-related question as to why Britain did not introduce more democracy earlier if it was genuine about political reforms. In particular, the revelation of the diplomatic documents showed how the proposing of the Omelco model by the Hong Kong government in 1989 was in fact a fraud, betraying the trust and hope of the people at that time. Putting into doubts Britain's sincerity about political reforms, this account also underlined a sense of suspicion about the motivation of Patten, who was introducing reforms at the so-called eleventh hour. Indeed but for this kind of retrospective understanding, the paper could have shared the view that the present Governor was 'right to be entirely open with the public about his proposals before he went to Beijing'; however, in making such a retrospective configuration, it tended to be suspicious about rather than supportive of the Governor. Looking further back from the present and then looking ahead, the paper was worried that there might already have been some deals struck behind the back of the Hong Kong people during the long process of Sino-British negotiation since 1982, and that there might still be some secret deals made at the present time that would determine the future of Hong Kong. As such, it expressed the disappointment and the anger that since the Hong Kong people's right to know and to participate had never been respected, there was no way for them to judge who was right and who was wrong in this tension-filled time. Further drawing on the 'democracy' or 'self-reliance' code, it urged the people neither to be led by the nose by China, nor to be used by Britain as the bargaining chip. Instead, it called for a due respect for the will of the Hong Kong people, advised against any more secrecy in the negotiation process, and urged the people for an active self-positioning in case of Sino-British negotiations on political reforms.

Clearly, these calls for transparency and participation were lending force to a new narrative around the theme of autonomy, which, as we have seen, had its germ in the call for the release of the documents immediately after Lu Ping's allegation of the existence of a secret deal. The structure of codes that underlay this new thematic plot was one like this:

'Autonomy' Suppressed	vs. 'Autonomy' to be Respected
Secrecy	Transparency
Exclusion	Participation
Being used as pawns	Self-reliance.

In terms of characters, both China and Britain were seen as the villains suppressing the autonomy of the Hong Kong people and secretly trading on their political future. This understanding had earned the two governments increasing distrust from the Hong Kong people. For the pursuit of a new possibility, the paper was proposing a new narrative of fighting against the suppression of the autonomy of the Hong Kong people. This new narrative, obviously, would have the people themselves, rather than Patten, be the protagonist in the fight. In other words, this new understanding constituted a shift not only in the narrative theme and the structure of affect, but also the identification of the chief actor.

On a deeper level, the theme of 'autonomy' would find its strongest emotional foothold in a situation where the people could trust neither Britain nor China. Indeed Lu Ping's allegation hit home because people had always suspected that some secret agreements to their detriment had been made by the two governments. While anti-China feelings had been rooted in a strong sense of fear and hostility about Communist totalitarianism, anti-colonialism expressed itself primarily as a deep sense of distrust about Britain's moral commitment to the society. That was what the democrats meant by Britain 'selling Hong Kong down the river' within the narrative frame of 'British betrayal and concessions'. Compelled with this surge of suspicion, they were therefore angry that Britain and China might have hatched a top-secret deal to curtail Hong Kong's democratic development. This feeling of anger, however, was mixed with a sense of fear that if Patten failed to weather this storm and went down, the liberal cause would go with him, and that in the triumph of Beijing, Hong Kong would read its own defeat. Caught in this dilemma, the more cynical democrats began to separate the democratic cause from Britain:

> For whatever Britain may or may not have promised, it remains a fact that Hong Kong people want democracy ... Whether the blame lies with Beijing or with London, the cause should continue to be supported. (Ng, *SCM Post*, 27 October 1992)

Although Patten did not come out 'polluted' i.e. proved to be doing dishonest politics, in a context of increasing distrust about the British, neither could he emerge all clean and innocent. Indeed within the 'autonomy' frame, to the extent that the Governor being a British took on the thematic significance of colonialism, the detachment of the democratic cause from the Governor, as we will see later, would be further required by the logic of this new narrative configuration.

The Image of the 'General Public'

From public discourse, we have seen how China's allegation failed to make a convincing enough case to seriously discredit the Governor's proposals, hence giving a finishing note to the 'breach' question. Still, the significance of the incident was two-fold. First, as the revelation of the documents raised doubts about Britain's commitment and sincerity, the question about Patten's motivation was then made a recurrent theme in public discourse. Secondly, that China continued to insist on a breach, despite the lack of conclusive evidence for such a claim, showed its firm opposing stance. Indeed in the press conference on October 23, Lu of China not only alleged the existence of a secret Sino-British deal, but also pronounced in his strongly-worded speech that the Chinese government would be ready in 1997 to unmesh the reforms it disapproved of. From this harsh warning, the people further learned of the degree of ferocity of the Chinese government about Chris Patten's reform proposals. This would certainly add strength to the undercurrent of worry about a possible disruption of smooth transition.

In terms of opinion polls, there was a slight increase (6.1%) in the disapproval rating for the proposals as well as a decrease (8.2%) in the undecided proportion (see appendix). While the increase in the disapproval rating might indicate increasing doubts about Patten's integrity or increasing alertness to China's opposition, the proposals were still able to garner more support than opposition. The image of the 'general public' was one of majority support for the reform proposals on the one hand, and one of relative calm, despite a sense of unease, regarding China's threats and entrenched opposition on the other. The following passage, while itself bespeaking an awareness of the potential problem of widespread worry, highlighted the absence of any notable signs of sustained panic:

> (That) the stock market reacted only most temporarily and no sustained panic was discernible ... The usual campaign of attack in the press and public forums through the usual well-known Beijing supporters plus some new blood was mounted again. But this time it has left the community cold. (Ng, *SCM Post*, 3 November 1992)

The Chinese government appeared to be a ferocious villain who could respond only with threats. It might have wanted to see the intended effect of its threats, yet to the contrary, it had instead, as it was understood, alienated itself further from the people:

The threats uttered so passionately (by Mr Lu Ping) against not British interest but Hong Kong's well-being, amounting to vengeance for disobedience, deeply alienated the community. (Ibid.)

In view of Mr Lu Ping's strongly-worded speech, the Hong Kong people lost much greater confidence in the Chinese government's policy over Hong Kong than Mr Patten's governership. (*Ming Daily*, 26 October 1992)

Still, although it had become a 'public' fact that the Hong Kong people in general aspired to more democracy, they had not been all portrayed as fearless heroes for the democratic cause. Rather, they were understood to be also concerned about the question of stability and prosperity, and hence the desire to avoid having confrontation with China. Indeed in the context of China's active opposition, the force of realism was making itself felt in public discourse, finding an anchorage point in the idea of conditional support for the romantic project. Drawing on the findings from an opinion poll, *Ming Daily* concluded as follows:

The majority of the Hong Kong people are in favour of Mr Patten's political reform proposals and the Hong Kong government's airport policy; but most of them think Hong Kong-China confrontations must be avoided and insist the two sides should continue to seek to iron out differences through discussions. (25 October 1992)

Thus conceived, the force of the 'public' became one of having to strike a delicate balance between people's conflicting desires for democracy and stability/ smooth transition:

Most people in Hong Kong would be willing to accept a slightly curtailed version for peace with Beijing. The balance will be extremely delicate, in that if Mr Patten accepts anything like a token concession, he will cease to command the support he still can count on at the moment. (Ng, *SCM Post*, 3 November 1992)

Caught between the conflicting demands, the Governor would be expected to make some concession with China without, however, turning it into a surrender. Nevertheless, so long as the implications of confrontation did not seem to be disastrous, he would still have every reason to stand firm.

China's Threats and Narrative Polarization of Political Conflicts

In public discourse, China's challenges and threats provided a niche for the consolidation of the countervailing forces of ironic realism, which had its roots in a culture of *pragmatism* and *mild anti-colonialism*. More and more people, realists and cynics alike, put into spotlight the critical relevance of the three questions concerning Patten's motivations, the charge of a breach of agreement and the prospects for smooth transition. The scenario as it developed was that, to the extent that Patten was not able to assure the public of the purity in his motivation and the sustainability of the project, he as a heroic character underwent a process of *de-heroization* and the narrative itself of *de-romanticization*. These processes allowed for and were themselves founded upon the simultaneous construction of alternative narratives by the realist conservatives and the cynical critics. At the same time, nevertheless, to the extent that Patten was not found polluted and China showed itself instead to be the angry and damaging villain, some romantic democrats demonstrated their support for the reform proposals with even greater perseverance, though they were themselves having a hard time struggling with the 'pro-British' label which carried a colonialist tinge. In such times of cultural and social tensions, where the people were trapped in a situation of divergent and intensely conflicting yet intersecting narrative accounts/ actions, the force of narrative progression was altering the meaning of the situation and putting new demands on the political actors in a most complex and delicate way.

Within the Legislative Council, the positions between the conservatives, represented by the Co-operative Resource Centre, and the few pro-democracy groups and individuals became polarized in the process of voting. Their conflicts were dramatized through the political act of voting; yet the deep symbolic differences between them were represented through narrative constructions. The pro-democracy legislators supported the proposals; they stressed the importance of 'autonomy', making themselves the hero in a new romantic narrative. On the contrary, the conservative group as well as a few other legislators voted against the proposals as they were concerned that it would not be in Hong Kong's interest to adopt a package of reforms that had no hope of surviving 1997. Here, while they were not putting themselves in any heroic posture, they were in a way mocking the heroic posture by the democrats by making their romantic narrative look rather impractical and imprudent. As the shapes of the two different narratives became more and more distinct, there developed less and less space for a middle position. The enlarging differences between the two sides were further polarized through China's strategy of threats and retaliation in the second stage.

In the face of China's threat of retaliation, there was great anguish among the people, who were left to wonder what had happened to all those oft-repeated pledges to preserve prosperity and stability. While many, especially democrats, were indignant to find China's retaliations 'drastic beyond all bounds of reason or necessity', the public also found fault with Patten's style of politicking and his way of handling the problem, which could be summarized in one word – arrogance. (In fact, this attitude of arrogance had been noted with caution in the first stage as a two-edge sword – being both the correlate of romantic courage and a likely cause for trouble.) As far as narrative construction was concerned, the former position lent itself to a deepened sense of China being the all-out villain in a romantic struggle whereas the latter, as an expression of ironic realism based on a distrust of colonialism, raised doubts as to whether Patten was acting in the interests of the Hong Kong people.

Of Hope Crumbling to Fear – Facilitating a Shift to Comic Action through Ironic Realization

As we have seen in chapter nine, in numerous accounts, the Hong Kong people were likened to helpless pawns in other people's power games. In the context of fear, helplessness and uncertainty, the discourse on 'public opinion' showed a primary concern with the decreasing support for the Governor's proposals. In a situation of hopes turned sour and heat turned cool, the public would need much more reassurance from the Governor than his same old words could offer. However, it seemed to the people that he was unable to drum up the much needed public confidence:

> So far, the Governor has stood by his line that ... The trouble is that this has turned into something of a monologue, and is beginning to sound dangerously like inertia. (*SCM Post*, 22 November 1992)

> ... but unless he can refresh the debate with a new more forceful message, he may find that whatever upturn in support he enjoys today could be eroded by the fickleness of public opinion tomorrow. (*SCM Post*, 14 December 1992)

Accordingly, in terms of narrative construction, even the democrats portrayed him in a different light – not so much as an invincible hero as a 'superstar' dangerously standing on its own without building up solid comradeship with the Hong Kong people. At the very beginning of his governorship, M. Ng wrote in her *SCM Post* column, there was a strong sense of hope, confidence and power in the public about the way the Governor would lead them through, 'If the heavens had chosen to fall in, people felt his broad shoulders would prop them up' (29 December 1992). In general, the public were at that time very much carried away by his charisma – his brilliance, courage and elegance – which outshone all his predecessors, the local politicians, and the Chinese officials. This amounted to a kind of personal worship. In such a context, he could 'fire half of his Exco and withdraw it from the public view with immunity' (ibid.). In retrospect, however, it was realized that this was a dangerous way to proceed: 'It was unsafe to depend on the goodwill of the public to one man, even if he was a superstar'. His honeymoon ended when China insisted that he was the prime trouble-maker:

> Then Government House showed itself to be the lonely place it had always been ... Only then did Mr. Patten learn of the fear and insecurity in his rank and file. As the silence deepened among his senior officials and Executive Coucillors, public confidence crumpled ... British administration will never succeed in Hong Kong unless it has the co-operation of the community. And co-operation does not mean just support for what Britain proposes, or a superficial response to charisma, but co-operation in the true sense of partnership, involvement and mutual respect. (Ibid.)

It was in this situation of hopes turned sour among the general public that the conservatives and the pro-stability press forged a narrative of comic versus ironic action whereby they took up the role of mediator in their political actions. This included, most conspicuously, the preparation for a less democratic proposal for motion debate in the final legislative process as an alternative to that by the Governor.

Anger and Fear for Betrayal – Consolidating the 'Autonomy' Plot

However, to the democrats, in view of China's downgrading the status of the highest legislative body in the society, the problem harped back on the issue of 'autonomy'. As *SCM Post* understood it, since the Legislative Council members had twice come out in support of the broad principles of the package, if Patten withdrew them at this stage, it would 'sabotage the status of the legislature, at the very time when he had been exhorting councilors to take their responsibilities seriously and decide their position on his planned reforms' (2 December). Similarly, E. Lau believed that if the Chinese government succeeded in forcing Patten to withdraw or dilute his proposals, the morale of the colony would be dealt a devastating blow. Within the frame of 'autonomy', most of the Legislative Council members were not ready to back down.

Holding such a strong belief in the principle of autonomy, some of them thus expressed a cynical attitude of disbelief and ridicule about those 'well-meaning' people who were paving way for the backdown of the Governor. In their view, these people not only side-stepped the issue of what was right and what was wrong, but also failed to see the futility in their acts – no matter how good a compromise proposal might be, it was certain to be dismissed out of hand at present. On the one hand, since China wanted to show it had the upper hand, it was in no mood to countenance anything less than the complete withdrawal of the Governor's package: 'Even a set of amendments which effectively neutralizes all the elements that the Chinese Government does not like would be unacceptable if it contrived to give face to Mr Patten' (Ng, *SCM Post*, 22 December 1992). On the other hand, it was highly unlikely that the Governor would climb down, for a retreat from a position that had been publicly maintained and that had got the stamp of strong public support would mean to the public a disgraceful surrender. Thus only 'fools' would ask for it whereas intelligent people would uphold the position of strength:

> If Mr Patten is unlikely to climb down, what would be the point of sending a go-between? Only a fool would ask for negotiations when he is in the weakest position, with declining popular support, because it can only mean a surrender. If Mr Patten is ready to surrender, why do it through a go-between? (Ng, *SCM Post*, 24 December 1992)

The 'fools' here referred to the conservatives who sought to propose a reform package with fewer democratic elements than the Patten package as a way to secure China's blessings. (This will be discussed in greater detail in the next chapter on the discourse of stability.) With such a strong assertion of the dividing line between the morally right and the morally wrong, the democrats and the conservatives were being increasingly polarized into two opposing camps.

For one thing, while the democrats defined China as the villain and the conservatives as the fool, they did not see Patten as an unflawed hero. The situation, as we have discussed in chapter eight, had been somewhat complicated by the underlying culture of nationalism versus colonialism. In the general climate of mild distrust of British colonialism, the democrats were struggling with the 'pro-British' label. From the vantage point of autonomy, the challenge for them was one of disassociating themselves from the British side without forsaking the democratic cause. Among the democrats, while a few non-party-affiliated legislators wanted to break loose from the apparent grip of Britain by making their own more radical proposals, the leading pro-democracy parties saw themselves as cautious allies with the governor.

Stage III: Different Pathways to Ironic Turns in Public Discourse

Conceivably, the intent for a narrative of romantic heroism may fail, in varying degrees, to stand up to its challenges. The theory of narrative progression postulates that the complications of the middle will make the ending open to various other possibilities. In this case, the ending turned out to be paradoxical and hence ironic in that the initial quest was completed, but since too much irony had preceded and would follow, it lost much of the romantic color it once entailed and passed into the collective memories of the Hong Kong people as an ironic blessing.

In the previous stage, there had existed deep divisions between the conservatives who, holding onto a comic-realist frame, were anxious to see the restoration of Sino-British co-operation through their mediation, and the democrats who, sticking to the heroic-romantic frame, were firm in their support for the cause of democracy they believed in. Structurally, the beginning of stage three (February 1993) was marked with some significant development from both the romantic and the comic-realist perspectives. At one end, the democrats sought to see the furtherance and completion of the romantic-heroic action i.e. the legislation of the reform proposals as scheduled. (The legislative process was in the stage of the Executive Council's final scrutiny of the draft bills giving effect to the proposals before they were formally introduced to Legislative Council in mid February.) At the other end, a comic turn took shape within the comic-realist frame when sudden and continued news reports about secret diplomatic contacts between Britain and China, and softer rhetoric on both sides, fuelled the belief among the people that a breakthrough in the deadlock was imminent. In terms of plot development, the two parallel processes — the Government's schedule to gazette the proposals and pass them into law (the local legislative process), and the continual diplomatic meetings between the two sovereign powers — got tightly intertwined in that China demanded that the proposals be dropped altogether if Sino-British negotiations were to be resumed whereas the Governor insisted that Legislative Council would have the final say over the proposals. In such a situation, the Patten administration was believed to be facing a fundamental dilemma. The force of the 'public', in narrative terms, was that if Patten did not concede at all, he would be regarded by the conservatives as a villain who posed to be an obstacle to the restoration of Sino-British co-operation; if, on the contrary, Patten conceded, he would be making himself a mock hero in the eyes of the democrats .

At this juncture, Patten's public credibility would rest on its ability to show that he was both genuine about his reforms and willing to have negotiation with China. Patten sought to strike a balance by delaying the introduction of his proposals while assuring the Legislative Council members that they would not be asked merely to 'rubber stamp' any Sino-British agreement not acceptable to Hong Kong people, but could amend legislation put before it. Over time, however, the talks dragged on with little progress rounds after rounds, showing themselves to be nothing but a series of ironic proceedings. The newspapers in the 'comic-realist' category expressed their increasing frustration in their hope for a Sino-British agreement so much so that indifference was bred. To both the democrats and the cynical critics, the numerous fruitless rounds of talks indicated that Britain might be playing into Beijing's hands. In this phase, the ironic mood was getting thicker and thicker in public discourse. It was in this context that opposition against the furtherance of the legislative process was weakened while the more radical stream among the democrats made its first organized appearance overshadowing the 'heroic' posture of their counterparts.

Ironic Cracks with the Heroic Romance — A Tragic Configuration

Within the heroic-romantic structure, the government's delaying strategy provided an 'opportune' moment whereby a tragic turn was configured and a cynical counter-narrative became full-fledged, both of which served to undermine the initial narrative of heroic romance. Worried that the legislative delay might indicate a tendency to yield to China's pressure, some newspapers warned the government of dwindling credibility in showing stagnancy, indecisiveness and powerlessness as opposed to the romantic traits of progress, activeness and strength:

> Further delay can easily be construed as weakness and indecision, indicative of a Government anxiously seeking compromise. There is a fine line between withholding the bills indefinitely, and withdrawing the Patten package altogether. The longer the bills are put back to entice the Chinese to the negotiating table, the more it begins to look as though Chinese preconditions for the talks have been met (*SCM Post*, 25 February 1993)

> Although the Government declares that it will give a due explanation about the delay, that it has failed to keep the promise of meeting the deadline, which in the eyes of the democrats shows nothing but moral retreat and irresponsibility, has tremendously undermined its credibility and especially that of Governor Patten. (*Economic Journal*, 1 March 1993)

Ironic cracks emerged from within the romantic structure, which was a sign of growing public impatience with the government's inaction. In a few weeks' time, the introduction of the proposals had been delayed thrice; as it was delayed time and again, opposition to any further delay gathered momentum. In the first place, the continual delay had been marked unusual in news and commentaries – unprecedented or even 'history-making' (*Express Daily*, 12 March), making further delay a less and less justifiable act. Adding further pressure on the government in the same direction, secondly, there were news highlighting how even some of the Hong Kong and British government officials believed Britain's concessions to China had already dealt a blow to the government's governing credibility. In other words, the insiders' view was that it did not find the government's continual delay as defensible. In fact, from the romantic perspective, the delay aroused the suspicion of a 'sell-out' by Patten and therefore provoked anger from the democrat-legislators:

> It is true the people of Hong Kong want to see negotiations between Britain and China; at the same time, they also want more democracy. It is a fallacy to assume that because the people of Hong Kong want negotiations they therefore would accept a sell-out. (M. Lee, *SCM Post*, 7 March 1993)

With this imagery of 'sell-out,' the democrats made a testimony to their beliefs in democracy and autonomy by means of a voice of protest. Likewise among the newspapers, seeing that the Patten government was about to fail their expectation, some insisted on respecting the autonomy of the society in general, and that of Legislative Council in particular:

> Legco must have say; there is a growing impatience over the way the political reform issue is being handled. It appears as though Patten is playing directly into the hands of Beijing. Patten needs to stand firm in insisting it would be unthinkable for Hong Kong not to have a say in talks affecting its future. (*SCM Post*, 6 March 1993, 12 March 1993)

> Either Patten has lost all power to push through his own package, or he and the British Government have buckled under Chinese pressure. Seeing that Government House is about to fail the people of Hong Kong, hopes must now be pinned on Legco and the ordinary men and women of this community who care enough not to be afraid of standing up for their own rights and the rights of their children. (Ng, *SCM Post*, 9 March 1993)

Within the same overarching romantic frame, while warning the government of its dwindling credibility, *Economic Journal* nonetheless diverged from *SCM Post* and the persistent romanticists in that it began to configure *a turn of tragic foreboding* from the initial romance. Specifically its portrayal of Patten put him well into the role of a 'tragic hero' – one who had been great but then looked less and less so – evoking a pathetic image among the audience. In terms of characterization, *Economic Journal* described Patten as wearing a tired look, which was a far cry from the extremely self-confident posture impressed on the public in his early governorship. It was through the temporal contrast in mimetic description that a sense of pathos was created about the fall of a once great and still respectable hero. Indeed among the newspapers, *Economic Journal* was the most sympathetic with the Governor, and in terms of plot development, it went so far as to suggest that Patten was himself a victim in Sino-British politics:

> In the hands of the government, the carefully worked-out grandeur of the reform proposals is going to pale off into a dismal existence ... Conceivably, the British side are just using the Patten package as a bargaining chip in the negotiation with China; they are prepared to sacrifice Patten. (9 December 1993)

The idea of a tragic turn had its roots, firstly, in an attitude of distrust about the two sovereign governments. From the perspective of romantic development, the paper had little faith in the Sino-British talks, because Britain would be a self-interested Machiavellian who was going to use the Patten package as a bargaining chip for more economic interests for Britain itself, whereas China had always shown itself to be unreasonable and authoritarian.[7] While the tragic turn was forced into being by the two villainous powers, it was facilitated, secondly, by the people's loss of romantic courage. According to the paper, the people's romantic sentiments, which had once been very strong, were being eroded in the face of China's threats and were now, rather ironically, replaced with the spirit of pragmatism:

> The Hong Kong people (particularly the businessmen) now have the sole aim of making more money. Their 'pale' souls show nothing but the lack of moral judiciousness ... When Patten becomes an obstacle to their money-making activities, they will turn against him with no regard to any moral considerations ... This is Patten's misfortune; this is the tragedy of the human species. (2 March 1993)

The paper's lament over the loss of romantic support for Patten or the democratic cause strengthened the sense of tragic foreboding about Patten's defeat. Remarkably, it was with this profoundly tragic re-configuration of the events that the old romantic notes never quite came back in this paper.

The prevailing sense of irony was in no way uplifted by the government's decision to gazette the bills. The reality was that since the resumption of Sino-British talks was close to an impossibility, the deteriorating relationships between the two sovereign powers would only cast a dooming shadow over the future of the society. The tragic-ironic aspect about the gazetting of the bills was that no matter how good the reform would be, the cherished 'through train' would be derailed by China. As such, *Economic Journal* had ended the story about the initial romance with its lament about a lost cause. Beyond the tragedy, a dark irony lay in that in the context of China's totalitarian governing tradition, democracy would have a very dim prospect in the society. Torn between nationalistic feelings and the cherished belief in democracy and justice, the paper expressed a sense of deep agony:

> Our present agony is not simply about the issue of political reform. Like all those who have not forgotten justice and who worship liberty, we experience an indescribable agony about having to support the political reform by a colonialist at this time. From the perspective of nationalistic

sentiments, there should be no good reason that we do not feel overjoyed about the freedom from colonialism ... Moreover, Patten is after all just a British colonial governor who must have no heart for and no sense of belonging to the society, and we cannot tell whether he has covered up any ulterior motives. Nonetheless, since the Communist Chinese government has displayed nothing but totalitarianism, our only rational choice is to support Patten's political reform. (*Economic Journal*, 5 April 1993)

The mood was indeed very painfully depressing. The ironic turn figured prominently in this account, with its tragic twist pointing to a dark, satirical picture of the post-1997 scenario.

The tragic account, together with a satirical projection of the future, became complete in itself, leaving little space for any retrospective modifications thereafter. Noticeably, it was with this sense of completion of one story that the paper began to develop another one in its shift to a new, more pragmatic concern with smooth transition over other matters, especially those relating to the economy. The narrative structure became one of comic-ironic, with a diction showing less passion but more cold analysis:

It will not be in China's interest to see instability or a jeopardized economy in Hong Kong. Looking from this angle, after some cool-headed calculations, China must be careful with the economic part in the second stove ... If both sides do not bicker over the economy, despite political non-convergence, it is not necessarily a bad thing to have two stoves. (*Economic Journal*, 18 March 1993)

From the perspective of comedy, the situation was far less dismal than it had been from a tragic perspective. However, very ironically, the present situation depicted by *Economic Journal* was still one of absurdity. Regarding the people's political orientations, the trend had become one of flattering the future sovereign power, which many believed to be a rational thing to do. In this connection, the Preparatory Committee formed by China for the making of the second stove was a lousy and showy existence. China's intent, as the paper conceived it, was not so much to solicit advice from the Committee as to map out its local power basis. As such, the people selected into it were happy about being just the yes-sayers among themselves while the Hong Kong people got increasingly confused about what these people were doing. In brief, the picture painted by the paper was one of showing a carnival in the midst of a confused and non-participating crowd. This was *an ironic parody of comedy*, conveying a strong sense of dissonance and absurdity. For one thing, it was in no sense that the tragedy was contained within a larger comic-ironic scheme. Rather, the paper was writing its editorials on two parallel but separate tracks – democracy and economy – within two different narrative structures. Although the latter began to be foregrounded against the former, the sombre, tragic mood from the background nonetheless lingered on and would override any sense of passionate joy that might arise from within a comedy. The *double irony* was that while the development of one had been a tragic irony, that of the other was tilting towards the ironic pole on a comic-ironic axis.

An Ironic Twist in A Comic-Realist Discourse

Having experienced some comic-ironic frustrations with the secret diplomatic talks between Britain and China, *Express Daily* began to show decreasing faith in the two governments in their efforts to restore co-operation. In terms of characterization, as we have seen, Patten as a mimetic character was further de-heroized, and Patten as a functional character was seen as contributing more and more to a comic-ironic state of disorder and deterioration. At the same time, China was re-interpreted as a fool with a villainous appearance whereas the pro-China 'toadies' were found to be the real villain from the Chinese side:

> There were bits and pieces of evidence that Patten was playing little tricks. China's way of handling the problem had been very poor – its outrageous reactions at the beginning and the threats of 'making an earlier takeover' made by those power-hungry opportunists had had a lot of negative effect on China's image and thereby alienated the Hong Kong people ... Conspicuously, the pro-China forces had been advising China to act against the wishes of the people. (*Express Daily*, 15 March 1993)

While China appeared to be the villain who had been uncompromising and inflexible, it was actually a stupid and inadequate fool who had been ill-advised by the behind-the-scene toading opportunists. It was the latter group who had advised China to go against public opinion in order that the situation would be favorable for them to gain more advantages. (With the construction of these people as the real villains, the image of China might look a little less wicked than it was supposed to be.) With this understanding of the major actors as being either villains or fools, the Hong Kong people were depicted as feeling fed up and less confident about the promise of stability and prosperity by the two sovereign powers. The mood was clearly one of pessimism.

As it developed, the talks had shown themselves to be a series of ironic proceedings. Rounds after rounds, the talks dragged on with little progress. By mid June, two months since their resumption, the talks were noted as 'making little headway' – so little so that 'a complete standstill seems likely'. (*SCM Post*, 18 June 1993). In particular, it was understood that China showed no incentive whatsoever to push the talks along. Regarding the difficult issue of through train, it toughened its position over which legislators could serve beyond 1997 by reaffirming that the SAR Preparatory Committee must have power to vet them. To the romantic critics, the numerous fruitless rounds of talks indicated that Britain might be playing into Beijing's hands. For the 'comic projection' groups, they experienced increasing frustration in their comic projection or hope for a Sino-British agreement. In this phase, the ironic mood, be it comic-ironic or romantic-ironic, was getting thicker and thicker in the society.

For those who were concerned about the question of resolving the Sino-British row, most of them were not very optimistic about the talk. *Express Daily*, having experienced a time of great frustrations with talk failure in the last phase, showed a desperate hope for a comic development. On the one hand, it expressed its wish to see the resumption of Sino-British co-operation; on the other hand, the reality of an ironic situation became more and more the dominant theme in its narrative. On the first two days after the news of talk resumption was broken, *Express Daily* expressed its comic hope with an ironic undertone of worry:

> Let the Patten package and China's second stove be put aside ... Regarding the 'through train' issue, China should give due consideration on it ... Those who make noises against their co-operation are rash and imprudent trouble-makers. (14 April 1993)

> The resumption of talks is unexpected but mostly desired ... Whether Britain or China wins should not be the issue; our greatest worry is that the Hong Kong people will lose the most. The pre-condition should be one of mutual trust, despite the ground for distrust. (15 April 1993)

Express Daily suggested both sides put aside their own proposals and resume talks on the basis of mutual trust. Within this 'comic projection' frame, those who sought to work against their co-operation were characterized as 'rash and imprudent trouble-makers' making obstacles to a comic development. Yet at the same time, the paper was aware of another, more important obstacle, which was the distrustful relationship between Britain and China. In its next editorial, a gloomy picture of a worrying situation was painted:

> Despite their consensus for prosperity and stability, Britain and China, because of their interests, had put the Hong Kong people into a state of anxiety - like ants on a hot pan. Unconcerned about the people's feelings, they did nothing reassuring until they had explored each other's bottom line. They resumed talks in the name of the Hong Kong people's interests, but their deep mutual distrust as well as their disregard for the Hong Kong people was shown through their mutual accusations and China's news-blackout policy. (16 April 1993)

Following its earlier line of characterization, it explained how the mimetic traits in the characters – Patten, China and those self-seeking opportunists – led to the current situation of absurdity. Both China and Britain were self-interested so much so that the Hong Kong people were thrown into a state of anxiety. In its characterization, Patten was an arrogant and unconcerned trouble-maker rather than a true romantic hero; the local self-seeking opportunists were the behind-the-scene villains who were adding oil on the fire regardless of the harm done on others; and China was too distrustful of Britain to resist any conspiratorial thinking:

> Patten is like a rash bull, destroying the 'harmonious' relations between China and Britain, which shows nothing but the unconscious pride of a colonizer. He is simply working on a self-complacent show before Britain retreating from the colony. Real democrats would not give applause to his proposals. (Ibid.)

> China's confidence in Hong Kong people drops – the fear for British conspiracy increases, plus, those who are close to China, for the sake of becoming the future political elites, further mislead China into believing such a conspiracy, by fanning the flame of nationalism and the flame of anti-colonialist sentiments. (For example, they spread the rumour that Britain was going to empty the Budgetary.) (Ibid.)

In short, the paper's experience with the negotiation was that the kind of hope once generated was one quickly dispelled as a false one.

As time went on, various papers of this position expressed their impatience about the slow progress of the talks. *Express Daily* warned of the limit of the Hong Kong people's patience and pleaded for more substantial progress.[8] Even the most optimistic paper, *Ming Daily*, queried the sincerity of both Britain and China: 'We cannot possibly find out what is in the minds of the Chinese or the British, but we know that few Hong Kongers relish seeing them play little or big tricks' (14 July 1993). Further to their disappointment, the two sides, instead of heading for an agreement, had been devising their own contingency plans in case of talk failure:

> The gulf is still wide enough between the two sides that each is preparing for contingencies should no agreement be reached. (*SCM Post*, 30 August 1993)

On the part of Britain, in July, Patten warned that if no agreement could be reached, he might still be prepared to go ahead unilaterally on further democracy for the territory. In his early October policy address, Patten hinted at a deadline for the end of the talks, which was 'weeks, rather than months, away'. On the part of China, it claimed that it was taking steps to minimize political and economic instability in the society if talks failed. In this connection, it was speeding up of the work of the Preparatory Working Committee. It was true that a small surprise turn of event took place in mid October when Patten, upon the suggestion of Liberal Party (which had played the role of mediator in sending a delegation to Beijing in mid October), appeared ready to split talks on the 1994/95 elections.[9] However, the surprise turn turned out to be another 'false dawn' – the bitter truth for the public to swallow was that the two sides could not reach an agreement even on what were considered the less contentious issues concerning the voting method:[10]

> It is less than three weeks since a new optimism enveloped the talks between China and Britain on Hong Kong's political system. Less than three weeks since Britain thought it had picked up Chinese hints that it might agree on the 'simple' elements of reform. Less than three weeks since Britain decided to speed up the talks by picking up China's suggestion of splitting discussion of the 1994 and 1995 electoral arrangements ... Now, two almost fruitless rounds of talks later, that dawn at the end of the long black night of dogged confrontation looks to have been false. (*SCM Post*, 29 November 1993)

By October, *Express Daily* was the first among this group to give up hope on the talks. In its several retrospective accounts published in October and November, the paper spoke of the experience of a *double irony* of hopes turned into despairs – first from a romantic response (to the

Governor's reform proposals) to an ironic realization of the impossibility of democracy, and then from a comic projection of Sino-British co-operation to a comic-ironic despair. Upon their release a year ago, Patten's proposals did put the Hong Kong people into a state of romantic fantasy about democracy, but then the romantic construction about Patten was quickly eroded in the process through a number of ironic encounters. The first of such encounters was with the force of realism – China's fierce opposition, which resulted in a decrease in public support for the Patten package:

> The Hong Kong people's crave for more democracy originates from a lack of trust in the 'one country two systems' policy, which explains why the people supported Patten's proposals last year ... However, after one year, the reality to the people is that (i) the British have their own interests to take care of, and (ii) China is worried that democratization in Hong Kong may spill over into China ... So, the people give up the dream about democracy and opt for the second best: the maintenance of the status quo, while hoping for changes in China by 1997. (7 December 1993)

In other words, the comic hope was a hope for 'the second best' – the maintenance of the existing order of stability and prosperity – which was generated from an ironic realization. The second set of ironic encounter was in the form of a satire – the discovery that Patten was an untrustworthy 'romantic hero' who was prepared to concede and abandon his democratic allies. In this later reconstruction, the democrats were portrayed as the unthoughtful and wavering fools who had misplaced their trust in Patten:

> Patten's grand proposals last year was just a strategy for compromise ... The democrats should not have supported the proposals, which was far behind their own model. Ironically, their support for the proposals not only gave China an excuse for repression/ intervention, but also gave the public the impression that their action for more democracy was nothing more than a strategy rather than an unwavering adherence to moral principles. (*Express Daily*, 11 October 1993)

The Hong Kong people actually wanted both more democracy, and stability and prosperity, but the ironies were that they could not have both due to China's fierce opposition to democracy, and they could not rely on Patten for democracy because he was unreliable. It was through these ironies that they turned to configure a probably more realizable comic hope of Sino-British co-operation as a means of safeguarding stability and prosperity:

> If we cannot have both democracy and 'stability and prosperity', at least should keep the latter, given that the present way of getting democracy through Patten is an untrustworthy pursuit because he is being dishonest and insincere ... We prefer a realistic consideration of gradual democratization to a way of fighting for democracy which would play into the hands of untrustworthy politician. (Ibid.)

In essence, the narrative development in the paper was not simply a clear-cut movement away from romance/irony to comic projection; rather, the comic projection itself contained an irony – the irony that it was itself a compromised second best to the initial romance. It was with this reconstruction that a somewhat romantic-ironic element was retained even in this late stage forming a small incoherent part of the narration within a comic-ironic frame:

> The circumstances are too irresistible for the Legco members to stand firm; so, how could the reform proposals be passed without modification? ... In other words, whether the talks succeed with an agreement or they fail, political development in Hong Kong will fall within China's orbit ... The democrats and Patten are in the same pitiful state, looking pensively helpless. (*Ming Daily*, 6 November 1993)

Instead of its previously sarcastic tone, the paper showed an attitude of *sympathy* towards the democratic fighters as well as Patten. In the same editorial, the paper also lamented that it was unfortunate that the people had to choose between democracy only and prosperity and stability only. (This would have seemed odd and rather incomprehensible if the narration had been a comic projection right from the very beginning.) The sense of structural and emotional incoherence bespoke the underlying irony.

The next ironic development was a 'downward' movement from the comic hope to yet another despair. After rounds of fruitless talks, the paper realized that the two sides, especially China, had not tried their best to arrive at a resolution:

> If both sides had been sincere about the talks, it should not have been too difficult for them to iron out their differences. However, the fact is they are not having a real two-way dialogue but are just talking past each other, being too much preoccupied with the question of strategic defence and attack. In particular, China, from the very beginning, has been making an all-out effort to be the sole winner, with no intention of conceding or compromising. (*Ming Daily*, 1 October 1993)

Moreover, with their respective contingency plans already mapped out in case of talk failure, they would be making a self-fulfilling prophecy. The sense of despair about the two sides was conveyed more and more explicitly. For example, on 4 October, the paper published an editorial titled 'Both China and Britain are indebted to the Hong Kong people for their expectation':

> Both China and Britain are talking about their self-interests rather than the interests of the Hong Kong people. It must not be beyond our imagination to realize how disappointed the people must be, because for the past six months, the people have paid the price of 'anxious patience' for nothing rewarding in return. (*Ming Daily*, 4 October 1993)

By late November, the paper believed that the Hong Kong people must be seeing clearly that 'both sides are just playing political games, wasting time over trivial matters' (26 November 1993). Regarding the virtual collapse of the Seventeenth round of the talks, the paper called it 'a ridiculous outcome'. (1 December 1993) Thus in a bitter tone, *Express Daily* suggested the two sides stop the talks, because (a) a break-up at that moment would not make a severe blow to Hong Kong and (b) the people were getting tired of this kind of non-constructive political game. With despair verging on indifference, the paper began to adjust to an easy-going attitude of 'come what may, no big deal'. The tone of repugnance was easing off to one of resignation:

> Even if the talks fail, and Britain and China will be making their own arrangements respectively before and after 1997, so long as there is not going to be any harm on the economy and our livelihood, it should not be a big problem. In any case, whichever arrangement they are going to make, it will not have any necessary relationship with Hong Kong's democratic development. (3 December 1993)

The response was ironic in mood, but it was put in a comic form with an attitude of ease. With the heavy sense of ironic despair somewhat made light of, the paper was able to find a little comfort in what it considered to be 'a fortunate encounter amidst misfortunes' – in deciding to solve the transitional problems on its own, China seemed to be inclining to a more pragmatic, problem-solving approach.[11]

Cynicism on the Rise – The Romance on the Brink of Collapse

The force of the 'public' as generated from the romantic structure was still at work. With a romantic beginning, a Sino-British agreement entailing unwarranted concessions by Britain would mean a public disgrace:

> If we can find no or very little trace of the Patten package in the outcome of the Sino-British talk, it means that Britain comforms to China's explanation of 'three accords' for the sake of national interests, even at the expense of Patten. (*Economic Journal*, 24 April 1993)

Likewise if Patten allowed himself to go with the pragmatic wind, he was certainly dwindling his 'heroic' image himself. The positions among the democrats ranged from one of believing that the romantic forces would override the ironic ones to that of believing the reverse, with the latter gaining wider currency. Among the latter group, moreover, positions differed as to whether the situation was regarded as a tragic turn from romance (tragic irony) or an ironic reversal of romance (satirical irony).

One of the widely believed ironic forces was that China was resorting to the old tactic of using the talks to fight against Britain. This might put Britain at its mercy:

> The numerous rounds of 'talks' were little more than China restating its predetermined position, until time and hopelessness drove the British to give way ... (Ng, *SCM Post*, 20 April 1993)

> Is Britain playing directly into the hands of Beijing? Is China just using the talks as a stalling tactic to keep Patten's reform bill from being tabled in Legco? (*SCM Post*, 1 June 1993)

Political critic Ng was one of the few who believed that given the weight of the heroic-romantic development, it was unlikely that Patten would concede as his predecessors did:

> (But) for the first time a breakdown of the talks is a real possibility – If one bears in mind that the British were playing to a world audience all agog; they could afford neither utter secrecy nor be seen to weaken in their championing of democracy. If they accept a paltry settlement, the world will jeer and British honour will suffer. It will be a humiliation made all the more public by the increasing interest in Hong Kong generated by Patten's high profile. (*SCM Post*, 20 April 1993)

Nonetheless, since she also realized that the cost in confidence would be tremendous when a breakdown happened, she suggested a number of things be done in order to minimize that cost. In other words, she was urging the public to get prepared for a successful but less than triumphant battle. As such, a weighty sense of caution was conveyed, which would overshadow any sense of romantic celebration that might arise in the end even in the case of victory. Another, more ironic aspect was related to the prospects for 'through train'. Ng seemed to come to the sudden realization that 'it will avail Hong Kong little to gain the whole Patten package if it loses the through train' (*SCM Post*, 25 May 1993). This marked an unmistakably clear change in her attitude from romantic optimism to a romantic-ironic worry:

> What (the public) fear is the totalitarianism which has always underpinned it, the intolerance of criticism and dissent, the ruthless pursuit of power and control over the lives of the people, the mystique which is the Party ... the vengeance of an intolerant officialdom. The phrase that symbolizes it came from the Tiananmen Square tragedy: 'settling the accounts after autumn'.... But to the general public, the main significance of the through train is that it would show China is prepared to be tolerant and allow HK people to continue their lives without interference. (Ibid.)

Ng expressed the fear that the dark forces of totalitarian intolerance and vengeance would make a satirical reversal of or triumph over what the democrats had been struggling for. With so much irony going with it, the Patten package had looked less and less a sustainable project even from the perspective of romance.

Finally, there was an ironic realization among the critics that Patten was conceding, either because he was weak vis-à-vis China (a tragic or a mock hero), or because he had been insincere about the reform right from the beginning (a villain in the guise of hero). The prevailing view was that Britain was backing down under China's pressure:

> There is a growing expectation within local political circles that Britain must eventually bow to pressure from China. (Ho, *SCM Post*, 30 April 1993)

> (T)here is little hope that Patten's plan for limited democracy will survive. China's negotiators are determined to string the process out through boredom, irritation and a conviction that they hold the highest cards ... Beijing dribbles a bit to its favourite reporters in Hong Kong's Chinese-

language press, which hints that the British are slowly giving in. (Mirsky, *SCM Post*, 4 June 1993)

News headline read 'Patten reforms wither on vine of Beijing talks' (*SCM Post*, 4 June 1993). In such an account, the heroic image of Patten shrank to one of relative powerlessness. This was contrasted with China's unyielding position in its intent to 'humiliate' Patten (Lau, *SCM Post*, 1 November 1993). In a more satirical way, the democrat-cynics suspected that Patten's democracy package was a 'sham' or a 'smokescreen' – nothing but a bargaining chip in exchange for something less or something else. This cynical parody of romance (farce) gained wider currency in October after it was made known to the public that Britain had proposed a much watered-down version at the nineth round of talks. In such accounts, Patten was found polluted – a self-interested and deceiving politician who, representing Britain's interests, had betrayed the trust of the local democrats:

> Now, with the partial disclosure of the secret talks, the people will be more interested in knowing Britain's political motivation ... Patten's package is a smokescreen, a bargaining chip in exchange for Britain's long-term interests in Hong Kong. In view of Britain's recent insistence on 'convergence' or 'through train', the narrative of the extension of British colonialism beyond 1997 has more credibility today. (Bug, *Economic Journal*, 14 July 1993)

> Even though the Patten package has been 'shrunk' in exchange for an agreement ... On the surface, Britain is retreating from its principles, but in reality, there is no difference between retreating and not retreating. As everybody knows it, unless a reform proposal is put into practice, it will remain an illusory construction or a fleeting existence, just like the firework displayed at night. The fact, however, is that in this political row, the Hong Kong people's interests have been used as the gambling chip. It is for everyone to see that Britain is the winner and the Hong Kong people the loser. (Bug, *Economic Journal*, 17 October 1993)

> Despite the reduction of Patten's proposals into something less, Britain is winning - it's democracy' which is losing ... The consensus, after one year's politics, is that Britain is targeting for something else ... (On, *Economic Journal*, 10 October 1993)

> With China playing the upper hand and Patten having nothing to explain to the public, the people will be disillusioned from the myth of Patten bringing more democracy to Hong Kong ... Patten's proposals could only deceive those politically unwise ... The greatest price paid for Patten's proposals is

234 Narratives, Politics, and the Public Sphere

> the democrats, who are used to getting along with situations rather than taking the initiative. (Wong, *Economic Journal*, 1 October 1993)

> Patten's proposals is nothing but a bargaining chip ... Patten is backing down and abandoning the Hong Kong people ... I have always believed that Britain is thinking about its own economic and political interests rather than fighting for more democracy in Hong Kong. But people attracted to its culture cannot see it through. (Wong, *Economic Journal*, 9 October 1993)

The above quotations showed in common the view that since Britain had been aiming at something else, probably its long-term interests in Hong Kong, Patten was not really sincere about the reform but had been secretly planning for a 'sure win' with his reform proposals serving as a bargaining chip. In most of the passages quoted above, there showed a strong ironic projection that many of those who had earnestly supported the Patten package, especially the democrats, were about to find themselves fooled or betrayed. Indeed from the perspective of 'autonomy,' it seemed to many that the democrats were just making themselves the passive and unquestioning supporters of Patten, rather than the active, independent and far-sighted political leaders of the public. In short, they had been led by the nose by Patten. Indeed from the perspective of 'autonomy,' the greatest irony lay in the truth that with all the enthusiasm shown about the Patten package upon its release, the package in turn 'pre-empted an agenda for Hong Kong's self-rule' (On, *Economic Journal*, 8 June 1993).

Pragmatic Shifts of Concern among the Comic-Realist Category

Regarding the deterioration in Sino-British relations, the newspapers in the comic-realist category had experienced a great deal of frustrations so much so that they began to give up hope on the diplomatic negotiations. In a bitter tone, *Express Daily*, for example, suggested the two sides stop the talks, because (a) a break-up at that moment would not make a severe blow to Hong Kong and (b) the people were getting tired of this kind of non-constructive political game. With despair verging on indifference, the paper began to adjust to an easy-going attitude of 'come what may, no big deal'. The tone of repugnance was easing off to one of resignation:

> Even if the talks fail, and Britain and China will be making their own arrangements respectively before and after 1997, so long as there is not going to be any harm on the economy and our livelihood, it should not be a

big problem. In any case, whichever arrangement they are going to make, it will not have any necessary relationship with Hong Kong's democratic development. (3 December 1993)

The response was ironic in mood, but it was put in a comic form with an attitude of ease. With the heavy sense of ironic despair somewhat made light of, the paper was able to find a little comfort in what it considered to be 'a fortunate encounter amidst misfortunes' – in deciding to solve the transitional problems on its own, China seemed to be inclining to a more pragmatic, problem-solving approach. In the meantime, a number of papers in this category shifted their focus to the work of the Preparatory Working Committee formed by China. This shift in focus reflected an underlying continuation with the main narrative line around the theme of smooth transition. With this shift, disappointed though they were about the outcome of the talks, they were able to put behind the talks and, as we will see later, dwell on the future with the same kind of comic-realist or pragmatic outlook.

It was with their loss of faith in the talks that these realists were able to accept with ease the idea of tabling the reform bills to the Legislative Council. As a result, opposition against the furtherance of the legislative process was being toned down. With the weakening of such opposing forces, the initial heroic-romance did not look as 'great' as it once appeared, taking away the sense of courageous quest that went with it at the beginning.

In a much less bitter tone, the other papers in this group shared *Express Daily*'s further watered-down hope that both China and Britain would still co-operate on other issues despite talk failure, or, in their words, separate the economic issues from politics. Specifically, quite a number of papers shifted their focus to the work of the Preparatory Working Committee formed by China[12]:

In case of talk failure, Hong Kong people would like to see a good seconc stove set up for the sake of smooth transition. (*Economic Journal*, 13 July 1993)

Wherever possible, the two sides should make sure politics will not affect the economy. (*Ming Daily*, 1 December 1993)

Now that the prospects for talk success look dim, it is not for us to play the 'blame' game. As a constructive thing to do, Hong Kong people should help PWC in its work, making sure that Hong Kong people's interests are being well looked after in the process of establishing the second stove. If Patten is really for the well-being of Hong Kong rather than just Britain's glorious withdrawal, he must help in the work of PWC. (*Ming Daily*, 13 December 1993)

Notes

1. According to the media, it might be more a sign of international confidence in the economy: 'While it is tempting to think that the money pouring into Hong Kong suggests outside investors approve of Mr. Patten's tough no-nonsense style, it seems clear that regardless of the bickering, there is a lot of international confidence in Hong Kong's role in the economic success story taking place in the Pearl River Delta' (*SCM Post* 23 October 1992).
2. A source quoted in *SCM Post* said, 'If Mr Patten does not care about converging the political development with the Basic Law, why should China care about changing all those legislators who are not returned in conformity with the provisions of the Basic Law?' In retrospect, this statement, being tantamount to saying that there would be no through train, was actually a prelude to the sub-plot of China setting up a second stove that would emerge in the next stage of the drama. However, at that time, it was not foregrounded in the press and the people did not see it as particularly threatening.
3. See Wong's article in *SCM Post*, 21 November 1992. In fact, this understanding was not without support. For instance, Zhou, the Hong Kong director of New China News Agency, had told the Hong Kong delegates of the National People's Congress and the Chinese People's Political Consultative Conference that Mr. Patten was attempting to turn the territory into an 'independent or semi-independent state'.
4. 28 February 1993.
5. British and Hong Kong government statements accompanying the letters said Britain had made clear repeatedly its dissatisfaction at the Chinese proposals for the number of directly elected seats in the Legislative Council, and '(a)t the end of these exchanges, the question of electoral arrangements in Hong Kong up to 1997 remained open ... The final version of the Basic Law was not satisfactory on this point because it did not spell out, as we had asked, the five principles agreed between the two sides as a framework for an Election Committee system'.
6. See *SCM Post*, 22 November 1992.
7. *Economic Journal*, 6 March 1993.
8. See *Express Daily*, 21 May 1993.
9. Patten wanted to press China to endorse the 'simple things' – voting age, voting method and the district board and municipal council elections - so that negotiations could proceed to more important issues.
10. The Chinese government insisted on separating talks of the Legislative

Council voting method from that of elections for district boards and municipal councils and criticized Britain for creating new demands by extending the single-seat, single-vote method from lower level polls to the Legislative Council elections. The Hong Kong government, however, rebutted that it would irresponsible to accept anything other than that method for it had been endorsed by the Legislative Council and the public well before the Governor's political reform proposals were announced.

11. See *Express Daily*, 18 March and 19 March 1994.

12. Although the formation of PWC was not in accord with the wishes of the public, most of the political groups and newspapers began to come to grips with the reality that it would inevitably have an important role to play.

11 The Romance to Strike Back?

The closing phase of the event saw the structural completion of the initial romantic action of legislating the Patten package. However, as we have seen and will see below, in the different public accounts, a kind of ironic texture was in the making, giving rise, not to an emotion of cheerful joy, but to an attitude, at best, of relief, or of resignation verging on indifference, at the final 'victory' of the reform package.

Back to Legislative Politics – A Romance That Never Quite Was ...

As the Sino-British negotiation was developing into a farce, the political actors, in demand for their different desired narrative closures, began to embark on some new courses of action. These different paths taken by the actors nonetheless were finally to converge on the same anchorage point – Legislative Council voting – with the Council becoming the battleground for the competing narrative discourses and actions. On the part of the local government, towards the last few rounds of the talks, it was seen as beginning to take back some of the initiative lost to the chinese government during the protracted negotiation. By the end of November, the government was considering an option of tabling a partial bill on the 1994/95 electoral arrangements in the next month. While the British side claimed that the partial bill might act as a gesture that there was still room for the continuation of negotiations, China had warned repeatedly that tabling Patten's package to the legislature would be tantamount to declaring an end to the talks. Notwithstanding China's warning, the public sentiment was that the numerous rounds of talks had shown themselves to be a mere farce, with the effect of draining them of their patience and lowering their expectation for an agreement to come out. In various accounts, the public were described as feeling bored or fed up about the meaningless talks (*Ming Daily*, 26 November 1993). Losing their faith in the talks, more and more people urged that there was no ground for their continuation:

In any case the talks have gone beyond the old heavyweight boxing rule of a maximum of 15 rounds. There seems little purpose in carrying on to a 17th or 18th. (*SCM Post*, 29 October 1993)

(T)here can be no doubt that the British side has lost too much already in the present talks. Because it is now too late for it to turn back, the only hope must lie in a total breakdown to free us to do our own thing. (Ng, *SCM Post*, 2 November 1993)

On the eve of the 17th round, both sides were again bickering over words and putting the blame on each other ... As such, it will be better to have a clear-cut breakdown and have them go their separate ways rather than let the talks drag on. (*Express Daily*, 26 November 1993)

With the talks becoming a fruitless proceeding, the force of the public dictated that there should be no compelling reason to further suspend the legislative process. Thus the public's reception to the government's idea of tabling a partial bill was almost one-sidedly favourable. While the comic realists considered it as understandable or being in line with public opinion,[1] some democrats believed it was time for the romance to strike back. Earlier on, when the talks had just started, the democrats had been calling for a due regard for the legislative schedule concerning the reform bills. The problem, as they saw it, was not so much with the fate of the Patten package as with the principle of autonomy:

To give Legislative Council less than a month to debate a bill of such complexity is nothing short of contempt. It will be no less than the sober truth to describe this as making rubber stamp of the Legislative Council ... The time of the dilemma has arrived ... To hesitate, to be afraid to do what is clearly necessary because of what is merely wishfully possible, will cost this government its hard-earned initiative and control, and the people their new-found autonomy. (Ng, *SCM Post*, 1 June 1993)

What is at stake is not so much whether Patten will have his way about democracy, but whether the Hong Kong Government can be allowed to run Hong Kong on the basis of the support of the community through Legislative Council ... Patten's job ... is rather how to make a break acceptable to this community, in case no acceptable agreement is forthcoming ... (Ng, *SCM Post*, 22 June 1993)

Later in view of the imminent collapse of the Sino-British talks, the democrats criticized that in a situation where China would not concede at all whereas Britain could concede no more, those Legislative Council members (the conservatives) who still proposed continuing the talks were shedding their responsibility. They propagated instead the view that the Hong Kong people should decide their own fate. Among the newspapers, *SCM Post* was the one who began to foreground the once submerged heroic-romantic theme. By October 1993, given the realization that China was not sincere about the talks, the paper, which had earlier on called for caution when the talks were underway, changed its stance and instead urged Patten to stand firm:

> The public expects Britain to be sliding towards some new inglorious compromise. But the Governor must be able to show he still has the backbone to be defiant. (*SCM Post*, 2 October 1993)

While the paper believed the public was expecting an ironic situation in which Patten gave in and settled for an inglorious or dishonorable compromise, the paper itself had faith in the credibility of Patten's course of action, showing the tenacity of the romantic narrative:

> Britain has embarked on a course of strengthening Hong Kong's political institutions both before and, if possible, after 1997. It should not be diverted by such threats (by China). (*SCM Post*, 29 October 1993)

> Patten's course of action has a sense of inevitability about it, given his very public commitment to democratic reform and the community support for his proposals concerning the 'simple issues' on the negotiating table. (*SCM Post*, 13 December 1993)

> He has nothing to gain by prolonging the agony until the spring and nothing to lose by championing arrangements that have wide public support. (*SCM Post*, 29 December 1993)

Among the more radical democrat-critics, however, some of them had lost faith in the Governor and the leading democrats so much so that their accounts surfaced an element of mockery of the initial romance. Looking back, critic Ng wondered how much the Governor had achieved for Hong Kong from the perspective of 'autonomy'. Specifically, she found Patten having been channelling the influence of the British administration into Hong Kong rather than consolidating the groundwork of the local government/ society for 'self-rule' in its genuine sense. As such, it was further to her ironic realization that Patten-the-strong-leader had won the trust of the democrats so much so that the latter forfeited their presumed leadership in local politics:

> One does not see a greater consolidation of the Hong Kong Government, inclusive of administration and legislature, as an autonomous governing apparatus. Rather, the Hong Kong Government is increasingly indistinguishable from the concept of the 'British administration in Hong Kong ... At a time when Hong Kong should be building its own core of officials and politicians, to give its autonomy a stronger basis, an increasing reliance is being placed on Mr. Patten, who is at best a transient phenomenon. The growing dependence on Strongman Patten is not only among the civil service but also within the liberal camp in the several tiers of representative government. The United Democrats seem to have entrusted the future of democracy to Mr. Patten. Even Mr. Martin Lee Chu-ming seemed until recently to have been content to play the second fiddle, to act as the trusted confidant rather than an independent and wary player in the all-important field ... Ironically, Lord Wilson (Patten's predecessor), by appearing pro-China, had nurtured his opponents. Mr. Patten, by winning their trust, has disarmed them. (Ng, *SCM Post*, 23 November 1993)

It was in this context of increasing cynical distrust in the Governor as well as the local leaders that the 'Full Democracy in 95' movement was formed as a more radical split from within the pro-democracy camp. The movement group was comprised of about 40 individual and group members, including a few members from the United Democrats, a number of Christian pro-democracy clerics, several trade unions, women's and pro-democracy political groups. To them, full democracy should not be compromised. What was proposed by the mainstream democrats was far from being true democracy, and what the Governor was offering in his package was, in their words, 'nothing'. As the leading member, liberal legislator Emily Lau explained,

> For a long time, those of us who want full direct elections to the Legislative Council in 1995 have tended to work with groups who support a slower pace of democratic change. These people have argued for 30 directly-elected seats, instead of 20, in 1995. But strictly speaking, asking for 30 directly-elected seats is the same as asking for 60. Both are in breach of the Basic Law ... You either have full democracy or you don't. Thirty directly-elected seats is not full democracy. (*SCM Post*, 15 July 1993)

As she recounted, the idea took off after the Ko Shan rally on 8 May 1993: 'A lot of the speakers talked about the 1995 elections. During my speech, I asked why we could not have 60 directly-elected seats. The stadium just erupted. We suddenly realized that the masses were so much more progressive than we thought and this emboldened us' (*SCM Post*, 15 July 1993). At the same time, they had no faith in the Sino-British talks. Their feeling was that Britain and China were just 'playing a numbers game, which, in the end, might result in two more seats in Legislative Council'. Frustrated by the talks, they finally decided to put their proposal on the agenda for Legislative Council discussion,

> Let's stop this mucking around and put full democracy for Legislative Council to the people. It's never been there to be debated. Let's put it on the agenda, and it can attract reaction. (Ibid.)

Thus these more radical democrats began to take a more active role in the political process in setting their own agenda for Legislative Council discussion while putting their case to the public. They were making themselves the hero and heroines in a new romance of 'autonomy' and 'full democracy'.

In contrast, among the political parties, the Liberal Party (the former Co-operative Resource Centre) had always adopted a comic mode of understanding and assumed the role of a mediator. In mid October 1993, as the talks showed little progress, the Party sent a delegation to Beijing whereby they portrayed themselves as acting as a courageous mediator required to bring about a comic turn in the ironic stage of a desired comedy. However such optimism was later replaced by a regretful feeling that the Party had been too optimistic to realize the 'deep mutual distrust' between the two powers. In view of the problem of political discontinuity in 1997, and realizing that Hong Kong could not rely on the two powers for its own well-being, A. Lee appealed to the public for self-help. Persisting with their cherished hope for smooth transition, they played a more active role in the legislative process, trying to bring about what they believed to be a semi-comic ending of something close to political convergence even in the absence of Sino-British agreement.

On 24 February 1994, the partial reform bill was passed by Legislative Council as expected, despite two attempts to block it. In particular, the Liberal Party's attempt to block the bill was regarded as redundant and naive.[2] Public's responses to the voting result varied from romantic applause to ironic indifference. *SCM Post*, continuing with its romantic narrative, was the only newspaper which celebrated the outcome as a first victory brought about by those who held onto their beliefs with courage and integrity:

> Hong Kong's legislators are to be commended for a mature, responsible and
> fearless first step on the long and troublesome road of democratization ... Mr
> Patten, too, deserves a fair share of the praise. It is after all, his name which is
> attached to the reforms. He has defended them relentlessly and effectively
> both at home and abroad. Moreover, he possessed the courage and, it must be
> added, the sense to trust them in the hands of the legislature. That trust proved
> well-founded. (*SCM Post*, 25 February 1994)

In this account, not only were the legislators found commendable, but
Patten remained to be the praise-worthy and triumphant hero. However, the
pro-democracy cynics believed such an account to be a myth. As an effort
to demystify it, critic Bug insisted that Britain had not been consistent in or
genuine about its democratic stance.

> Britain's democratic turn was forced into being by history – by China's
> refusing to accept the watered-down proposal by Britain ... If Britain had
> really wanted democracy for Hong Kong, there would have been no Sino-
> British talks at all. For once there were talks, the reform proposal would
> become only a bargaining chip. Indeed Britain did concede in the 8th round ...
> (Bug, *Economic Journal*, 27 February 1994)

Keeping on with these demystifications, other critics ridiculed the leading
democrats as lacking real leadership and yet indulging in self-heroism:

> Instead of thinking about progress, the democrats stuck to the populist
> mentality of moral politics in the aftermath of June 4th while letting the
> pragmatic culture get strengthened among the people resulting in a strong
> sense of impotence and helplessness vis-à-vis China ... They get trapped in a
> game set by the power-holders while feeling pleased with the label of
> 'moderate democrats' upon the moderate-radical dichotomy. They fail to get
> united and maximize the space for democratic development for Hong Kong in
> the process of bargaining, and instead stop complacently at indulging in
> heroism. (On, *Economic Journal*, 18 March 1994)

The attitude was one of cynicism, which nevertheless bespoke a stronghold
of romanticism in the higher romantic vision of autonomy. As such, it put
added strength into the 'Full Democracy Movement' formed by the more
radical democrats. However, while this brand of cynicism – *romantic
cynicism* – was elaborated by the few articulate critics, what was found in
the editorials of most of the newspapers was a kind of *cynical indifference*.

As we have seen before, *Economic Journal* had already turned into tragic despair about the initial romance whereas *Express Daily* had been frustrated to learn that the heroic romance was a mere illusion. For *Ming Daily*, the political order expected to come, albeit not one of chaos or deterioration, was one rid of dreams and direction. Under the given constraints, the best to hope for was therefore a political development no more regressive than that already prescribed in the Basic Law:

> Without convergence, any reform can only be short-lived ... The Hong Kong people have no dream about democracy, and only hope that Sino-British row would not rock the society to its foundation ... China's second stove should fall within the confines of the Basic Law - if the Basic Law can be put into practice, even though the pace of political development slows down, it would not be a big problem. (*Ming Daily*, 25 January 1994)

Having come to terms with the reality, the paper resigned to an attitude of indifference about the legislative process in that it advised the legislators not to make a fuss about it but to simply finish the legislative process as scheduled.[3] Likewise, *Economic Journal*, failing to rekindle its past romantic enthusiasm about the reform, had receded to a position of passionless pragmatism and indifference about the legislative process:

> Presumably, what the Hong Kong people are concerned about or hope to see is a resolution in the form of a Sino-British agreement for the sake of smooth transition. Now that the sides are going their separate ways, the people should not be expected to feel interested in a reform plan that will have no bearing on convergence ... For those legislators fighting for democracy, they should constructively work for smooth transition in the absence of official convergence rather than do anything in the name of democracy that may cause worry to the ordinary citizens, who aspire to a simple stable and prosperous life. (*Economic Journal*, 26 February 1994)

On the part of the legislators, having embarked on their courses of combat, they would of course decide that the fight over the first partial bill was but a small part in the larger struggle yet to come. Thus immediately after the first partial bill was approved, they quickly prepared to put foward amendments to the remaining items of the Patten package. The major competing alternatives to the Patten package included the 'full direct election' proposal by E. Lau, and the '1994 package' by the Liberal Party. While the former was meant to go beyond the offer of limited democracy in the Patten package, the latter, containing fewer democratic elements than the Patten package, was devised to obtain China's (implicit) blessings so as to secure some kind of unofficial convergence. By late June, after much lobbying, the chances of the Liberal Party holding sway in Legislative Council took a sharp turn for the better on the eve of the Legislative Council meeting, when seven pro-China legislators indicated they would lend their support to the '1994 package'.[4] With this, it was to the ironic realization of the public that the fate of Patten's electoral reform package would lie in the hands of the few wavering independents. As such, *the already meagre sense of romance retained about the event was further overlaid with a mundane look of mere politicking.* Further taking away from the event any possible romantic colour, some newspapers – *Economic Journal* and *Ming Daily* – continued with their ironic or tragic-ironic mode of understanding and showed an attitude of indifference about the outcome:

> If the Patten package had not been rejected by China, 29 June 1994 would have been Patten's day of marked achievement in Hong Kong ... Since it is going to be short-lived, whichever reform plan will be passed by Legislative Council is of no relevance or importance. (*Economic Journal*, 30 June 1994)

In a more positive tone, *Express Daily* affirmed an attitude of respect for the legislative process but showed indifference, rather implicitly, to the outcome:

> No matter which proposal is passed, it should be well-taken by all the legislators because this means a due respect for the practice of parliamentary politics. (30 June 1994)

With this attitude of resignation, none of the reform proposals would look outstandingly credible and worth-supporting, even though none of them would look particularly abhorable.

On 30 June 1994, as it turned out, the councilors (including 3 ex officio members) voted 32 to 24 in support of the final reading of Patten's electoral bill, whereas the two other competing packages – the '1994 package' by the Liberal Party and E. Lau's private member's bill of full direct election – suffered the same fate of defeat by one vote. In the public, the press in general accepted the legislative outcome as fair, but they showed no sense of a glorious victory in the editorials and the commentaries (except for brief news about the cheerful responses of those democrat-legislators who had supported the Patten package) whilst expressing sympathy for the Liberal Party's narrow defeat.[5] As a matter of truth, full of cautious calculations and filled with a sense of uncertainty instead of enthusiasm and confidence, the experience of many other democrats with the final stage of the legislative process could be likened, at best, to one of *anti-climax of relief*:

> Sighs of relief, rather than ecstatic cheers are in order. Chris Patten's electoral reform package has passed into law ... (*SCM Post*, 1 July 1994)

> By a hair's breadth that disaster was averted ... No wonder there was, in the aftermath, no elation but only immense relief. (Ng, *SCM Post*, 5 July 1994)

There was no sense of a romantic fulfilment about the outcome. Rather paradoxically, the 'romantic' action was completed without bringing about a romantic mood. What was in place was a half comic and half ironic sense of having something worse avoided. With this, what ensued was a quick, clear-cut turn to the more mundane or pragmatic concern with other transition-related businesses:

> With the debate over, Hong Kong has a chance to concentrate on the work of the transition. (*SCM Post*, 1 July 1994)

> Now that the row over political reform is over, let it be over. The Hong Kong people are glad to know that Sino-British co-operation on other issues has been underway. (*Express Daily*, 1 July 1994)

Worse still, the more cynical democrats found little solace but showed the greatest disappointment at the outcome. What they found ironic and even humiliating about it was that the local leaders had not had the moral courage to stand up for an uncompromised belief in democracy but stayed in their easy role of faithful supporters of Patten. In this regard, critic Ng's comments were worth quoting at length:

> Indeed, people who support democracy have reason to be deeply disappointed in the feebleness of their champions ... They seemed totally unable to do more than what the British Government was prepared to do anyway. It is absurd and humiliating that, if anyone had emerged as the hero of the hour, it was a British colonial administrator, not a local champion of all that is right, just and noble.
>
> The narrow defeat of Emily Lau's private member's bill is a bitter pill to swallow for the same reason. Not because it was defeated, but because it was defeated more or less by default - because many of those who purported to believe in true democracy did not have the guts to ask for it, the spirit to

believe it possible or the fight for it even if victory was improbable.

For them it was enough that the Governor had said he would not sign the assent even if the bill was passed. This was sufficient excuse not to take the bill for democracy seriously. But to take a defeatist attitude with the British is no more laudable than taking a defeatist attitude with the Chinese. (Ng, *SCM Post*, 5 July 1994)

Other critics showed a similar attitude of puzzled disappointment at the performance of the leading democrats, taking also into account the diminished relevance of the element of Sino-British relation for a credible romantic pursuit:

If, as it was in the earlier stage, the Patten package could be used to force China to accept it, it was all right that they gave the package their full support. However, as Sino-British relations later broke down and China insisted on building up a second stove, the democrats still lacked the courage to affirm the symbolic meanings of full direct election. (On, *Economic Journal*, 3 July 1994)

Indeed in the whole episode concerning the Governor's reform package, these cynical democrats had experienced great disappointment, despair and disillusion, not only about the once romantic hero – Patten, but also about what their local leaders had done and what they themselves could do.

In sum, a heavy sense of irony prevailed in public discourse over the event of the final Legislative Council vote. *SCM Post* was the only critic which saw a completion of the initial heroic romance, but even in its account, the dominant note was one of relief rather than victorious joy. For those who experienced the greatest irony, *Economic Journal* and *Express Daily* had shown indifference to the event itself whereas the democrat-critics and the democrat-cynics responded with bitter cynicism over the voting result. The initial sense of romantic heroism had diminished tremendously.

Finding a Little Solace in Revived Hopes

Nevertheless, looking at the event from a different narrative perspective, the event could mean quite different things. To the comic realists, the Legislative Council voting, when taken in a prospective manner, did mean a stride forward in the political history of Hong Kong. Despite uncertainties and foreseeable difficulties, there were images of a growing Legislative

Council and of persistent struggles on the part of the people. Among the press, *Ming Daily* and *Success Daily* affirmed the value of the Legislative Council voting and adopted a forward-looking view vis-à-vis the event. *Success Daily*, without showing either optimism or pessimism, believed that the biggest test was yet to come - whether the 1995 elections would turn out to be a success causing no instability in the society.[6] In a much more optimistic tone, *Ming Daily* saw the Legislative Council voting as an occasion for celebration in that in the one and a half centuries of British rule, it was the first time the Hong Kong people's representatives could directly participate in the process of deciding the pace of democracy in the society. Moreover, it urged the people to bury their past conflicts, look forward and actively participate in the election, for 'if the people indicate their support for the model passed by Legislative Council through their action, China may also have to consider such expressions of public opinion when designing the second stove' (30 June 1994). Still, despite its optimistic faith, the paper struck a note of pessimistic worry: 'China is not prepared to listen to divergent views in designing the model of the SAR government. Unless the Hong Kong people get united in getting China to be more open to different views, Hong Kong may be going the way backward on this road to democracy' (Ibid.). The deep message nonetheless was that the Hong Kong people had to get united rather than give up on the democratic cause.

Among the (once) romanticists, *SCM Post* and the democrat-critics were the first to put the event behind them and shared with the comic realists a sense of hope and faith in the soon-to-be-reformed system. *SCM Post* which started its editorial with a mundane appeal concluded with the speculation that within the government it might not be business as usual, for Legislative Council 'will feel emboldened, having just played the central role in democratic progress' (1 July 1994). Likewise in a newspaper article, the democrat-critic, Ng, at the end suddenly switched from her cynical remarks to a position of persistent romanticism, urging the democrats to fight on with perseverance. To her, the event was just the beginning of a new battle to come:

> The passage of the Patten package is not the end of the difficulties but the beginning. One glance at the contents shows that there will be many elections to fight. Candidates will have to be found and campaigns organized. The system will be far more open, the battle fought on a much wider field ... Democrats will have to gain much greater strength within a very short time in order to secure anything like a useful majority. Any more defaults will mean

that last Wednesday's work was no more than paving the way for the forces it was meant to hold at bay. (Ng, *SCM Post*, 5 July 1994)

The heroic romance might belong to the past, but the rhetorics of heroic romanticism stayed strong.

Notes

1. According to *Success Daily*, 'If Britain did have a conspiracy, it would need to get an agreement with China ... It stands to reason that Patten made the decision out of urgency and out of the belief that China will not formally terminate the talks' (5 December 1993). According to *Express Daily*, 'The government's decision has been expected ... It is believed to be acceptable to the people ... This seems to be Britain's only choice ...' (3 December 1993).
2. See *SCM Post*, 23 January 1994; *Express Daily*, 25 January 1994; *Success Daily*, 24 February, 1994.
3. See *Express Daily*, 25 January 1994, and 26 February 1994.
4. See Chapter 10.
5. See *Success Daily*, 30 June 1994.
6. *Success Daily*, 30 June 1995.*

12   Conclusion

This book has as its general theoretical aim an explanation of the interplay between culture and politics in the public sphere. It seeks to devise a framework as well as a method to analyse the cultural and political processes that come to define and re-define the public meanings of a political event. Pertinent to the empirical case in this book, I have limited my discussion to a specific instance in which a political event was first constructed as a heroic romance and then went through a process of de-romanticization and de-hero-ization – not so much in the structural progression of the event as in the cognitive and emotional-moral reception about the event on the part of the public. In this concluding chapter, I will first present an overview of the kind of theoretical generalizations that we may arrive at out of the empirical study. This will include a critical discussion of the theoretical and methodological limitations and promises of the research. In addition, I will reflect on the case in hand with a view to teasing out its larger implications on the cultural-political context of the Hong Kong society: the role of the public sphere in the political process, and the cultural boundaries that shape and are shaped by the materiality of politics.

Theoretical Generalizations

In my theoretical chapters, I have argued that the formation of public opinion must be analysed in relation to the notions of 'public' and 'narrative'. The public is posited on the structural, institutional and symbolic levels whereas narrative is conceived to be constituting the discursive context for the operation of the symbolic public. A public is formed through a common communicative space within a political community i.e. the public sphere. The theoretical import of the notion is two-fold: first, it directs us to focus on the intricate relationship between politics and public opinion by highlighting the very interface between state and society, and between culture and politics. Secondly, it marks out a sphere of politics of public credibility which incorporates and yet goes beyond the legitimate-versus-illegitimate distinction.

A large part of public discourse takes the form of narrative; public opinion is embedded in public discourse which embeds narratives. Narrative is a discursive form which is meaning-laden in itself while allowing an intertwinement with different thematic structures to produce the meanings of an event in all its structural, thematic and emotional specificities. As such, narrative analysis provides a much overlooked clue to unravelling a society's cultural formation and the actors' experience with specific events. As an attempt to explain the continuous interaction between politics and culture, I integrate the theory of the public with a theory of narrative progression that attends to both the structured quality and the experiential dynamics in the development of an event. The following will discuss a few tentative theoretical generalizations – as well as their meta-theoretical implications – that may be drawn from the empirical study. The discussion will be followed by an evaluation of the limits to such generalizations.

Structure and Agency

The occurence of an event is a structural consequence, mediated by agency, of the narrative construction of the pre-existing situation. In a situation perceived as romantic-ironic, a heroic romance will take shape in the event of charismatic mobilization. In a situation perceived as comic-ironic, action will be oriented towards a comic resolution by means of pragmatic intervention.

In terms of structural development, a narrative construction both presupposes a specific state that comes before it and predisposes subsequent development to particular patterns. Agency plays a role in constructing particular narrative frames out of a cultural repertoire, and in mediating between the particular structural predisposition and actual happenings. In the case under study, the pre-existing situation had been understood by a portion of the public as falling short of the democratic ideal. The predisposing forces were there, but it needed Governor Patten's charismatic appeal and innovative formulation to turn the ironic situation into a narrative of promise. The heroic-romantic aspect of the act hinged on a context where on the one hand, the Hong Kong people had been aspiring to more political democracy, and on the other, the all-powerful Chinese government was always frustrating their aspirations and attempts whereas the British had adopted a policy of passive submission and moral retreat with regard to the democratic cause in Hong Kong. It was against this background that tremendous courage and innovativeness were seen in Governor Patten's political reform proposals.

As far as agency is concerned, while the Governor's charisma, public relations exercise and reform plan all contributed to his success, the public critics played a no less important role in the narrative construction of the event. Specifically, the 'heroic' sense was imparted through three inter-related narrative practices in public discourse, namely thematic emplotment, characterization and mood construction. In this regard, the democrat-critics, *Economic Journal*, *SCM Post* and the polling agents projected a hopeful picture of a new order around the twin themes of democracy and autonomy and showed general faith in the Governor as a strong and tough (but not flawless) leader.

At the same time, there were those – the pro-China forces and the conservatives – who had initially constructed a narrative of comedy about the pre-existing situation and instead believed the Governor to be an arrogant trouble-maker disrupting the order of smooth transition. In other words, they had endowed upon the event quite different meanings within their own comic-ironic frame. Their narrative frame both determined their reactions to the event and structured the lines of action they would take. Nonetheless, the specific strategies adopted and the specific actions taken were matters of agency – the actors' positions differed, for instance, as to whether to oust the Governor from office or to provide him with a ladder to step down with grace. Moreover, the actors' discursive construction, rather than a mere mechanical reaction to the structural tension, took time to develop (through episodes) from doubts, reservations and oppositions into a specific, coherent and more forwarding-looking narrative. For instance, it was towards the end of the second stage that comic-realist actors (the pro-stability press and the conservatives) began to forge a narrative of comic versus ironic action whereby they defined not only the locus of blame, but also the desired order of reconciliation as well as the course of action to be taken for a comic resolution. More specifically, the conservative elites proposed a more conservative model for political reform which they believed to be more acceptable to the Chinese government.

As a matter of fact, the role of agency lies not only in mediating between structure and action but also in the process of change. The idea of 'moving structure' in narrative development is to capture the relationship between structure and change through counter-actions. This will be discussed below.

Structure, Contingency and Change

(a) Given a specific narrative beginning about an event, the subsequent unfolding of the event is open to a few structural possibilities, the closure of which is contingent upon actions and counter-actions, whether intended or not, that make up episodes. Where the episodes could further the development of the narrative of heroic romance/ comedy, the event will develop into a fulfilled romance/ comedy. Where the episodes bring about significant turns in narrative development, a heroic-romantic beginning will develop into a tragedy or irony whereas a comic beginning will develop into a comic-irony.

(b) While the progression of an event towards a particular ending is impelled by the structural logic in a developing narrative, the experience of the event may change in the midst of episodes so much so that the discrepancy between structure and meaning may generate a sense of irony, which in turn brings about a change in the structure of the narrative.

The Patten event started as a heroic romance, but it ended as a light irony. The irony did not lie in it being an unfulfilled romance – the fact was that the Patten proposals were passed into legislation – but that the meaning as well as the emotional experience about the structural progression of the event had changed. It was the growing discrepancy between structure and experience, as a result of a number of episodes, that shifted the narrative structure.

As we have seen, the meaning of the Patten event underwent subtle changes through a number of episodes whereby ironic turns were made and new narrative themes or new heroic figures were constructed. The 'secret deal' controversy was the first of these episodes. Although Patten did not come out 'polluted', neither could he emerge all clean and innocent. The calls for transparency and participation further lent force to a new narrative around the theme of autonomy, the logic of which required a detachment of the democratic cause from the Governor. Later as a result of the Chinese government's retaliations, the heroic-romantic plot backfired, allowing the undercurrents in the first stage to develop into serious undermining forces. Irony set in when it was suspected or believed that instead of fulfilling the promise of romance the people had expected of him, Patten the hero was actually leading them to chaos and victimization. The public then became divided into two opposing blocs, with the democrats holding firmly to the narrative of heroic-romance whilst struggling with the 'autonomy' theme and the conservatives pursuing a comic line of action. With so much irony coming along, while the structure of heroic-romance still lingered, it had already lost much of its emotional flavour.

At the beginning of stage three, when Sino-British talks intertwined with the legislative process over the reform proposals, one bloc's source of joy became the reason for worry for the other. However, as the diplomatic talks later showed themselves to be a series of fruitless proceeding, a thick sense of irony developed in both camps – regarding Patten's plausible concession/ defeat among the democrats and the diminishing likelihood for reconciliation among the conservatives. It was at this juncture that the narratives in *Economic Journal* and *Express Daily* featured a decisively ironic turn of the events within their respective frames – the former turning from heroic-romance to tragedy and the latter from comic hopes to ironic disappointment. Importantly, these narrative shifts generated an attitude of indifference regarding the legislative process, which contributed to the structural completion of the heroic-romance while undermining a possible sense of victorious joy about the final outcome.

It is interesting to note that the heroic romance, once established, carried the force of fulfilling its expected mission, but the structural completion of the action was accompanied and facilitated by different kinds of emotion. On the one hand, the last stage was supposed to see the furtherance and completion of the romantic-heroic action i.e. the legislation of Patten's reform proposals as scheduled. On the other hand, the situation towards the end of stage three was that, some had turned into indifference; the pro-stability press (comic-realist category) began to give up hopes on the diplomatic talks; the mainstream democrats stuck to the initial narrative of heroic-romance about the governor's reform proposals; and the more radical democrats sought to construct an alternative heroic-romantic narrative of democracy and autonomy. Under such circumstances, the force of the public dictated that there should be no compelling reason to further suspend the legislative process. In the last minute, as the radical democrats dared the legislators to give support to a higher ideal by proposing a more aggressive model, the initial heroic-romantic quality about the Patten proposals looked diminished against the higher standard. Finally, within the divided legislature, the legislative politics over the reform bills was overlaid with a mundane look of mere politicking, further thinning out the already meagre sense of romance retained about the event. In retrospect, the final development of irony presupposed a romantic or comic projection at the beginning or in the middle, and the subsequent experiences of frustration and disillusionment over a widening gap between ideal and reality.

Politics and Culture

(a)   The force of narrative progression as the force of the 'public', which changes the significance of an event or a figure over time, will incline the actors to continually re-position themselves with regard to the new situations. When a romantic or comic narrative gains ground, the task of the heroes/ heroines and their supporters is to carry the plot forward to a desired end, and the burden for those labelled as villains, cowards and/ or mock heroes (heroines) is to assume either a supportive role in the prevailing narrative or a heroic role in an alternative narrative. When an ironic narrative gains ground, the burden for those labelled as villains, cowards and/ or mock heroes (heroines) is to assume a heroic role in a comic or romantic narrative. When two competing narratives equally hold sway, the burden for those labelled as heroes (heroines)/ villains is to strike a balance between the two while subtly consolidating one over the other.

(b)   In the midst of competition among the different narrative constructions by the conflicting actors, the likelihood that a narrative will prevail over the others depends on the weight of ironic forces thrown upon it by the opponent, and the narrative cultures (e.g. romanticism) among the public. The stronger a particular narrative culture and the bigger the challenge by the opponent, the more likely that the public will hold steadfastly to a narrative genre corresponding to their narrative culture. The weaker a particular narrative culture and the bigger the challenge by the opponent, the more likely that the public will shift their narrative positions.

In politics of public credibility, political actors seek to incorporate the sacred symbols into a narrative of heroic romance or comedy about themselves while associating their opponents with the symbols of profanity or mediocrity in ironic or satirical narratives. In particular, political actors are symbols for public identification in an order of moral relationships – between hero/ heroine, villain, coward and victim. In the case under study, the Governor at first successfully established himself as a heroic figure in a romance vis-à-vis the Chinese government. Further as a step to advance the plot of heroic quest, he prepared to put together the legislation that would be needed to implement his reform package. In this connection, the Legislative Council's endorsement of the proposal on the Election Committee gave added weight to the public credibility of the heroic-romantic cause symbolized by the Patten package. The Chinese government, in response, mobilized every cultural and material resource available to discredit Patten and to trap him in a difficult or fragile position. Specifically, by means of its revengeful actions, it put into question Britain's trustworthiness and spelt out to the Hong Kong people the harsh reality they might face without its blessings. To a large extent, the Chinese government's challenges and threats provided a niche for the consolidation of the countervailing forces of ironic realism, which had its roots in a culture of pragmatism (comic realism) and mild anti-colonialism (cynicism). More and more people, realists and cynics alike, put into spotlight the critical relevance of the three questions concerning Patten's motivations, the charge of a breach of agreement and the prospects for smooth transition. The scenario as it developed was that, to the extent that Patten was not able to assure the public of the purity in his motivation and the sustainability of the project, he as a heroic character underwent a process of de-hero-ization and the narrative itself of de-romanticization.

In the face of an erosion in the heroic romance, the public critics responded by consolidating and modifying certain parts of their narrative accounts on the one hand and developing new narrative lines of action on the other. As we have seen, the strand of romanticism was strong among the pro-democracy critics including *Economic Journal* and *SCM Post*. To them, the Chinese government appeared to be a ferocious villain who abused power over weaker subjects. It might have wanted to see the intended effect of its threats, yet to the contrary, it had instead alienated itself further from the people. Thus instead of retreating from the cause they had supported, they stood firm on their principles. Nonetheless, seeing character flaws in Patten – due in part to a sense of growing distrust about a colonial figure and in part to the public ridicule of a 'pro-British' label, the romantic critics as well as the democrats found themselves fighting a tough battle on two fronts – a need to continue supporting the Patten package as a symbol of extended democracy, and a need to advocate autonomy from both China and Britain. The democrats were somewhat divided on which front to give priority to.

In the meantime, *Ming Daily, Express Daily and Success Daily,* implanted in a culture of comic realism, began to forge a narrative of comic versus ironic action. Among the legislators, the conservatives, which had been ridiculed as cowards and waverers by the romantic critics in the first stage, struck back by undermining the credibility of the heroic romance with a discourse of ironic realism – a stress on the impracticality of the project. Amidst the growing desire for reconciliation, these conservative elites assumed the role of mediator in a comic narrative. This started a process of local struggles in which the conservative groups sought to replace the Governor's proposals with their more conservative models.

In the face of setback, the romanticists could ill afford to back down from the romantic cause because if they did so, they would be making a mockery of what they themselves had been advocating. However, as public criticisms against the Governor increased, the romanticists also faced the pressure of being ridiculed as naive idealists or rash fools. At such a crossroad, while a few of them chose to withdraw from the pro-democracy camp, most of them played the role of the unyielding supporter/ ally of the Governor and some others kept their distance from the Governor yet without giving up on the democratic cause.

At the beginning of stage three, amidst the two major competing narratives between the romanticists and the comic-realists, the government was trapped in a position where it sought to strike a delicate balance. If Patten did not concede, he would be regarded by the conservatives as a villain who posed to be an obstacle to the restoration of Sino-British co-operation. If, on the contrary, Patten conceded, he would be making himself a mock hero in the eyes of the democrats. As a result, the Patten administration adopted a two-pronged approach by delaying the introduction of his proposals to the Executive Council for gazetting on the one hand and setting deadlines for their gazetting and assuring the Legislative Council of its final legislative power over the proposals on the other. However, as the Sino-British negotiation was conceived as developing into a farce, the different newspapers and critics had shown different attitudes about the situation. Some indicated diminishing faith in their respective pursuits whereas the others embraced contradictory desires between them. As such, the public credibility of the Patten government was being maintained on rather fragile grounds.

Regarding the relative public credibility of the different narratives, the heroic romance gained ground in the first stage, reflecting and at the same time consolidating a culture of romanticism among the public. However, while this narrative culture was quite firmly rooted among the democrats and the pro-democracy critics, it did not seem to be deeply implanted among the general public. Thus in the second stage, in the face of the Chinese government's threats and revengeful actions, while the pro-democracy group held steadfastly to the heroic romance, the romantic aspirations of a good portion of the public were eroded by more pragmatic considerations so much so that an alternative narrative of comic-irony could develop in full swing. In the third stage, the pro-democracy forces were divided among themselves as they embedded different strands of romanticism – pure romanticism, tragic romanticism (tragic realism) and cynical romanticism (cynical realism) – which resulted from the interaction among their respective ideals, the weight of challenging forces and their narrative responses to the challenging forces. For one thing, although the initial heroic romance was somewhat undermined by the ironic and even cynical forces, it had not been effectively reversed or thoroughly discredited. It was in this political-cultural context that the Legislative Council voting took place. Within the Legislative Council, the legislators were divided into the conservative/pro-China camp, the democrats and the more radical democrats who held three different narrative positions. While the voting result could be taken as a matter of 'numbers' of the different camps, it was also to be understood against the political-cultural background – as the interactive product of 'voting numbers' and narrative dynamics. With the legislation of the Patten proposals, the event came to a structural end, but the public's experience with the event was to continue to play a part in future political processes.

Theoretical and Methodological Issues

I began this book with partial knowledge of the promises and limits of this study. After conducting the empirical research, I become more alert to the limitations of my theoretical construction and also the possible areas for further expansion. In the first place, I must profess that the theory of politics of public credibility is neither intended to have universal applicability nor meant to be a comprehensive theory about politics. One of the central questions about the 'public' concerns whether there exists in a political community a public sphere which stands relatively independent of the state and is strong enough to confront it by means of open criticisms. In principle, it is in a democratic society where the people could speak for themselves and with the state that an autonomous sphere for public discourse will be in operation. In a totalitarian society where the state speak to and for the people as subjects, an autonomous public among the citizenry simply does not exist. That is to say, in presupposing the existence of a public sphere, the theory of politics of public credibility is, strictly speaking, applicable only to democratic societies.

Nevertheless, while suggesting that the theory is applicable to certain types of society and not quite to others, it would seem to be an over-simplification to assume that a political community plays an all-or-nothing role vis-à-vis the state. I hazard the argument that politics of public credibility not only assumes a central place in a democratic system, but also plays an important part in the process of struggle for democracy. In a non-democratic society, the structural prerequisites for the emergence of a debating public, as Habermas suggests include the development of a modern state, the growth of a market economy as well as a strong communicative infrastructure. While the first two structural factors facilitate the development of a non-state-controlled domain of activity which takes on a public relevance, the last factor makes possible frequent communication among citizens with different socio-economic backgrounds. On top of this, I would stress also the role of the middle class in the struggle for political inclusion and democratic accountability, which effects the formation of a public that is to get increasingly involved in a politics of public credibility. In other words, a public is not a structural given, but has to emerge through struggles. As such, the theory would have relevance to both democratic societies and societies struggling for democracy, even though its relative importance may differ in the two cases.

Still, the theory is not a comprehensive theory about politics. The reason is that in every political system, politics have two dimensions, one public and the other non-public. To the extent that it is played out in the public, it is regulated by the culture of the public – the norms of public decorums, the store of sacred symbols and the symbolic representations of public opinion. However, to the extent that politics is conducted behind closed doors, it does not come under the scrutiny of the public. Insofar as the non-public dimension of politics is not quite accessible to the researcher, the theoretical as well empirical focus in this study is limited to the role of the public in the politics of public credibility. By way of conclusion, I would say that the more open the political system is, the weightier the politics of public credibility will be, and hence the greater the role of the public in politics will be.

The second set of issues concerns the theoretical conception of public opinion as well as the methodological approach to the problem. 'Public opinion' is an ambiguous and controversial (and even dubious) concept. It is true that people in a community do talk with one another about political issues in coffee-houses, living-rooms, the market, work-places and so on. It is also true that opinions expressed in these various lived contexts of the people, which bear significantly on the formation of public opinion, do not necessarily have an adequate representation in the mass media. However, while it is technically rather infeasible to probe into what the people say in these more private or diffused settings, it is also beyond the theoretical intent of this research to study how public opinion is constructed out of these more private and diffused opinions. As far as the present research is concerned, public opinion refers not so much to the summation of the opinions of private individuals as to the symbolic force of the 'public' that regulates the material aspect of politics, which includes the various symbolic representations of public opinion in public discourse. The symbolic force of the 'public' is constructed through the public sphere, which is institutionally located in the non-state-run mass media. In limiting public opinion to public discourse and further limiting public discourse to media discourse, the empirical findings concerning the opinions of the public in this study may not be generalized to the opinions of the community at large.

Regarding the construction of 'public opinion', a question may arise concerning the validity of the public interpretations of opinion polls. For example, in the first stage of the event, as the hard data showed, the 'don't know' portion actually outweighed the number of those who supported the proposals, hence raising doubts as to whether the proposals did carry wide support from the general populace. Put within the present theoretical framework, however, this question would not pose as a detrimental methodological flaw as it might first suggest. There have been many ways of defining the concept of public opinion, and for present purposes, I have conceived it as a discursive construction and hence a symbolic force over politics. It therefore matters less as to whether the opinion polls could have been interpreted in a different light than how they are interpreted in the actual public discourse. The strength of this approach lies in a greater sensitivity to the basis for collective self-understanding among the public, but one of its major limitations is that it does not take as its central task to track down and analyse those changes in public opinion that might have been overlooked or deliberately ignored in public discourse.

In my framework, public discourse has been equated with media discourse. In this regard, the question concerns the relative autonomy of the mass media as the public sphere. The post-Marxist approach to the mass media conceives the modern media as enjoying relative autonomy which allows for the politics of signification among the conflicting forces. It nonetheless insists that the commercial media operate within the boundary of the hegemonic consensus and a structure of differential accessibility. The post-Marxist approach is right on both counts, but in emphasizing the latter over the former, this approach lends itself too quickly to a position that underrates the extent that the public may shape the political process whereby the dominant interests are challenged in varying degrees. This study does not intend to simply do the reverse by emphasizing one over the other. Rather, it is one of the aims of the research to affirm the role of the meaningful experiences of the people in political processes by encompassing the full range meaning of the 'public' as expressed in the media. It must be acknowledged that the research has not dwelled on the concept of 'hegemony'. Nevertheless, the concept of centre-periphery and the idea of irony are used to highlight the tensions involved in the political process. In this connection, a theory of narrative development is elaborated to explain the different kinds of ideal-reality gaps that both the political actors and the public experience and have to continuously respond to in one way or another.

Still, under the present conception of the public, one of the methodological limitations of the empirical research is that it has confined the study of public discourse to that conducted in the newspapers, and hence excluding media discourse in the radio, television and magazines. In particular, in recent years, with the emergence of several new programmes in the former two media that accommodate more daring political criticisms, radio and television seem to constitute an increasingly important part of the public sphere in the society. It is in part out of practical considerations and in part based on certain theoretical and methodological assumptions that I take the newspapers – five newspapers – as my empirical referent. (Theoretically, it is assumed that public dialogue proceeds by means of intertextual references; and therefore the different media will be connected to one another in some intricate ways. Methodologically, I have included in my sample a relatively broad range of narrative positions to safeguard representativeness.)

As such, this study may not have taken into adequate account the vast range of media discourses, especially those conducted in the newly-developed radio and television programmes. Based on my impressionistic observation, nonetheless, I have not found any major discrepancies between the discourses in the different media, and I hazard the guess that an inclusion of all these different media in my study would have enriched but not necessarily contradicted my empirical analysis.

Regarding the question of sampling, moreover, there is a technical difficulty in this research. I have intended my sample to be a representative one – in terms of the range of narrative positions shown at the beginning of the event. The problem is, since this study started long before the event ended, and since narrative position is a matter of development rather than fixed structure, it is beyond our ability to predict how some similar narrative positions in stage one would develop into very different narrative structures in the end. For instance, it has not been foreseen that among the romantic and the comic-realist critics, respectively, *Economic Journal* turned into tragedy and *Express Daily* into irony towards the end of the event. In this light, a major methodological problem with the design of the research is that I could have excluded certain types of narrative positions which were marked with a beginning similar to those I chose but then departed significantly from them in later stages. In this research, it is fortunate that I have included a wider range of narrative positions than I intended and that the present sample happens to be able to exhaust the different structural possibilities within romance. Still, there is the question of weighting between the newly developed sub-categories. It will be discussed in relation to the third issue below.

The third set of issues concerns the question of incoherence. In chapter three, I have included 'coherence' as one of three validity criteria. As we can see from the study, there are certain places of incoherence. For instance, it has been found that the construction of heroic romance in the first stage was not without its challenges. I have sought to resolve this seeming incoherence on two levels, one theoretical and the other methodological. On the theoretical level, the incoherence in narrative construction is explained as part of the dynamics involved in the public sphere of cultural politics. The narrative development of an event is seldom without incoherence for there always exist some undercurrents that may undermine the prevalent narrative in one way or another. The fact about the larger cultural formation was that, while some common value frames are essential for social integration, conflicts usually take place at the sub-cultural and the social levels. A society's general values are subject to different narrative interpretations by different social actors with divergent interests. As such, there certainly exist a portion of people who, having taken a non-ironic view about the pre-existing situation, will not respond to the event of charismatic mobilization with romantic enthusiasm but with cautions, reservations or oppositions. The theoretical importance of the concept of undercurrent is to underlie the ways the challenges may bear on the development of public discourse and of the event.

On the methodological level, the question is about the weight of evidence. In this research, I have combined a qualitative approach with a simple quantitative measure by including seven categories of public critics in my sample. In a nutshell, the greater the number of category of critics adhere to a particular narrative, the greater the force of the 'public' that the narrative is supposed to carry. The question is, *had I picked a different sample, would my analysis and conclusion about the public's narrative experiences of the event have been different?* Now that more is learned about the narrative positions of the different critics, let me re-examine the issue of representativeness of the sample. At the outset, I chose the newspapers according to the class background of their target readers and their editorial positions (along the liberal-centrist-conservative continuum). Two other types of public critics were added into the sample for the purposes of creating equal weight between the liberal category and the centrist-conservative category on the one hand, and enhancing the representativeness of the sample (by including a non-mainstream position on the other). As it turned out, since narrative positions changed in the course, there developed sub-categories within each category, hence possibly creating the problems of biased sample and unequal weighting between the sub-categories. The issue of sampling has been discussed already and will not be repeated here. As regards the question of weighting, some qualifications have to be made. First, for the research question in hand, 'representativeness' does not necessarily mean having equal numbers in each sub-category; rather, it is the difference in the size of the categories as they develop that provides more useful information about the public weightiness of particular narratives. Secondly, as it turned out that a sense of irony developed and thickened across all the categories and sub-categories towards the end, albeit at different paces, the issue of weighting does not constitute a problem as far as the conclusion of irony is concerned – it may matter, though, on the question of the kind of irony that prevailed in the public at that time. That is to say, while I may conclude with good confidence that public discourse developed into ironies at the end, I might not be able to make empirical generalizations about the relative weight of the different kinds of irony that were generated.

Finally, the fourth set of questions concerns the adequacy of the theory of narrative progression that draws on the four-fold distinction of narrative genres in the Western tradition. Basically, the idea of narrative is used to underline the part-whole relationships between episodes and characters. More specifically, the notion of 'moving structure' in terms of the theory of narrative genres is found to be useful in that it explains the relative tenacity of a narrative structure and at the same time allows the possibility of change from within the narrative structure. Indeed it is the major theoretical aim of this research to demonstrate the underlying structural logics and patterns of variation in discourse and in action. Still, agency has been overlooked and is conceived as playing an important role –not only in mediating between structure and action but also in the process of change. For example, the persistence of the narrative construction of heroic romance among the romanticists in stage two and the ironic turn from romance to tragedy in *Economic Journal* in stage three constitute very strong evidence in support of the claim. (This has been discussed in the previous section.) In this connection, the four-fold distinction is found to be useful in highlighting the common ground while making nuances between these narrative experiences from within the structure of romance. Moreover, the typology is useful in drawing a dividing line between the different kinds of ideal – those of a comic, romantic and cynical nature – which help explain the cultural bases for political mobilizations and conflicts.

While the theory gives a quite convincing account of the structural logic of change within a narrative structure, it is, however, found to be rather weak in explaining changes or shifts from one narrative structure to another. The need to explain such changes does not arise until the third stage of the event in which the critics put closure to their old narrative account and developed new themes in new narratives. Indeed the strategy of closure seems to attain a more important theoretical status than has been expected. As we have seen, in most instances, actors sought to discredit their opponents by means of ironic reversal of and alternative narrative construction parallel with the opponents' narratives. Nonetheless, it has been noted that in a few other instances, say at the beginning of stage two when the 'secret deal' controversy put into question Patten's honesty, the romanticists, in the face of unconvincing evidence, resorted to the strategy of closure to end the debate on the episode. Over this episode, with the heroic romance still carrying the force of the public, the romanticists' practice could be explained within their own narrative position and therefore did not create a theoretical problem. However, in stage three, the strategy of closure was used for narrative shifts. This, I would say, did not contradict but posed a challenge for the theory.

In stage three, there were two notable examples of inter-genre shifts. In both cases, the critics put closure to the Patten event itself within their own narrative structures whereby they developed new thematic narratives about 'another' event. The key lies therefore in the definition of the beginning and the ending of an event. As a matter of fact, just as one episode may be meaningfully connected to another to make up an event, an event may also be connected to another to make up a larger event. In this light, there is in theory no end to the development of one event, and the definition of the boundary of one event is subject to *the researcher's judgment on the relative coherence of the narrative experience of the actors*. The first instance of inter-genre shifts was found in *Economic Journal*. The tragic account about the Patten event became complete in itself, leaving little space for any retrospective modifications thereafter; and it was with this sense of completion of one story that the paper began to develop another one in its shift to a new, more pragmatic concern with smooth transition over economic matters. The narrative emphasis was then embedded within a comic-ironic frame. In terms of structure, the tragic account was overlaid with rather than replaced by a comic-ironic account, with the tragic theme, as well as emotion, of regret lingering over its new narrative. For one thing, the tragic account developed in part out of a gap between romantic ideal and the ironic reality of deteriorating Sino-British relations. In other words, the comic-irony had its germ in the tragic account whereas the tragic narrative had a lingering effect over the comic-irony. Given the high degree of consistency and continuity between the two accounts, the theory of narrative progression is not refuted; but in face of the gap, the theory certainly needs to be further expanded. In this research, I suggest that it was the touch of pity within a tragic account rather than of bitterness within a satirical account that helped ease the shift from a romantic mode to one that embraced a more pragmatic thematic concern. This is a tentative explanation which needs to be substantiated with more solid support.

Another instance of inter-genre shifts was found in stage three when the event 'ended' with the Legislative Council voting. Most of the critics responded to the outcome with an attitude of indifference, disappointment or bitterness, giving an ironic touch to the event as a whole. Notwithstanding such narrative constructions, when taken in a prospective manner, the Legislative Council voting signified instead a positive turn in a larger narrative context – a stride forward in the political history of Hong Kong and a beginning of a new romantic battle to come. Again, this example illustrated the importance of the idea of closure as a strategy to mark one event off from another by the actors. At this point, one question may arise as to why the romanticists and the comic-realists, given their opposing stands, should share the same optimistic outlook at the end. In relation to this, what we observe from the empirical case is that despite the ironic closure to the Patten event, the notes of romantic and comic optimism re-appeared, respectively, among the romanticists and the comic-realists. How should we explain this pattern of re-appearance? Moreover, why did the others not follow suit and resort to the narratives of comic/ romantic optimism? These questions finally lead us to re-think about the nature of the different narrative cultures.

A particular narrative culture will incline the actors to construct a particular narrative about their situation accordingly. Corresponding to the four-fold typology of narrative genres, narrative culture is conceived as consisting of four strands, namely romanticism, comic realism, tragic realism and cynicism. In terms of their orientations to the ideal-reality gap, romanticism presents itself as a strong conviction in the spirit and conduct of combating for the ideal. It sees a distinct line between the sacred and the profane worlds and condemns those who show a lack of moral courage to affirm the dividing line. Realism, in contrast, points to the force of reality. As a variant of it, comic realism celebrates flexible pragmatism and regards compromise and co-operation as the most desired attributes that will bring about a result of reconciliation and/ or restoration of order. It is true that romanticism and comic realism both embrace an ideal, but the former strives for liberation whereas the latter strives for order, partly as an ideal in itself and partly as a pragmatic consideration. Tragic realism (defeatism), as another variant of realism, presents itself as an expectation of defeat. It entails a romantic ideal but prones to give way to the force of ironic realism in a way that emotionally blurs the moral distinction between the just and the unjust. Finally, cynicism bespeaks either a stronghold of romanticism in an even higher ideal or a disbelief in any kind of optimism.

Following the above exposition, we now come back to the questions previously raised. As it has been explained, both romanticism and comic realism, in contrast to tragic realism and cynicism, entail an optimistic outlook or spirit about their respective aspirations and concerns. Specifically, for combative romanticism, it means never giving up even in the face of difficulties; for comic realism, it celebrates flexible pragmatism and is therefore quick to adjust to new situations. In other words, implanted in the cultures of romanticism and comic realism, the romanticists and the comic-realists should be expected to be able to quickly put behind the past event and revive their hopes for a desired end. This explains why the democrat-critics and the comic-realists showed a similarly optimistic tone and were able to shift from their ironic accounts to the new narrative positions immediately after the Legislative Council voting. On the contrary, the tragic-romanticists and the cynics, having lesser faith in the reality, did not strike any high notes at the end of the event.

The above analysis brings us to the position that narrative culture is the most fundamental determinant in narrative constructions. While narrative constructions about particular events may change over time, narrative culture explains the more deep-rooted and persistent cultural force that shapes the specific narrative constructions. In this light, I would conclude that the more events we study, the more episodes we include in an event, or the longer the time span is involved, the more revealing the empirical case will be. On top of this, an analysis of whether and how the actors change their narrative frames upon the completion of an event is also essential to a more profound understanding of the socio-cultural dynamics involved in narrative construction.

An Overview of the Public Sphere in Hong Kong

On the structural-institutional level, the question about the 'public' concerns whether there exists in a community a relatively autonomous public sphere which institutionalizes the practice of open discussion about political matters. As Habermas has pointed out, the development of an independent public sphere is not a universal given, but is brought about by very specific historical processes. In the case of Hong Kong, a public sphere of general accessibility began to emerge in the 1970s and the 1980s. The brief historical study in chapter four has highlighted the structural and conjunctural factors that gave rise to the general public sphere, which sheds light on a few aspects about the socio-cultural context of the Patten event. The detailed analysis of the event in turn illuminates the political and cultural dynamics involved in the public sphere in Hong Kong. The following will summarize a few observations about the development and operation of the 'public' in the society, with particular attention to the possibility of democratic practices through the public sphere.

As we have seen, the growth of a capitalist economy formed a structural prerequisite for the development of a public sphere whereas political and cultural processes shaped the specificities of political struggles that were to have a great impact on the character of the public sphere. In more specific terms, the state entailed a closed polity; the economy produced different classes, which had differential power and hence different strategic orientations to the state. It was in the struggle for political inclusion by the different classes that conflicts were continually generated at the state-society interface, which finally marked out a sphere of politics which increasingly stressed the role of the public. In the early days, the merchants, with their growing economic power, engaged themselves in the practice of open criticisms and later in the struggle for (exclusive) inclusion into the political centre. The government's acquiescence to the merchants' demand brought about a decrease in public criticism among the commercial elites while reinforcing a political division between the mercantile capitalists and the bulk of the working class. In other words, a closed polity generated public criticisms and a struggle for inclusion by the dominant class; the consequence of partial and privileged inclusion by means of appointment, however, deepened the tie between the state and the dominant class while keeping the majority of the people outside the centre.

All along, the government had not built up adequate institutional mechanisms to channel and respond to public opinion. The practice of consultation by the government since the early 1970s was embedded within an authoritarian political structure. This system of political co-optation and channelled consultation failed to accommodate increasing challenges from the periphery. The 1970s already saw a growth of incidents of strikes against state policies. In the 1980s, the system cracked up in the face of increasing political mobilization in the society, especially among the middle class, who demanded general or universalistic (versus sectional) inclusion into the political centre.

While the growth of a local-born middle class was explained as the product of economic and demographic changes, their increasing mobilization was attributed to pre-existing associational infrastructure, political events and crises, and cultural factors. Their participation in the political process in turn have brought about changes in their organizational patterns, the political scenario and the political culture of the society. In particular, in their struggles for political inclusion, a new conception of the 'public' is seen in the making, which poses a fundamental challenge to the one adhered to by the government. The new set of values/ codes governing the public conduct of the actors in the public sphere, including state officials and citizens, are 'public accountability', 'representativeness' and 'transparency'. As these codes become more and more important as the normative guides to the politics of public credibility, 'democracy' gradually acquires the status of a sacred value symbol in public discourse.

Importantly, the rise of the new culture of the 'public' has had significant bearing on the role of the media as the public sphere and on the narrative construction of the Patten event. As we have discussed, the increase in social protests in the 1970s, the struggles over political reform in the 1980s, and the introduction of direct elections to the Legislative Council in the early 1990s have re-shaped the play of politics in a way that leans more and more towards media publicity. A major reason for adopting publicist strategies in the 1970s and the 1980s was that since the Hong Kong people had been denied the right to participate in the formal decision-making process, it would be the civil society, and more specifically the media within it, rather than the state that was more accessible to the people as a field of struggles. In particular, regarding the political groups formed in the 1980s, since they intended to voice out their concerns and opinions in the public rather than seek for political power in any immediate way, their participation in politics mainly took the form of open discussion and debate through the media. All these consolidated the role of the media as the political public sphere in opposition to the political centre.

The introduction of direct elections to the Legislative Council in 1991, which signified the beginning of a process of increasing societalization of the state, brought in the dawn of a politics of public credibility within the political centre. Political groups and individual activists who had been kept out of state power jockeyed for inclusion into the state through public elections. The 1990s has seen the formation of political parties within each political camp. While some – the pro-China forces and some business elites – prefer exercising their influence through private lobbying to participating in electoral politics, those who have formed into parties adopt a high profile in the public arena, taking every chance to enhance their own public credibility in the new political game.

In this context, the mass media serve as an important part of the political public sphere in the community in various ways. First, as agents of news-making, they provide an open discursive space for both state and non-state actors to engage in some kind of 'dialogue' and speak to the public through various kinds of public campaign. Secondly, the editorial column in each paper is itself an expression of the opinions and positions of the paper, which belongs to the public of private citizens. Today the major newspapers all carry daily editorials, even though not all of them are of high quality. Thirdly, besides editorials, most of the newspapers have columns for political commentaries by free-lance writers and for letters from the readers, which form an arena for vigorous debate among the public, including academics, politicians, political activists, columnists, and ordinary citizens. (Recently radio phone-in programs have become more and more popular, which reflect active responses and quality opinions by program hosts, guest speakers and audiences from different ranks.)

The autonomy of the media from the state is a matter of degree. There are limits to complete press freedom on the one hand and some offsetting factors on the other. The limits include the practice of confidentiality by the political centre that curtails the scope of publicness and a growing tendency of self-censorship among the press vis-à-vis the Chinese government. These constraining forces are indeed making partial inroads upon press freedom, but they are currently being offset by three major factors, namely (a) the need to take into account the market environment and the flux of public opinion, (b) the presence of a competitive market which has made possible relative diversity among the press, and (c) increasing political mobilization within the society and increasing societalization of the state which keep alive a politics of public credibility. In this light, the scope of 'publicness' in Hong Kong is not a given but stays in constant flux in the process of political struggles.

In the event studied, the media were shown to be playing an indispensable role in the development of the force of the 'public'. It was in part a matter of political expediency and in part due to the normative force of the new culture of the 'public' that the actors kept turning to the media. For instance, upon his arrival, Governor Patten kept a high profile in the public through media publicity. As a result of his populist skill, he was able to secure largely favorable media coverage, which established for him a public image of an energetic, accessible and charismatic leader. Moreover, introducing the Westminister-style of political campaigning to the society, not only did he meet with the public face-to-face, he also took part in live television forums about his policy speech. It was in the context of a growing cultural emphasis on the values of 'transparency' and 'public accountability' that the Governor's open style as well as populist strategy was effective in summoning strong support from the public, especially the democrats. It was, moreover, in the context of a growing emphasis on 'democratic representativeness' that his proposals mustered popular support when they were released. As such, the culture of the 'public' showed a strong inner connection with the master narrative of democratic struggle, as a result of which the specific narrative of heroic-romance around the theme of democracy carried high public credibility in the first stage.

The role of the media as a sphere for open politics was also reinforced, for a large part of politics between the Governor and the Chinese government were conducted through the media, especially in the first two stages of the event. The reasons being that, firstly, the Governor, who took initiative in this event, resorted to publicist strategies over and above the traditional practice of closed-door diplomacy as a more effective way of mobilizing public support. Secondly, the Chinese government, holding a grudge against the Governor's style, refused to have any direct contact with him and sought instead to discredit him openly. In the 'secret deal' controversy, for instance, the Chinese government dared the government to make known to the public the diplomatic exchanges between Britain and China. As a result, much politicking developed around the issue of publication. The public's urge for the right to know finally resulted in the publication of the letters in the media. In the third stage of the event, although the Sino-British talks were conducted under the principle of confidentiality, the 'progress' of the talks were indirectly reported, hinted at, guessed about and even commented on in the media so much so that the finally publicized details of the talks became stale news. It was in part due to the media reporters' informal connection with the political centre and in part due to the two governments' strategic considerations – to put the blame for talk failure on the other party – that media publicity still formed part and parcel of the political process. Apparently, the less able the political actors were to resolve their conflicts through non-public means, the more likely they would resort to publicist means. (In a recent article (Ku 1998a), I have focused on the question of openness/ secrecy regarding the event.)

On the part of the public, the newspaper editors, the columnists, the political parties, individual legislators and various many other professional and community associations joined in the fierce debate about the Patten proposals in the media. In particular, at the beginning of stage two, even the Business and Professionals Federation, which had always kept a low profile in the public, came out in opposition against the Patten proposals. Certainly, there was a non-public dimension about politics such as the private visits to Beijing by a few local leaders. None the less, these private visits also bore a public dimension in that these leaders brought news to soothe the Hong Kong public and/ or went ahead with their alternative proposals which they believed to be more acceptable to the Chinese government. In other words, the non-public dimension of politics often (but not always) entailed a public presentation in one way or another. (In retrospect, these public mediators all participated in the following elections, which bespeaks an inherent relationship between election and the politics of public credibility.) Moreover, opinion polls became rife since the 1991 elections and their results were often drawn on in media discourse as indicating the public opinion of the day. This was also the case in the Patten event, especially in the first two stages when 'public opinion' was closely attended to as reflecting the flux of public sentiments.

It was difficult to prove whether politics influenced public opinion or vice versa, and it was equally difficult to measure how much one influenced the other. What I have attempted to show in this study is that the two interacted in a continuous manner, with the political actors trying to win over public opinion by means of narrative practices (which were translated into both discursive and material actions), and the public formulating specific narrative responses to their changing political environment. In the first stage of the Patten event, the Governor's political strategies worked effectively upon the aspirations of the public, whose reactions then played a central role in the construction of heroic-romance so much so that the Governor could justify the act of propelling the legislative process forward. In this context, the force of the 'public' appeared to be paramount and irresistible. However, when the materiality of interest politics made its force in the later stages, the public seemed to be too powerless to change the situation. Indeed in the face of the Chinese government's threats and Patten's rashness, in the face of secret diplomacy between the two governments, and in the face of the Chinese government's setting up of a 'second stove', the public found themselves pressed into the role of helpless victim. The thickening sense of irony in public discourse bespoke a frustrating experience of a widening ideal-reality discrepancy. Public opinion changed as the different portions of the public developed new narratives in response to the widening gap. Nevertheless, it would be an oversight to conclude that the public played a passive and negligible role in politics. The fact was, the public did play an important part in the process – in the least, the Patten proposals were legislated despite the Chinese government's opposition. The final outcome might not be the most desired ending, but undeniably, it marked a sign of self-determination in a very tough situation. The public sphere has been and will continue to be an arena for political struggles and identity formation amidst the dynamic mixture of romanticism, comic-realism and cynicism.

Looking Ahead – Narrative Cultures, Credibility Bases, and Political Struggles

In this study, I have identified three sets of generic codes and three modes of narrative construction as characteristic of the symbolic structure of public discourse in Hong Kong in the transitional years, namely the coded discourses of sovereignty/ nationalism, democracy/ autonomy, and stability/ prosperity, and the narrative modes of comic-realism, romanticism and cynicism. Within the pro-democracy camp, the struggles for democracy were couched in romantic-ironic terms wherein the Chinese government was seen as a powerful oppressor, the British government a morally uncommitted hypocrite, and the local elites a group of amoral opportunists. Under British colonial rule before 1997, rather unfortunately yet perhaps quite inevitably, the struggles for/ against democracy had been articulated onto the discourse of 'nationalism versus colonialism' and the discourse of 'autonomy versus colonialism', whilst the former nationalist discourse was further intertwined with the comic-realist discourse on stability. Within the discourses of democracy and autonomy, given Governor Patten's introduction of political reform as well as a new political culture in the final transitional years, the democrats had to struggle among themselves as to whether to take the governor as a strategic ally or as an untrustworthy politician carrying colonial vices. Within the discourses of sovereignty and stability, the democrats were warned against maintaining a confrontational relationship with the Chinese government. Different fragments in the pro-democracy camp took different positions. Apparently, under the discursive power of a competing narrative from their radical counterparts, the leading democrats, in showing full support for the governor's reform proposals in the final legislative process, suffered a setback on moral grounds. Their pragmatic concessions on the democratic cause, despite their confrontational stance toward the Chinese government, raised questions in the public sphere about their leadership credibility. Thereafter the challenge for them was to consolidate or re-establish their 'heroic' posture by standing firm against further concessions. In this light, their decision not to ride the Beijing-manipulated political 'through train' in 1997 might be understood as an act of narrative repair to restore their public credibility. In contrast, their milder counter-parts represented by the Association for Democracy and People's Livelihood was unable to keep up public credibility in taking an ambiguously conciliatory stance toward the Chinese government.

Among the democrats, it appeared that so long as there was some willed obstruction to democratization by the power centre, their discourse would remain romantic-ironic in structure. After 1997, democracy and human rights continue to be important issues on the democrats' political agenda. For example, the lousy formation of the provisional legislature – part of the 'second stove' set up by the Chinese government – became an object of much cynical criticisms in public discourse, by the democrats, media critics, and general citizens. The difference perhaps lies in that, without the British, the struggles for democracy could be somewhat 'liberated' from the nationalist discourse of 'nationalism versus colonialism' and the anti-colonial discourse of 'autonomy versus colonialism'. Stripped of an anti-colonial reference, political contestation is now shaped basically in terms of the discourse of democracy as opposed to the discourse of stability. (Nationalism is another important theme but it is juxtaposed against globalization rather than colonialism). In this context, the leading democrats (represented by the now Democratic Party which resulted from a merge between United Democrats and Meeting Point) and the more radical democrats (such as the now The Frontier) seem to be able to join hands together for the democratic cause for the time being.

After 1997, on the part of the power centre, the first Special Administrative Region government draws on the discourse of stability/ prosperity with all the more vigour in order to legitimate its authority while keeping down the issue of democracy. At its inception the SAR government already suffered slashing attacks by the democrats on the issues of civil liberty, rule of law and democracy. Toward the end of 1997, no sooner had the new government made its public pledge to better the society in administrative, economic and welfare terms than the public credibility of the government was severely put into test. A series of unprecedented incidents and crises within the local milieu and across the Asian region had taken the whole society by surprise. The government contributed to its diminishing public credibility by making numerous administrative blunders, by responding with habitual and mechanical references to the narrative of stability and prosperity, and by showing an extraordinary insensitivity to public sentiments. For the first time, the master narrative of stability and prosperity, which has dominated political and popular discourses for more than two decades, has faced a severe challenge. The economic crisis is perhaps just at its beginning, the intensity of which is yet to be known. Whether the master comic-realist narrative of success will stand the test of the challenge or whether it will evolve into a counter-discourse that lends force to the discourse of democratic accountability is a matter for us to wait-and-see, think about, or even act upon.

Bibliography

Abbott, A. (1992), 'What Do Cases Do? Some Notes on Activity in Sociological Analysis', in C. C. Ragin and H. S. Becker (eds), *What is a Case? Exploring the Foundations of Social Inquiry*, Cambridge University Press, Cambridge, pp. 53-82.

Adorno, T. And Horkheimer, M. (1947), 'The Culture Industry – Enlightenment as Mass Deception', extracted from their *Dialectic of the Enlightenment*, in J. Curran, M. Gurevitch, and J. Woolacotts (1977) (eds) (1977), *Mass Communication and Society*, Edward Arnold, London.

Alejandro, R. (1993), *Hermeneutics, Citizenship, and the Public Sphere*, State University of New York Press, Albany.

Alexander, J. C. (1988), 'Introduction: Durkheimian Sociology and Cultural Studies Today', and 'Culture and Political Crisis: "Watergate" and Durkheimian Sociology', in J. C. Alexander (ed), *Durkheimian Sociology: Cultural Studies*, Cambridge University Press, New York, pp. 1-22.

—— (1990), 'Analytic debates: Understanding the relative autonomy of culture', J. C. Alexander and S. Seidman (eds), *Culture and Society: Contemporary Debates*, Cambridge University Press, New York, pp. 1-30.

—— (1991), 'Habermas and Critical Theory: Beyond the Marxian Dilemma?' in A. Honneth and H. Joas (eds) *Communicative Action*, Polity Press, Cambridge.

Alexander, J. and Smith, P. (1993), 'The Discourse of American Civil Society', *Theory and Society*, 22, pp. 151-207.

Anderson, B. (1983), *Imagined Communities*, Verso, London.

Arendt. H. (1985), *The Human Condition*, The University of Chicago Press, Chicago.

Barthes, R. (1975), 'An Introduction to the Structural Analysis of Narrative', *New Literary History*, vol. VI, no.2.

Baudrillard, J. (1985), 'The Masses: The Implosion of the Social in the Media', M. Maclean (trans), *New Literary History*, vol.16, no.3, pp. 577-89.

Bellman, B. L. (1981), 'The Paradox of Secrecy', *Human Studies*, 4, pp.1-24.

Bendix, R. (1978) *Kings of People? Power and the Mandate to Rule*, University of California Press, Berkeley.

Benn, S. I. and Gaus, G. F. (1983), 'The Liberal Conception of the Public and the Private', *Public and Private in Social Life*, St. Martin's Press, New York.

Bobbio, N. (1989), *Democracy and Dictatorship: The Nature and Limits of State Power*, P. Kennealy (trans.), Polity Press, Cambridge.

Bogart, L. (1972), *Polls and the Awareness of Public Opinion*, Transaction Books, New Brunswick and Oxford.

Brubaker, R. (1992), *Citizenship and Nationhood in France and Germany*, Harvard University Press, Cambridge.

Brooks, P. (1984), *Reading for the Plot: Design and Intention in Narrative*, Harvard University Press, Cambridge.

Bruner, J. S. (1986), *Active Minds, Possible Worlds*, Harvard University Press, Cambridge.

Calhoun, C. (1992), 'Introduction: Habermas and the Public Sphere', in C. Calhoun (ed), *Habermas and the Public Sphere*, The MIT Press, Cambridge, pp. 1-50.

—— (1994), *Social Theory and the Politics of Identity*, Blackwell, London.

—— (1995), 'Nationalism and Difference: The Politics of Identity Writ Large', *Critical Social Theory – Culture, History, and the Challenge of Difference*, Blackwell, Cambridge, USA.

Carr, D. (1986), *Time, Narrative, and History*, indiana University Press, Bloomington.

Chambers, R. (1984), 'Story and Situation', in *Story and Situation: Narrative Seduction and the Power of Fiction*, University of Minnesota Press.

Chan, J. M. (1987), *Shifting Journalistic Paradigms: Mass Media and Political Transition in Hong Kong*, Occasional Paper No.20, Centre for Hong Kong Studies, the Chinese University of Hong Kong, Hong Kong.

Chan, J. M. and Lee, C. C. (1991), *Mass Media and Political Transition: The Hong Kong Press in China's Orbit*, Guilford Press, New York.

Chan, M. K. (1994), 'Introduction: Hong Kong's Precarious Balance – 150 Years in an Historic Triangle', in *Precarious Balance – Hong Kong between China and Britain, 1842-1992*, Hong Kong University Press, Hong Kong, pp.3-8.

Chan, W. K. (1989), *The Making of Hong Kong Society – A Sociological Study of Class Formation in Hong Kong, 1841-1922*, Ph.D. Dissertation, the British Library Document Supply Centre, West Yorkshire.

Chan, Y. Man E. (1998), 'Structural and Symbolic Centres: Centre Displacement in the 1989 Chinese Student Movement', a paper presented at the World Congress of Sociology, Montreal.

Chandhoke, N. (1994), *State and Civil Society – Explorations in Political Theory*, Sage Publications, London.

Chaney, D. (1993), *Fictions of Collective Life: Public Drama in Late Modern Culture*, Routledge, New York.

Chang, K. S. (1982), 'Hong Kong', in J. Lent (ed), *Newspapers in Asia: Contemporary Trends and Problems*, Heinemann Educational Books.

Cheah, P. (1994), 'Violent Light: The Idea of Publicness in Modern Philosophy and in Global Neocolonialism', *Social Text* 43 (Fall), pp. 163-190.

Chiu, S. (1994), *The Politics of Laissez-faire*, Occasional Paper no. 40, Hong Kong Institute of Asian-Pacific Study, Hong Kong.

Clayton, C. C. (1980), 'Hong Kong', in John Lent (ed), *The Asian Newspapers' Reluctant Revolution*, The Iowa State University Press, Iowa.

Cohen, J. L. and Arato, A. (1994), *Civil Society and Political Theory*, MIT Press, Cambridge.

Couto, R. A. (1993), 'Narrative, Free Space, and Political Leadership in Social Movements', *The Journal of Politics* 55 (1), pp. 57-79.

Culler, J. (1975), 'Defining Narrative Units', in Roger Fowler (ed), *Style and Structure in Literature*, Cornell University Press, New York.

Dalgren, P. (1994), *Television and the Public Sphere – Citizenship, Democracy and the Media*, Sage, London.

Davis, S. N.G. (1977), 'One Brand of Politics Rekindled', *Hong Kong Law Journal,* 7, pp.44-80.

Dewey, J. ([1927] 1946), *The Public and Its Problems*, Gateway, Chicago.

Durkheim, E. ([1912]1965), *The Elementary Forms of Religious Life*, Free Press, New York.

Eley, G. (1992), 'Nations, Publics and Political Cultures: Placing Habermas in the Nineteenth Century', in C. Calhoun (ed), *Habermas and the Public Sphere*, MIT Press, Cambridge, pp.289-339.

Fahey, T. (1995), 'Privacy and the Family: Conceptual and Empirical Reflections', *Sociology,* vol.29, no. 4, pp. 687-702.

Fisher, W. (1987), *Human Communication as Narration: Toward a Philosophy of Reason, Value and Action*, University of South Carolina Press, South Carolina.

Fiske, J. (1986), 'Television: Polysemy and Popularity', *Critical Studies in Mass Communication,* vol.3, no. 4, pp. 191-408.

Fraser, N. (1993), 'Sex, Lies, and the Public Sphere: Some Reflections on the Confirmation of Clarence Thomas', in J. Leonard (ed), *Legal Studies as Cultural Studies*, State University of New York Press, Albany, pp. 175-196.

Frye, N. (1957), *The Anatomy of Criticism*, Pinceton University Press, New Jersey.

Fussell, P. (1975), *The Great War and Modern Memory*, Oxford University Press, Oxford.

Garcelon, M. (1997), 'The Shadow of the Leviathan: Public and Private in Communist and Post-Communist Society', in J. Weintraub (ed), *Public and Private in Thought and Practice*, University of Chicago Press, Chicago, pp. 303-332.

Garnham, N. (1992), The Media and the Public Sphere', C. Calhoun (ed), *Habermas and the Public Sphere*, MIT Press, Cambridge, pp. 359-376.

Garmanikow, E., Morgan, D., Purvis, J. and Taylorson, D. (eds) (1983), *The Public and the Private*, Heinemann, London.

Geertz, C. (1973), *The Interpretation of Cultures*, Basic Books, New York.

Gitlin, T. (1978), 'Media Sociology: The Dominant Paradigm', *Theory and Society*, Vol.6, pp.205-53.

Goffman, E. (1959), *The Presentation of Self in Everyday Life,* Anchor Books, New York.

Goldfarb, F. (1991), *The Cynical Society: The Culture of Politics and the Politics of Culture in American Life*, The University of Chicago Press, Chicago.

Gould, M. (1987), *Revolution and Rebellion in the Early Modern World*, University of California Press, Berkeley and Los Angeles.

Gramsci, A. (1971), 'Modern Prince', *Selections from the Prison Notebooks*, International Publishers, New York.

Habermas, J. ([1962]1989), *The Structural Transformation of the Public Sphere: An Inquiry into a Category of Bourgeois Society.* The MIT Press, Cambridge, MA.

Hansen, K. (1987), 'Feminist Conceptions of Public and Private: A Critical Analysis', *Berkeley Journal of Sociology*, vol.32, pp.105-28.

Hall, J. A. (ed), (1995), *Civil Society – Theory, History, Comparison*, Polity Press Cambridge.

Hall, S., Tony, J., John, C. and Brian R. (1978), *Policing the Crisis: Mugging, the State, and Law and Order*, Holmes and Meier Publishers, Inc, New York.

—— (1982), 'The Rediscovery of Ideology', in Gurevitch, M., Bennett, T. Curran, J. and Wollacott, J. (ed), *Culture, Society and the Media*, Routledge, London and New York, pp. 56-90.

Harris, P.B. (1978), *Hong Kong: A Study in Bureaucratic Politics*, Heinemann, Hong Kong.

Hart, J. (1992), 'Cracking the Code: Narrative and Political Mobilization in the Greek Resistance', *Social Science History*, vol.16, no.4, pp.631-68.

Herbst, S. (1993), 'The Meaning of Public Opinion: Citizens' Constructions of Political Reality', *Media, Culture and Society*, vol.15, no. 3.

Hirsch, D.E., (1967), *Validity in Interpretation*, Yale University Press, New Haven.

Husserl, E. ([1928]1964), *The Phenomenology of Time-consciousness*, translated by J. S. Churchill, Indiana University Press, Bloomington.

Jacobs, R. N. (1996), 'Civil Society and Crisis: Culture, Discourse, and the Rodney King Beating', *American Journal of Sociology*, vol.101, no.5, pp.1238-1272.

—— and Philip S. (1997), 'Romance, Irony and Solidarity', *Sociological Theory* vol.15, no.1, pp. 60-80.

Kane, A. (1991), 'Cultural Analysis in Historical Sociology: The Analytic and Concrete Forms of the Autonomy of Culture', *Sociological Theory*, vol.9, pp.53-69.

—— (1994), *Culture and Social Change: Symbolic Construction, Ideology, and Political Alliance during the Irish Land War, 1879-1881*, Doctoral Dissertation, University of California, Los Angeles.

—— (1997), Theorizing Meaning Construction in Social Movements: Symbolic Structures and Interpretation during the Irish Land War, 1879-1882', *Sociological Theory*, vol.15 ,no.3, pp. 249-276.

Kerby, A. P. (1991), *Narrative and the Self*, Indiana University Press, Bloomington.

Kermode, F. (1979), *The Genesis of Secrecy on the Interpretation of Narrative*, Harvard University Press, Harvard.

Kertzer, D. (1988), *Ritual, Politic and Power*, Yale University Press, Cambridge.

Kessler, C. S. (1978), *Islam and Politics in a Malay State,* Extracted from David Kertzer (1988), p.5.

Klapp, O. E. (1962), *Heroes, Villains and Fools: The Changing American Character*, Prentice Hall, New York.

—— (1964), *Symbolic Leaders: Public Dramas and Public Men*, Aldine, Chicago.

Klapper, J. (1960), *The Effects of Mass Communication*, Free Press, New York.

Ku, A. S. (1998a), 'Boundary Politics in the Public Sphere – Openness, Secrecy and Leakage', *Sociological Theory*, vol.16, no.2, pp.172-190.

—— (1998b), 'The Public up against the State – Narrative Cracks and Credibility Crisis in Post-colonial Hong Kong', Presented at the World Congress of Sociology, Montreal.

Lam, J. T. M. And Lee, J. C. Y. (1993), *The Dynamic Political Actors in Hong Kong's Transition*, Writers' and Publishers' Cooperative, Hong Kong.

Lam, Yau Lan (1977), *The History of the Development of the Press in Hong Kong*, The World Bookshop, Taiwan.

Lang, G. E. and Kurt, L. (1983), *The Battle for Public Opinion: The President, the Press, and the Polls During Watergate*, Columbia University Press, New York.

Lau, S. K. (1982), *Society and Politics in Hong Kong*, The Chinese University Press, Hong Kong.

Lazarsfeld, P., Berelson, B. and Gaudet, H. (1948), *The People's Choice*, Columbia University Press, New York.

Leitch, T. (1986), *What Stories Are: Narrative Theory and Interpretation*, The Pennsylvania University Press, London.

Leung, B. K. P. (1990), 'Political Development: Prospects and Possibilities', in B. K. P. Leung, (ed), *Social Issues in Hong Kong*, Oxford University Press, Hong Kong, pp.143-63.

Lippmann, W. ([1922]1965), *Public Opinion*, The Free Press, New York.

Lopata, H. Z. (1993), 'The Interweave of Public and Private: Women's Challenge to American Society', *Journal of Marriage and the Family*, vol.55, pp.176-90.

MacIntyre, A. (1984), *After Virtue: A Study in Moral Theory*, University of Notre Dame Press, Notre Dame.

Marks, S. R. (1994), 'Intimacy in the Public Realm: the Case of Co-workers', *Social Forces*, vol.72, pp.843-58.

Martin, W. (1986), *Recent Theories of Narrative*, Cornell University Press, London.

Mayhew, L. (1984), 'In Defense of Modernity: Talcott Parsons and the Utilitarian Tradition', *American Journal of Sociology*, vol. 89, pp.1273-1305.

Mills, W. C. (1956), *The Power Elite*, Oxford University Press, New York.

Miners, N. J. (1986), *The Government and Politics of Hong Kong*, Oxford University Press, Hong Kong.

—— (1991), 'The Transformation of the Hong Kong Legislative Council 1970-1994: From Consensus to Confrontation', *The Asian Journal of Public Administration*, vol 16, no 2, pp.224-248.

Peters, J. D. (1993), 'District of Representation: Habermas on the Public Sphere', *Media, Culture and Society*, vol.15, no.4, pp.541-571.

Phelan, J. (1989), *Reading People, Reading Plots: Character, Progression, and the Interpretation of Narrative*, The University of Chicago Press, Chicago.

Polkinghorne, D. E. (1988), *Narrative Knowing and the Human Sciences*, State University of New York Press, Albany.

Prince, G. (1982), *Narratology: The Form and Function of Narrative*, The Hague, Mouton.

Pui, Y. Y. (1993), *Intraorganizational Power Distribution within the Newspaper Industry in Hong Kong*, Unpublished Thesis, The Chinese University of Hong Kong, Hong Kong.

Ragin, C. C. (1987), *The Comparative Method: Moving Beyond Qualitative and Quantitative Strategies*, University of California Press, Los Angeles.

Ragin C. C. And Becker, H. S. (Eds) (1992), *What is a Case? Exploring the Foundations of Social Inquiry*, Cambridge University Press.

Ricoeur, P. (1985), *Time and Narrative*, vol.1, University of Chicago Press, Chicago.

Robbins, B. (1993), 'Introduction: The Public as Phantom', in B. Robbins (ed), *The Phantom Public Sphere*, University of Minnesota Press, London, pp.vii-xxvi.

Scholes, R. (1982), *Semiotics and Interpretation*, Yale University Press, New Haven.

Schudson, M. (1982), 'The Politics of Narrative Form: The Emergence of News Conventions in Print and Television', *Daedalus*, vol. 3.

Scott, I. (1989), *Political Change and the Crisis of Legitimacy in Hong Kong*, Oxford University Press, Hong Kong.

Scott, J. (1990), *A Matter of Record*, Polity Press, Cambridge.

Sennett, R. (1974), *The Fall of Public Man*, Cambridge University Press, Cambridge.

Sewell, W. Jr. (1985), 'Ideologies and Social Revolutions: Reflections on the French Revolution', *Journal of Modern History*, vol.57, pp.57-85.

―――― (1992), 'Introduction: Narratives and Social Identities', *Social Science History*, vol.16, no.3, pp. 479-488.

Shils, E. (1972), *The Constitution of Society*, The University of Chicago Press, Chicago.

Skogerbo, E. (1990), 'The Concept of the Public Sphere in a Historical Perspective: An Anachronism or a Relevant Political Concept', *Nordicom Review of Nordic Mass Communication Research*, vol.2, pp. 41-46.

Smith, P. (1994), 'The Semiotic Foundations of Media Narratives: Saddam and Nasser in the American Mass Media', *Journal of Narrative and Life History*, vol. 4, no.1, 2, pp.89-118.

Somers, M. R. (1992), 'Narrativity, Narrative Identity, and Social Action: Rethinking English Working-Class Formation', *Social Science History*, vol.16, no.4, pp. 591-630.

―――― (1993), 'Citizenship and the Place of the Public Sphere: Law, Community, and Political Culture in the Transition to Democracy', *American Sociological Review*, vol. 58, no. 5, pp.587-620.

—— (1995a), 'What's Political or Cultural about Political Culture and the Public Sphere? Toward and Historical Sociological of Concept Formation', *Sociological Theory*, vol.13, pp.113-44.

—— (1995b), 'Narrating and Naturalizing Civil Society and Citizenship Theory: The Place of Political Culture and the Public Sphere', *Sociological Theory*, vol. 13, no.3, pp. 229-274.

Somers, M. R. and Gibson, G. D. (1994) 'Reclaiming the Epistemological "Other": Narrative and the Social Construction of Identity', in *Social Theory and the Politics of Identity*, Blackwell, London, pp. 37-99.

Stacey, M. (1981), 'The Division of Labour Revisited or Overcoming the Two Adams', in P. Abrams, R. Deem, J. Finch and P. Rock (eds), *Practice and Progress*, Allen and Unwin, London.

Steinmetz, G. (1992) , 'Reflections on the Role of Social Narratives in Working-Class Formation: Narrative Theory in the Social Sciences', *Social Science History*, vol.16, no.3, pp. 489-516.

Sum, N.L. (1995), 'More than a War of Words: Identity, Politics and the Struggle for Dominance during the Recent Political Reform Period in Hong Kong', *Economy and Society*, vol. 24, no.1, pp.67-100.

Tang, J. T. H. (1994), 'World War to Cold War: Hong Kong's Future and Anglo-Chinese Interactions, 1941-55', in M. K. Chan (ed), *Precarious Balance – Hong Kong between China and Britain, 1842-1992*, Hong Kong University Press, Hong Kong, pp.107-130.

Taylor, C. (1985), 'Self-interpreting Animals', *Human Agency and Language: Philosophical Papers I*, Cambridge University Press, Cambridge.

Thompson, J. B. (1990), *Ideology and Modern Culture – Critical Social Theory in the Era of Mass Communication*, Polity Press, Oxford.

—— (1994), *The Media and Modernity – A Social Theory of the Media*, Polity Press, Cambridge.

Turner, V. (1974), *Dramas, Fields, and Metaphors – Symbolic Action in Human Society*, Cornell University Press, Ithaca.

Vaughan, D. (1992), 'Theory Elaboration: The Heuristics of Case Analysis', in C. C. Ragin and H. S. Becker (eds), *What is a Case? Exploring the Foundations of Social Inquiry*, Cambridge University Press, Cambridge.

Walton, D. (1992), 'Making the Theoretical Case', in C. C. Ragin and H. S. Becker (eds), *What is a Case? Exploring the Foundations of Social Inquiry*, Cambridge University Press, Cambridge, pp. 121-138.

Warner, M. (1992), 'The Mass Public and the Mass Subject', in C. Calhoun (ed), *Habermas and the Public Sphere*, The MIT Press, Cambridge, pp. 377-401.

Weintraub, J. (1997), 'The Theory and Politics of the Public/ Private Distinction', *In Public and Private in Thought and Practice – Perspectives on a Grand Dichotomy*, The University of Chicago Press, Chicago, pp. 1-42.

Weintraub, J. and Kumar, K. (eds) (1997), *Public and Private in Thought and Practice – Perspectives on a Grand Dichotomy*, The University of Chicago Press, Chicago.

White, H. (1987), *The Content of the Form: Narrative Discourse and Historical Representation*, The Johns Hopkins University Press, Baltimore.

Williams, R. ([1958]1983), *Culture and Society*, Columbia University Press, New York.

Wuthnow, R. (1989), *Communities of Discourse*, Harvard University Press, Cambridge.

Zaret, D. (1994) , 'Literacy and Printing in the Rise of Democratic Political Culture in Seventeenth-century England', *Research on Democracy and Society*, vol. 2, pp.175-211.

―――― (1996), 'Petitions and the Invention' of Public Opinion in the English Revolution', *American Journal of Sociology*, vol. 101, no.6, pp. 1497-1555.